THE SHEEP OF HIS PASTURE

HARVARD SEMITIC MUSEUM

HARVARD SEMITIC MONOGRAPHS

edited by
Frank Moore Cross

Theology of the Program of Restoration of Ezekiel 40–48	Jon Douglas Levenson
Isaiah 24–27 and the Origin of Apocalyptic	William R. Millar
Late Biblical Hebrew: Toward an Historical Typology of Biblical Hebrew Prose	Robert Polzin
Textual and Historical Studies in the Book of Jubilees	James C. VanderKam
Studies in Lucian's De Syria Dea	Robert A. Oden
The Apocalyptic Vision of the Book of Daniel	John Joseph Collins
The Scripts of Ancient Northwest Semitic Seals	Larry G. Herr
Parallelism in Early Biblical Poetry	Stephen A. Geller
Rank among the Canaanite Gods: El, Baal and the Rephaim	Conrad L'Heureux
The Exile and Biblical Narrative: The Formation of the Deuteronomistic and Priestly Works	Richard Friedman
The Greek Text of Judges: Recensional Developments	Walter R. Bodine
The Assembly of the Gods: The Divine Council in Canaanite and Early Hebrew Literature	E. Theodore Mullen, Jr.
The Constitution of the Monarchy of Israel	Baruch Halpern
The Coinage and Mints of Phoenicia: The Pre-Alexandrine Period	John W. Betlyon
The Ammonite Language of the Iron Age	Kent P. Jackson
Textual Studies in the Book of Joshua	Leonard Greenspoon
The Sheep of His Pasture: A Study of the Hebrew Noun 'Am(m) *and Its Semitic Cognates*	Robert McClive Good
The Symbolic Vision in Biblical Traditions	Susan Niditch

Robert McClive Good

THE SHEEP OF HIS PASTURE

A Study of the Hebrew Noun ʿAm(m) *and Its Semitic Cognates*

Scholars Press
Chico, California

THE SHEEP OF HIS PASTURE
A Study of the Hebrew Noun *ʿAm(m)*
and Its Semitic Cognates

Robert McClive Good

Library of Congress Cataloging in Publication Data

Good, Robert McClive.
The sheep of His pasture.

(Harvard Semitic monographs ; 29)
Revised version of thesis (Ph. D.)—Yale, 1980.
Bibliography: p.
1. ʿAm (The Hebrew word). 2. Bible. O.T.—Language, style. I. Title. II. Series.
BS1185.G63 1983 492.4'2 83-9034
ISBN 0-89130-628-5

Printed in the United States of America

TABLE OF CONTENTS

ROBERT MCCLIVE GOOD is Assistant Professor of Religious Studies at Brown University. He received his B.A. from Princeton University and his Ph.D. from Yale University.

PREFACE

This volume is a revised version of my Yale Ph.D. dissertation (Near Eastern Languages and Literatures) submitted in 1980.

Research for the dissertation was made possible in part by a grant from the American Schools of Oriental Research for study in Jerusalem. I gratefully acknowledge their support. In Jerusalem progress on my research was greatly facilitated by the generous assistance of Professor M. J. Kister and his doctoral student Ophir Livneh. I presented material concerning the Covenant Formula at a public lecture in the spring of 1979 and benefitted from the responses of Professors Moshe Weinfeld and Frank M. Cross; to the latter I owe a special additional thanks for occasional comments and criticism offered in private discussion.

The dissertation was prepared under the direction of Professor Marvin H. Pope; I am grateful for his encouragement and criticism. During the final stages of thesis preparation I enjoyed the enormous benefit of careful readings of the entire thesis by Professors Franz Rosenthal and Robert Wilson. For much of the soundness of the manuscript I am indebted to their selfless labors. Professor Benjamin R. Foster has offered helpful criticism of my treatment of the cuneiform sources. It was Dr. Marten Stol who gave me initial direction in pursuing the noun *ʿamm* in Akkadian texts.

Some of the production costs of the published volume were offset by a Brown University faculty development grant, and I gratefully acknowledge the University's assistance.

For the support of my wife Kathleen there can be no adequate word of thanks.

LIST OF ABBREVIATIONS

ABR	*Australian Biblical Review*
AHw	W. von Soden, *Akkadisches Handwörterbuch*
AJA	*American Journal of Archaeology*
AJSL	*American Journal of Semitic Languages and Literatures*
al-Jāḥiẓ *Al-Bayān wat-Tabyīn*	al-Jāḥiẓ, *Al-Bayān wat-Tabyīn* (Beirut, 1976)
al-Jāḥiẓ *Ḥayawān*	al-Jāḥiẓ, *Kitāb al-Ḥayawān* (U.A.R., 1966)
al-Mufaḍḍalīyāt	Charles Lyall, *The Mufaḍḍalīyāt* (Oxford, 1918)
al-Muzhir	as-Suyūṭī, *Al-Muzhir fī ʿUlūm al-Luġa* (Būlāq, 1875)
AnBib	Analecta Biblica
ANET	J. B. Pritchard (ed.), *Ancient Near Eastern Texts*
an-Nasā'ī	an-Nasā'ī, *Sunan* (U.A.R., 1964-1965)
Antas	D. Fantar, "Les Inscriptions," in E. Acquaro et al., *Ricerche puniche ad Antas*
AOAT	Alter Orient und Altes Testament
AOS	American Oriental Series
Arad	Y. Aharoni, *Arad Inscriptions* (Hebrew; Jerusalem, 1975)
ARM	*Archives royales de Mari*
ArOr	*Archiv orientální*
aṣ-Ṣiḥāḥ	al-Jawharī, *Tāj al-Luġa waṢiḥāḥ al-ʿArabīya* (U.A.R., 1957)
ATANT	Abhandlungen zur Theologie des Alten und Neuen Testaments
BA	*Biblical Archaeologist*
BASOR	Bulletin of the American Schools of Oriental Research
BBB	Bonner biblische Beiträge
BDB	F. Brown, S. R. Driver, and C. A. Briggs, *Hebrew and English Lexicon of the Old Testament*

BETL	Bibliotheca ephemeridum theologicarum lovaniensium
BH^3	R. Kittel, *Biblia Hebraica* (3rd edition)
Bib	Biblica
BibOr	Biblica et Orientalia
BKAT	Biblisher Kommentar: Altes Testament
BSO(A)S	Bulletin of the School of Oriental (and African) Studies
BWANT	Beiträge zur Wissenschaft vom Alten und Neuen Testament
BZ	Biblische Zeitschrift
BZAW	Beiheft zur ZAW
CAD	*The Assyrian Dictionary of the Oriental Institute of the University of Chicago*
CBQ	*Catholic Biblical Quarterly*
CIH	*Corpus Inscriptionum Semiticarum* vol. 4, Inscriptiones Himyariticas et sabaeas continens
CIS	*Corpus Inscriptionum Semiticarum*
Cowley	A. Cowley, *Aramaic Papyri of the Fifth Century* (Oxford, 1923)
CRAIBL	*Comptes rendus de l'Académie des Inscriptions et Belles-Lettres*
CTA	A. Herdner, *Corpus des tablettes en cunéiformes alphabétiques*
Dīwān al-Farazdaq (Boucher)	R. Boucher, *Divan de Férazdak* (Paris, 1870)
Dtn	Deuteronomistic
EnJud	*Encyclopaedia Judaica* (1971)
Finkelstein Mem	M. Ellis, ed., *Essays on the Ancient Near East in Memory of Jacob Joel Finkelstein* (Memoirs of the Connecticut Academy of Arts and Sciences 19; Hamden, Connecticut, 1977)
FS Bertholet	W. Baumgartner, *Festschrift für Alfred Bertholet* (Tübingen: Mohr, 1950)
FS de Quervain	J. J. Stamm and Ernst Wolf, eds., *Freude am Evangelium* (*Beiträge zur evangelischen Theologie* 44; München, 1966)

FS H. G. May	H. T. Frank and Wm. L. Reed, eds., *Translating and Understanding the Old Testament* (Nashville: Abingdon, 1970)
FS Loewenstamm	Y. Avishur and J. Blau, eds., *Studies in Bible and the Ancient Near East Presented to Samuel E. Loewenstamm* (Jerusalem: Rubenstein, 1978)
FS Muilenberg	B. W. Anderson and W. Harrelson, eds., *Israel's Prophetic Heritage* (New York: Harper, 1962)
FS Nöldeke	Carl Bezold, ed., *Orientalische Studien Theodor Nöldeke...gewidmet* (Giessen: Töpelmann, 1906)
FS Procksch	*Festschrift Otto Procksch* (Leipzig: Deichert, 1934)
FS Rowley	*Wisdom in Israel and in the Ancient Near East* (SVT 3; Leiden: E. J. Brill, 1955)
FS Rudolph	A. Kuschke, ed., *Verbannung und Heimkehr* (Tübingen: Mohr, 1961)
FS von Rad	H. W. Wolff, ed., *Probleme biblischer Theologie* (München: Kaiser, 1971)
GAG	W. von Soden, *Grundriss der akkadischen Grammatik*
GLECS	*Comptes rendus du Groupe Linguistique d'études chamito-sémitique*
Ḥamāsa (Freytag)	G. G. Freytag, *Hamasae Carmina* (Bonn, 1828)
HAT	Handbuch zum Alten Testament
HUCA	*Hebrew Union College Annual*
Hudhayl (Kosegarten)	J. G. L. Kosegarten, *The Poems of Huzailis* (London, 1854)
Hudhayl (Wellhausen)	J. Wellhausen, *Skizzen und Vorarbeiten* I/2 (Berlin: Reimer, 1884)
Ibn Durayd	Ibn Durayd, *Kitāb Jamharat al-Luġa* (Hyderabad, 1925-1933)
Ibn Māja	Ibn Māja, *Sunan*
Ibn Qutayba, *ʿUyūn al-ʾAḫbār*	Ibn Qutayba, *ʿUyūn al-ʾAḫbār* (Cairo, 1964)
IM	Iraq Museum

JAOS	*Journal of the American Oriental Society*
JBL	*Journal of Biblical Literature*
JCS	*Journal of Cuneiform Studies*
JNES	*Journal of Near Eastern Studies*
JPOS	*Journal of the Palestine Oriental Society*
JQR	*Jewish Quarterly Review*
JTS	*Journal of Theological Studies*
KAI	H. Donner and W. Röllig, *Kanaanäische und aramäische Inschriften*
Kāmil al-Mubarrad	W. Wright, *The Kāmil of el-Mubarrad* (Leipzig, 1864)
Labīd (Brockelmann)	C. Brockelmann, ed., *Die Gedichte des Lebīd* (Leiden, 1891)
Lisān	Ibn Manṣūr, *Lisān al-ʿArab* (Būlāq, 1883-1891)
L.P.	Inscriptions of E. Littmann, *Safaitic Inscriptions* (Leiden, 1943)
MAD	Materials for the Assyrian Dictionary
Maymūn (Geyer)	R. Geyer, *Gedichte von Abū Baṣīr Maimūn ibn Qais al-ʾAʿšâ* (London, 1928)
MUSJ	*Mélanges de l'Université Saint-Joseph*
MVAG	Mitteilungen der Vorderasiatisch-ägyptischen Gesellschaft
NEph	R. Degen, W. Müller, and W. Röllig, *Neue Ephemeris für semitische Epigraphik* (Wiesbaden: Harrassowitz, 1972-1978)
OEC	Oxford Editions of Cuneiform Texts
OLZ	*Orientalische Literaturzeitung*
Or	*Orientalia*
OTL	Old Testament Library
OTS	*Oudtestamentische Studien*
Pauly-Wissowa	Pauly-Wissowa, *Real-Encyclopädie der classischen Altertumswissenschaft*
PBI	Pontifical Biblical Institute
PRU	*Le palais royale d'Ugarit*
RA	*Revue d'assyriologie et d'archéologie orientale*
RAO	(Ch. Clermont Ganneau), *Recueil d'archéologie orientale* (Paris: Leroux, 1888-1924)

RB	*Revue biblique*
RÉS	*Répertoire d'épigraphie sémitique*
Rev. Africaine	*Revue africaine*
RHR	*Revue de l'histoire des religions*
Rje	Redactor of J and E.
RSO	*Rivista degli Studi Orientali*
RSPT	*Revue des sciences philosophiques et théologiques*
RTP	*Revue de théologie et de philosophie*
SAHG	A. Falkenstein and W. von Soden, *Sumerische und akkadische Hymnen und Gebete*
Samaria	G. A. Reisner et al., *Harvard Excavations at Samaria* (Harvard, 1924)
SBT	Studies in Biblical Theology
Sefer Rendtorff	K. Rupprecht, ed., *Sefer Rendtorff* (Dielheim, 1975)
Sem	*Semitica*
SJSOT	Supplement, *Journal for the Study of the Old Testament*
Sousse	P. Cintas, "Le sanctuaire punique de Sousse," Rev Africaine 91 (1947):1-80.
StSem	Studi Semitici
SVT	Supplements to VT
Tāj al-ʻArūs	Murtaḍā az-Zabīdī, *Tāj al-ʻArūs*
TDOT	Theological Dictionary of the Old Testament
THAT	E. Jenni and C. Westermann, eds., *Theologisches Handwörterbuch zum Alten Testament* (München: Kaiser, 1971-1976)
ThSt (Barth)	*Theologische Studien*, ed. Barth
TM	Tell Mardikh
Trip	Tripolitana (see KAI, vol. 3:7ff.)
TZ	*Theologische Zeitschrift*
UF	*Ugaritische Forschungen*
Ugaritica	C. Schaeffer, *Ugaritica* (Paris, continuing series)
ʻUrwa (Nöldeke)	Th. Nöldeke, *Die Gedichte des ʻUrwa ibn Alward* (Göttingen, 1863)
UUÅ	*Uppsala Universitetsårsskrift*

VD	*Verbum Domini*
VT	*Vetus Testamentum*
WMANT	Wissenschaftliche Monographien zum Alten und Neuen Testament
WUS	J. Aistleitner, *Wörterbuch der ugaritischen Sprache*
YOS	Yale Oriental Studies
ZA	*Zeitschrift für Assyriologie*
ZAW	*Zeitschrift für die alttestamentliche Wissenschaft*
ZDMG	*Zeitschrift der deutschen morgenländischen Gesellschaft*
ZDPV	*Zeitschrift des deutschen Palästina-Vereins*
ZKT	*Zeitschrift für katholische Theologie*
ZTK	*Zeitschrift für Theologie und Kirche*

TRANSLITERATION AND ARABIC SOURCE CITATION

The system of transliteration adopted here is that recommended by the *Journal of Biblical Literature*. For epigraphic texts consonants not differentiated graphically are not differentiated here, thus *šn*ʾ for **śn*ʾ.

Editions for Arabic citations are noted in the list of abbreviations.

Chapter I

INTRODUCTION

In recent years Biblical lexicography has undergone methodological changes brought about in large measure by the publication of James Barr's *The Semantics of Biblical Language*.[1] Semantic analysis has begun to replace the comparative Semitic approach to the study of Hebrew words. John Sawyer's excellent monograph *Semantics in Biblical Research* typifies the new wave of word studies.[2] Sawyer finds apologetic justification for producing another study of salvation terminology in the fresh insights made available by the new method of investigation. The price paid for fresh insight is an enormous restriction of material made subject to inquiry. Indeed, so demanding are the requirements of semantic analysis that the reader of Sawyer's volume will sense a necessary incompleteness in his study. It is clear that a broad topic cannot easily be made subject to limited semantic treatment.

The present volume deals with a broad topic, an understanding of the Hebrew word "people." If by calling our topic broad we imply an apology for not using the methods of semantic analysis, we can at least forgo excusing the breadth of the subject. Although the Hebrew noun *ʿam(m)* is one of the commonest words in the Bible, and although the Biblical idea of a people has great significance, the word has never been the subject of a monograph.[3] A small literature of articles and an unmanageable body of incidental remarks have addressed the word's meaning, but this study has occurred without exhausting the potential for enlightenment from comparative Semitic research.

To designate our endeavor a comparative Semitic study does not satisfactorily introduce the approach inherent in the pages that follow. Pride of place and center of concern belong to the Biblical evidence. It will become clear that this is appropriate to the topic. Our thesis - it must be stated with the cautionary remark that its absolute proof is unattainable - is that the noun *ʿam(m)* represents the sound made by caprine beasts and originally signified "flock." The flock provides that natural group which in prehistoric times gave its name to the human group "tribe" or "people." Because linguistic evidence for such a thesis comes only from written sources and because the Semitic literatures are the product chiefly of urban civilizations, a special burden is placed on the two Semitic languages with close links to a situation in which men and flocks lived together, Hebrew and Arabic. The latter preserves an enormous vocabulary of camel nomadism at least some or which can be presumed a linguistic heritage from earlier kinds of nomadism. The lateness of the Arabic literature warns against drawing unbounded conclusions from its evidence. In Biblical Hebrew we possess the literature of a people who rendered account of themselves as the descendants of flock nomads. Precisely this point has become the focus of controversy. Especially C. H. J. de Geus has challenged the simple model of Israelite origins according to which pastoralists became a settled nation in a linear evolution. De Geus emphasizes Israelite continuity in the land and the compatibility of the Biblical data with the notion that Israel grew into existence in place in Palestine.[4] Although we recognize the implications of our thesis for such historical and sociological questions, we shall not address them here. The evidence used in evaluating events of prehistory and at the shadowy threshold of history must include the study of words, and it is here that the present investigation should have its place.

While it is true that Israel presents a picture of pastoral origins, it is also true that the records of those origins are later than the times they portray. From a literary standpoint Israelite writings are subject to a shortcoming shared by other Semitic texts. They are the product of an urban civilization. The obstacle thereby posed to the quest for a pastoral vocabulary is not insurmountable. Religious traditions and pious formulae can be resistant to change, and the advance of Biblical studies has brought techniques for retrieving early settings of such materials and for detecting changes in their meanings. In much of this work we shall be concerned to recapture early uses of the word *ʿam(m)*, and this necessitates investigative procedures not ordinarily employed in strictly philological studies. Our investigation will sometimes unfold information which seems at first to be only remotely germane to the topic, but the effort will in each case contribute something to a diachronic understanding of Israel's self-image as a people.

Our undertaking is potentially unmanageable, and the scope of the inquiry must be carefully restricted to permit progress toward the goal of understanding what is meant by people in the Old Testament. It would be impractical and only marginally useful to survey meanings of *ʿam(m)* and its cognates in the modern Semitic languages. Although linguistic fossils are retrievable from any layer of the history of a family of languages, the likelihood of recovering significant insight into the parent meanings of *ʿam(m)* declines with the historical advance of the Semitic tongues. We have therefore excluded from consideration modern Semitic languages; for each branch of the Semitic language family we shall restrict our attention to the early period. This exclusion leaves a still enormous undertaking, and further research priorities have been needed to promote progress. Occurrences of *ʿam(m)* in personal names are significant but provide minimal information about the meanings of the word. In order to interpret the evidence of names one must first know what *ʿam(m)* means, as a glance at studies of Semitic personal names will show. Moreover, the interpretation of individual names is fraught with difficulty, and for this reason the evidence of personal names alone cannot support weighty conclusions. Since the relevant personal names have often been studied, it is possible to rely on prior researches in this domain.

The task remains large, but the etymology and meanings of *ʿam(m)* have been the subject of remarks by a number of the greatest orientalists of our era, and the modern researcher is heir to a rich heritage of insights and information.

* * *

History of Research

The modern discussion of the word's etymology began in 1885 with the publication of W. Robertson Smith's *Kinship and*

Marriage in Early Arabia. Although agnatic relationship has been the dominant organizing theme of Arabian society in historical times, Smith believed that an era of social matriarchy preceded Arabian patriarchal society and constituted the primitive order of Semitic human relationships. The semantic development of words provided Smith with some of the evidence for his thesis. For example, the use of an Arabic word meaning "womb" *(baṭn)* to denote "tribe" points to an underlying principle of cognatic relationship. Smith discussed the word *ʿam(m)* because this word for "people" offered an apparent counterexample to words like *baṭn*. The Arabic word *ʿamm* most frequently designates the father's brother. A development of the word "people" from the noun "paternal uncle" would suggest a primitive agnatic basis for human organization, and so Smith sought to establish that the historical process moved in the opposite direction. That is, he insisted that the word "paternal uncle" derived from "people" and not vice versa. The fluid use of the Arabic words *ʿamm* and *ḫāl* ("mother's brother") supported this conclusion. According to Smith, the latter refers simply to an individual from the mother's group, the former is no more specific.[5]

Smith's view was immediately criticized. In 1886 Theodor Nöldeke reviewed *Kinship and Marriage* and made several observations about the word *ʿam(m)*. Treating the nouns *ʿamm* and *ḫāl* together, Nöldeke provided evidence to show both nouns as early Semitic in the respective meanings "paternal uncle" and "maternal uncle." The latter left traces in Aramaic both in Syriac and, to judge from a personal name, Palmyrene; the former in Syriac. But Nöldeke recognized a problem in the existence of a word *ʿamm* meaning "group." Noting its occurrence in a few verses of Arabic poetry, he inclined to the view that "paternal uncle" and "people" were not the same word.[6]

Julius Wellhausen approached the problem of *ʿam(m)*'s etymology from a different perspective. The topic was a natural outgrowth of his study of Arabian marriage practice, since the father's-brother's-daughter *(bint ʿamm)* pattern of marriage has been prevalent and favored in Arabian society. According to Wellhausen, in both Arabian and early Israelite society a man enjoyed a privileged right to the hand of his paternal uncle's daughter, the *bint ʿamm*. Wellhausen located the meaning of the word *ʿamm* in the polarity native:foreign. The *bint ʿamm* was a woman of the same tribe; those related on the paternal side formed the native, endogamous group. Although exogamy was permitted, a strong bias in favor of agnatic, endogamous marriage existed among the ancient Arabs, and in time of war martial obligations extended throughout the agnatic side and not as a rule the cognatic. Wellhausen recognized that the word *ʿamm* can mean "paternal uncle" in numerous Semitic languages - Arabic, Syriac, South Arabian, and even Hebrew.[7] But Wellhausen did not view this as the original meaning of the word. The unique original sense of the term was "people," considered as a relationship group. The meaning "paternal uncle" arose later. The Arabic noun *ʿaṣaba* provided an analogy for this development. This term means literally "band," secondarily "agnates." In Arabic, the original meaning of *ʿamm* survived in a verse from the *Ḥamāsa*, the scholiast to ʿUrwa, and in the loose use of the phrases *ibn ʿamm*, *bint ʿamm*, *banū ʿamm* (literally "male cousin," "female cousin," "cousins") to designate persons of quite distant relationship. Here the noun balances the senses "tribe" and "paternal uncle." The subtlety of Wellhausen's understanding must not be lost. He did not argue that the original word "people" carried a necessary connotation of agnatic relationship. Rather, he held that this connotation came to attach to the word historically at a time when patriarchal tribal organization was the rule. Only after a people was an agnatic group did the noun *ʿamm* develop the meaning "paternal uncle."[8]

Wellhausen's treatment won the qualified approval of Otto Procksch,[9] but in 1898 Fritz Hommel insisted on a reversal of Wellhausen's analysis, making "kindred group" an outgrowth of "paternal uncle."[10]

In 1901 Hugo Winckler published one of the most detailed and enigmatic treatments of the word *ʿamm* and its history. Winckler was concerned to account for several bits of information about the word and about the history of the Semites. First, the word has as attested meanings both "paternal uncle" and (in Nabatean) "forefather." But these kinship terms differ from the more common sense "people." Second, the primitive social order of the Semites was polyandrous, a fact Winckler had previously attempted to establish.[11] These data suggested to Winckler that an *ʿamm* was originally a *gens*, a blood fraternity that lived together and did not marry within itself. Each member of the group was also an *ʿamm*; together they shared a wife. In such a situation the father of a child sired by the fraternity would be unknown, and the offspring would not distinguish father from *ʿamm*, with the result that *ʿamm* and forefather could be confused. So, too, the notion would arise that a person's closest relative was his *ʿamm*. Winckler forged ahead, equating "love" with "sexual intercourse." An *ʿamm* is a sex partner in his reconstructed society, and so the word *ʿamm* and the word *wadd/wudd* ("love") became synonyms. Thus Hebrew may denote a tribesman "beloved" *(yādîd)*, and thus the South Arabian gods Wadd and ʿAmm may be equated.[12]

In 1906 Th. Juynboll dedicated a study of the meaning of the word *ʿamm* to Theodor Nöldeke. Unlike Nöldeke, Juynboll inclined to the view that the words "paternal uncle" and "people" are the same. He found Wellhausen's analogy of *ʿaṣaba* to be instructive. But he opposed much of the evidence used by Wellhausen and others to clarify the problem. According to Juynboll, the fluid use of *ʿamm* in expressions like *ibn ʿamm* does not justify the sense "people" for the term *ʿamm*, which always refers to a specific individual, whatever the degree of relationship joining him to the other. One does not say *ibn ʿašīra*, "son of a tribe." Further, Juynboll argued that the scholiast to ʿUrwa, cited by Nöldeke and Wellhausen in support of the primitive meaning "group," had not intended the alleged meaning. Rather, he meant by *ʿamm* a paternal relation. Juynboll allowed as possible the view of Smith and Wellhausen that "people" is the word's primitive signification. Whatever the truth of this assertion, he believed the noun to have had at a remote time the fundamental meaning "a member of the previous generation." This meaning accounts for the Biblical death euphemism "to be gathered to one's *ʿammîm* (i.e., ancestors)," the Genesis Ammonite name etiology, and the Arabic sense "paternal uncle."[13]

L. B. Paton was next to discuss the word. He concluded that *ʿamm* belonged to the stock of Proto-Semitic words and had the meaning "a male relative of the preceding generation." Following Winckler, he assumed that an era of polyandry played a role in the transformation of the noun's signification; in that era "father" and "paternal uncle" were undifferentiated, but thereafter the word could develop the specialized latter sense.[14]

Brenda Seligman's study of Semitic kinship terminology differed in its approach from previous investigations of *ʿamm*. For Seligman, the study of Semitic kinship was an extension of the study of a human group within the Tigre (Ethiopic) language area. She believed that a "classificatory" system of kinship reckoning prevailed among the earliest Semites. Roughly, such a system reckons human relationships in terms of classes rather than in terms of relationship to an individual. Thus, among the Semites the word "father" shows rather consistently a plural which is formally feminine. This allows the inference that "fathers" constituted a class, all those of the father's generation. In a classificatory system of kinship reckoning, a word for the specific relationship "father's brother" should be wanting. Such an individual would belong to the class of men known as the fathers. It was therefore important for Seligman that the absence of a common Semitic term for paternal uncle be demonstrated. She noted that for the Bani Amer, the Ethiopian group about whom she had a specialized knowledge, the word for paternal uncle is *yiba*, "my father," and not a separate word signifying "father's brother." She argued that the word *ʿamm* has only a very general meaning. In Arabic it refers to not only the father's brother, but also the grandfather's brother and other relatives. Outside of Arabic the evidence of personal names cannot be used to demonstrate the term's sense "paternal uncle." In personal names as in South Arabian, *ʿamm* represents a deity.[15]

It was natural for J. Pedersen to discuss the Hebrew word "people" in his epochal *Israel: Its Life and Culture.* He made a special contribution to the word's understanding by calling attention to a number of Arabic words in which collective and singular meanings alternate - *ʾahl* ("tribe," "wife"), *qawm* ("people," "an individual"). The Hebrew noun *ʿam(m)* balances the sense "kinsman" against the meaning "people." Like so many before him, he found the former signification in the idiom "to be gathered to one's *ʿammîm*."[16]

A new period of investigation began in 1928 with Martin Noth's study of Israelite personal names. Noth had been impressed by the theory that a society's inventory of words designating relatives falls into one of two patterns. Some groups possess a vocabulary organized by degree of kinship, while others possess a generationally oriented stock of words. Noth observed that the Semitic languages originally had only terms for generationally oriented relatives; parents ("father," "mother"); children's generation ("brother," "sister"); children's generation viewed from above ("son," "daughter"). There are no common Semitic terms "uncle," "aunt." Noth recognized that in historical times *ʿamm* meant "paternal uncle," but he insisted that this meaning derives from a more general concept "member of the tribe or family." He could point to the analogy of Hebrew *dôd*, which first meant "beloved" and only later "uncle."[17]

Noth's study became the point of departure for one of the most important investigations of the Hebrew noun *ʿam(m)*. Writing for the Procksch Festschrift, Leonhard Rost marshalled evidence pointing to a Proto-Semitic noun meaning "paternal uncle," a meaning which survived in Arabic, Aramaic, and Biblical Hebrew. "People," he argued, is an extension of the fundamental concept "father's brother." He rejected Noth's analysis of the issue, pointing out that the generalized replacement of *ʿam(m)* by *dôd* coupled with the continuing use of the former to denote "people" opposes the originality of "people" as the meaning of *ʿam(m)*. That is, if the word *ʿam(m)* first denoted "people" or "agnate," then its specialized replacement by the word *dôd* only in the sense "uncle" is a curiosity. More than this, Rost pointed out that without *ʿam(m)* Hebrew already had two words for "tribesman," *rēăʿ* and *ʾāḥ*. Although the noun *ʿamm* appears to have had a broad original meaning ("ascendant" or the like), this appearance results from a sociological phenomenon. At the death of an individual's father, his paternal uncle must assume the fatherly role of guardian (Arabic *walīy*). From this "paternal uncle" took on broader connotations.[18]

Studies by E. Dhorme bracketed Rost's essay in the 1930s. Dhorme insisted that originally *ʿamm* designated a close relative; *ʿammîm* constituted what in Latin would be called the *gens*. The grammatically singular noun *ʿam(m)* took the meaning of its plural secondarily and thus signifies "people" in Hebrew.[19]

W. F. Albright set forth views on the word's etymology in *From the Stone Age to Christianity*, where his remarks supersede a number of previous statements about the problem. He consistently resisted the temptation to give the noun a primitive meaning other than the collective sense "clan." His strictly empirical methods supported this. According to Albright, the earliest occurrence of the meaning "paternal uncle" belongs to the eighth century B.C.E. and the South Arabian language group. Biblical texts never offer this meaning, and the Biblical literature is generally older than the literature of South Arabia. Furthermore, an Akkadian tradition understanding *ʿamm* to signify "family" pushes the meaning "clan" still earlier. "Kindred group" was the original meaning of the word.[20]

H. S. Nyberg contributed to the ongoing discussion. He determined that the root meaning of the noun is "ancestor." Because ancestors are believed to participate in the life of their descendants, it is possible for the word "ancestor" to denote his collective descendants. A people is thus collectively the descendants of a single ancestor, a meaning represented by the rare English word sib.[21] In more recent times John Gray has promoted this understanding.[22]

By relying on the sense of the Arabic verb *ʿamma*, G. Ryckmans was able to insist in 1951 that the fundamental aspect of a people is its collateral nature. The Arabic verb means "to be extensive," and Ryckmans imagined an *ʿamm* as a horizontal organism.[23]

E. A. Speiser offered an etymological study of *ʿam(m)*. Working independently, he arrived at conclusions essentially identical with those of Leonhard Rost: the Proto-Semitic noun meant "paternal uncle," a meaning with broad support in the historical Semitic languages.[24] More recently, Richard Deutsch has expressed a similar understanding, making a close paternal relative the original signification of the noun.[25]

The investigation of the meaning of *ʿamm* in personal names has been a specialized aspect of the word's study. We shall give the enormous literature the problem has generated only an abbreviated summary. E. Nestle made early progress in understanding the relevant names when he compared Hebrew personal names like Abiel with corresponding names like ʿAmmiel. In a series of such names the elements *ʾāb* and *ʿam(m)* occupy the same position, and Nestle inferred that *ʿam(m)* can be construed a kinship term. On the basis of Arabic *ʿamm* he assigned the meaning "paternal uncle" to the word.[26] Although not every *ʿamm*-compounded name submits readily to such an analysis, the essential correctness of Nestle's insight has been recognized by subsequent scholarship.[27] Martin Noth's fundamental study of kinship terminology in personal names has brought further assurance of Nestle's results,[28] and while the precise definition "paternal uncle" is not to be recommended generally for Semitic names, it is at least clear that *ʿamm* often expresses a close relationship.

Attention quickly shifted to new issues and new problems. It is evident from a comparison of names like Abimelekh ("father is king" ?) and Elimelekh ("god is king" ?) that a kinship term may alternate with a divine name, whether proper or common noun. That this kind of alternation was general in Semitic names compounded around kinship terminology won widespread recognition at an early date. With the addition of *ʿamm* to the inventory of kinship terms, the problem of the use of the language of relationship in personal names acquired new dimensions. Matters were complicated by Glaser's discovery of a Qatabanian divine name written *ʿm*.[29] Glaser identified the name as a cognate of Arabic *ʿām*, "year," and suggested that the South Arabian god was a solar deity.[30] But prior and subsequent researchers have connected *ʿamm* and the divine name. The occurrence of a "full spelling" *ʿmm* was initially hailed as the proof of the connection, but better evidence comes from the early Arab author Ibn Hishām, who knew of the worship of a god called ʿAmm-anas, and from St. Nilus, who recorded the personal name Ammanes.[31]

Hommel observed that the Qatabanians styled themselves the "children of ʿAmm." This reminded him of the Genesis Ammonite name etiology where the name of the Ammonites is explained by contriving their descent from *ʿammī*. This could be taken quite literally (if not contextually) to mean that the Ammonites, like the Qatabanians, were the children of ʿAmm.[32] This curious Ammonite hypothesis attracted numerous adherents.[33] The close association of a people and its god was well-known. It was logical that the Ammonites should have a god, and it was satisfying that they should share the name of their god. One even noted that Rehoboam, whose name includes the element *ʿam(m)*, had an Ammonite mother. Thanks in part to the writings of C. C. Torrey[34] and especially G. B. Gray,[35] the Ammonite hypothesis was eventually abandoned for lack of real supporting evidence.

Along with the Ammonite hypothesis came the view that the element *ʿamm* is a proper noun in Semitic names even outside South Arabia. This notion was best supported by the fact that in cuneiform texts the name Hammurabi is sometimes written with a preceding divine name determinative.[36] But as Martin Noth observed, the determinative so used governs the entire name and not just the element **ʿamm*; the deity is the apotheosized king.[37] The worship of a god named ʿAmm appears generally to have been restricted to South Arabia.[38]

It is nevertheless appropriate to ask how *ʿamm* substitutes for a divine name, and what is probably the same question, how the word came to be a proper noun. A number of answers have been proposed. François Lenormant connected the word with the preposition *ʿim(m)/ʿam(m)* ("with") and understood the god to be with his devotees.[39] Lagrange interpreted the word as "paternal uncle," a proper metaphorical designation for a protector.[40] Bauer's similar explanation emphasized the protective role of the paternal uncle in Semitic societies.[41] Ditlef Nielsen denied that such metaphorical visions of the deity were possible for primitive man. By defining *ʿamm* as "father," he could argue that primitive men believed themselves to be physical descendants of the god. The father-god is referred to as any of a variety of kinsmen (father, brother, etc.), and this shows that within the divine family the specific ancestor god could assume a variety of stations.[42] E. Dhorme supported this peculiar view.[43] Gray made use of the theory of tribal totems to explain the concept of the kinsman deity. Men are descended from the tribal totem, and can look upon the totem-god as a close relative.[44] Praetorius and Winckler argued that the kinsman god was actually a kinsman - a deified ancestor.[45] Noth succeeded in reversing objections to the metaphorical understanding of kinship terminology by insisting that in the era when this terminology evolved men could relate to gods only in the framework of the gods' being relatives participating in the life of the tribe.[46] This is the view which has attracted the widest support. Most recently, however, Hermann Vorländer has challenged Noth's view by arguing that in historical times the requisite tribal sentiment cannot be thought in evidence. He imagines kinship terminology to reflect the personal relationship between god and named individual.[47] Noth's point, of course, was that tribal consciousness was prominent in those *pre*historic times when kinship names originated.

* * *

Directly through the study of the word *ʿam(m)* or indirectly through the investigation of related topics a mixture of enlightenment and confusion has been produced. Broadly, three options for understanding the genesis of the word's meanings are visible. A primitive term of relationship may have grown into a collective; a primitive collective may have acquired the meaning of a kinship term; or separate singular and collective nouns may have coexisted from the outset. The evidence for choosing among these options has not been interpreted with unanimity and requires careful attention. One striking fact does emerge, that the evidence can support any of these theses. Singular and collective meanings enjoy equally wide distribution among the Semitic languages. Part of our task will be to attempt to circumvent this deadlock.

The chapters that follow offer a new survey of the comparative Semitic evidence, a detailed investigation of the Biblical material, and a synthesizing conclusion that seeks to render account of the Israelite idea of a people against its Semitic and especially Syro-Palestinian background.

Chapter II

COMPARATIVE SEMITIC EVIDENCE

The historical background to the use of the Biblical noun *ʿam(m)* is provided by a comparison of the use this noun's cognates in other Semitic languages. That this is the case results not from a notion that the immediate linguistic antecedents of the word are at hand in any one or all of the Semitic tongues, but rather from the fact that when taken together the Semitic languages provide an indirect witness to historical events in the life of a word. If certain meanings of the word occur commonly in the Semitic languages, then it is not unreasonable to assume that these meanings were inherited from that nebulous era called Proto-Semitic. We may thus hope to learn something of the Hebrew word's semantic heritage from studying other languages. The use to which comparative information may legitimately be put needs to be specified. It would be improper to allow the supposed inherited meanings of the word to dictate the noun's meanings or nuances in Hebrew, for in Hebrew as in any language the word may have lost old meanings, preserved rare senses, or developed new ones. Each of the Semitic languages must be allowed to reveal the noun's meaning independently of the evidence of other languages, although comparative evidence may sometimes function to indicate a range of possibilities in defining a term which in context is ambiguous. But when the evidence has been gathered, it becomes possible to recover a picture of how the meaning(s) of the word developed. That which is common and that which is distinctive - a context for comparison and contrast of the Biblical notion of a people - come into view. Furthermore, something of the full history of the noun becomes evident. Now part of the evidence for sketching the early semantic history of *ʿam(m)* must come from Hebrew itself. Since that evidence is set forth in the chapters that follow this section, our immediate objective will be restricted. We hope to indicate that the singular and collective referents of the noun can be so closely related that it need not be doubted that a single noun is extant and not a pair of distinct words. We wish also to provide the necessary data for sketching the developments of the noun's meanings and locating the Biblical "people" in a broad context.

Simplicity dictates that the comparative Semitic evidence be arranged by language; the order in which languages will be examined is approximately chronological.

* * * * *

Ancient West Semitic
(Eblaite and Amorite)

If Mitchell Dahood is correct, the earliest occurrence of the noun *ʿam(m)* is to be found in the recently excavated texts from Tell Mardikh. A published administrative text refers to a palace at Ebla by the name *é-AM.*[1] G. Pettinato edited the text but was unable to decide the meaning of this name. He assumed the element *é* to be the common Sumerian noun "house," "palace." With *AM* interpreted as the Sumerian noun "bull," the palace name becomes "Bull Palace." But taken as a Semitic word, *AM* could be related to a root attested in the Akkadian noun *amtu* ("slave girl") and denote "service" or the like.[2] Dahood responds to these ideas by suggesting that *AM* is cognate with *ʿam(m)* "people." *é-AM* becomes the "people's palace."[3] It might be noted that the Old Testament refers to a "people's palace," *bêt haʿam*. Among several accounts of the fall of Jerusalem, that given at Jer 39:8 mentions the burning of this edifice. But we are not in a position to infer much from the existence of this Hebrew noun phrase, and still less in a position to connect it in any way with *é-AM*. The interpretation of the Eblaite palace name as "people's palace" must be set aside as mere speculation until enough Eblaite materials have been published to show that the newly found Semitic language had a noun **ʿam(m)* and that it spelled the noun *am*.

The word *ʿam(m)* is held by consensus to be foreign to Akkadian.[4] Its occurrences in Akkadian texts are restricted both in number and in date - the word is confined to the Old Babylonian and subsequent periods, a happenstance which

interpreted "who provides justice for the people."[19] As a collective noun, *ʿamm* was not always used with reference to kindred groups.

* * * *

Ugaritic

It is difficult to evaluate the position of *ʿam(m)* in Ugaritic. A preposition *ʿm* occurs frequently and has the sense "with, towards, like." This may be presumed to reflect an ancient noun "group."[20] Possible occurrences of a noun *ʿm* are discussed below. The existence of such a noun seems to be assured by the occurrence of *ʿm* in personal names. At an early date Charles Virolleaud collected and studied the pertinent names,[21] and his effort is now supplemented and superseded by Frauke Grøndahl's systematic treatment of the onomastic corpus.[22] The spellings of syllabic cuneiform texts indicate the vocalization *ʿamm*. There is no Ugaritic evidence showing the meaning of this word, and the neutral translation "kinsman" must be preferred to Grøndahl's "paternal uncle."[23] An Ugaritic noun *ḫāl* seems also to have existed,[24] and this may point to distinctions based on the difference between paternal and maternal relationship.

There is no doubt that in the alphabetic cuneiform texts *ʿm* most often represents the preposition and not a noun of the same spelling. In the recent literature *ʿm* has been interpreted as a noun in only a handful of instances. These require careful consideration.

In accordance with his theory that the noun can mean "wisdom," Mitchell Dahood divides and translates CTA 4.4.41-43 (cf. 3.5.38-39):

tḥmk il ḥkm
ḥkmt ʿm ʿlm
ḥyt ḥẓt tḥmk
Your message, El, is wise,
Your wisdom is eternal sagacity,
Life felicitous your message.[25]

Dietrich, Loretz, and Sanmartín have correctly opposed Dahood's suggestion.[26] The lines should be translated:

Your decree, El, is wise.

You are wise unto eternity.

A fortunate life is your decree.

ʿm is a preposition and not a noun meaning "sagacity."

In the context of the search for a god to rule in place of Baal, a certain *Ydʿ Ylḥn* is proposed to stand in the storm god's place. CTA 6.1.50-51 contains El's response to the proposal:

dq anm lyrẓ ʿm bʿl

lyʿdb mrḥ ʿm bn dgn ktmsm

Aistleitner understood both occurrences of *ʿm* to reflect a noun "tribe" and the passage to mean:

The one who is weak in powers, he will not subdue Baal's tribe;

He will not use the staff of the tribe of Dagan's son in authority.[27]

Most commentators have interpreted *ʿm* here as the preposition. This is correct, but errors in the stichometric analysis of the passage hinder its interpretation as a whole. Dietrich and Loretz divide:

dq anm lyrẓ

ʿm bʿl lyʿdb mrḥ

ʿm bn dgn ktmsm

This yields the translation:

The weakling cannot run,

before Baal he cannot wield the spear,

before Dagan's son he is on his knees.[28]

Like J. de Moor,[29] they have connected *ktmsm* and Akkadian *kitmusu*. The same incorrect stichometry brings Dennis Pardee to the translation:

One meager of strength cannot run,

like Baal cannot handle the spear,

like Ben-Dagan, one who lacks beauty.[30]

Pardee's "one who lacks beauty" follows proposals made by Gaster and Dahood,[31] who divide *ktmsm* into two words *kt msm*. *kt* is derived from a root $\sqrt{\text{ktt}}$ presumed to have passed through a semasiological development identical to that experienced by the root $\sqrt{\text{dqq}}$; both have as a primary meaning "to crush," by extension "thin, lacking." *msm* belongs to the root √wsm, well attested in derivatives signifying beauty.

The stichometry of the text is easily determined once its parallelism is permitted to speak for itself. The expression *ʿm bʿl* balances *ʿm bn dgn*, while *lyrẓ* parallels *lyʿdb mrḥ*. The passage may be divided:

dq anm lyrẓ ʿm bʿl

lyʿdb mrḥ ʿm bn dgn ktmsm

Despite proposed alternatives,[32] *dq anm* should be taken to mean "one lacking strength." The sense of *ktmsm* is still obscure. Gray leaves it untranslated.[33] Driver divides it into a particle and two words, *k tm sm* "for what is right is accomplished."[34] Ginsberg rendered "Glory Crown."[35] Caquot and Sznycer read *k.msm*, attach *msm* to Akkadian *asāmu*, and translate "as it suits."[36] There is, in short, no lack of alternatives for the understanding of this line, but also no certainty in interpretation. We may translate the passage, leaving *ktmsm* unexplained:

A weakling - he cannot run like Baal.

He cannot handle spear like Dagan's son - a *ktmsm*.

The word *ʿm* is the preposition which, as Moshe Held has shown, can signify "like."[37]

H. J. van Dijk finds a noun at PRU 5.63.9-12 in a letter from a certain Shipiṭbaal:

ʿbdk.b

lwsnd

[*w*?] *bṣr*

ʿm[.] *mlk*

Following and correcting an interpretation set forth by M. Astour,[38] van Dijk would translate, "Your servant in Lawasanda fortified the *fortress* of the king."[39] He justifies the meaning "fortress" by assuming a verbal root √ʿmm signifying "to be strong." The assumption is incorrect, as will be seen in connection with Hebrew *ʿam(m)*. Dietrich, Loretz, and Sanmartín have attempted to refute van Dijk's proposal by taking *bṣr* as a preposition governing a place name, "in *ṣr*."[40] Pardee follows this analysis, but the result is an awkward interpretation: "Your servants are (?) in *lwsnd* and in *ṣr* with the king."[41] The missive comes from an individual, and the plural "servants" is therefore unmotivated. What necessitates the plural is the belief that *bṣr* indicates a place, and since a single servant cannot have been in two places at once, a plural is devised. The problem lies in the break before the letters *bṣr*. Virolleaud restored the letter *w*, but his hand copy does not show sufficient space for the character. The graph *m* is to be restored, and the line taken as a noun *mbṣr*, "citadel." We translate, "Your servant is in Lawansandiya the citadel, in the presence of the king." *lwsnd* is to be equated with the independent city state Lawasant/diya in eastern Cilicia.[42]

In the midst of one of the most controversial Ugaritic passages, we read (CTA 17.2.16-17 // CTA 17.1.27-28 and CTA 17.1.45-46):

nṣb skn iliby
bqdš ztr ʿmy

The subject of these lines and those that follow is the ideal son, whose characteristic activities are itemized through line 23. His works are regularly indicated by active participles, the first of which is thought to be *nṣb* in line 16. The poetic line is widely understood to mean, "One who erects the stele of my ancestral god."[43]

A correct appreciation of *ilib* is vital to the accurate interpretation of the text. Following various proposals, the vocable may denote either a deified ancestor or a familial numen. The word is a compound of *il* and *ib*, the latter having been shown to be a phonetic mutation of *ab*, "father."[44] Etymologically, therefore, either understanding of the term is possible. But etymology is at best an approximate approach to lexicography. Contextual indications must be given priority in determining the precise sense of any word. Apart from its use in this context, *ilib* never demonstrably denotes a family numen or an ancestral god. In offering lists it designates a god whose place is alongside El, Baal, and the other great gods of Ugarit. Now in a cosmopolitan city like Ugarit it is difficult to imagine that *ilib* was thought the special god of a single family, or the apotheosized ancestor of a given sib. In CTA 17, *ilib* is mentioned before either El or Baal, and this priority matches the order of deities given in Ugarit's canonical god lists: *ilib*, later *il* and *bʿl*.[45] In our view, *ilib* is a high god, and the activity portrayed by *nṣb skn iliby* a votive act on behalf of Danel. We translate, "One who erects the stele of my *ilib*."

The continuing context supports this interpretation. The following line immediately refers to the sanctuary, by which is meant the place of worship for Danel's *ilib*. This is all that can be said with certainty about the line. The assumption that *ilib* refers to an ancestor god has led to definitions of *ʿm* as clan,[46] clan god,[47] ancestor,[48] race.[49] Tsevat equates *ztr* and Hittite *sittar* ("sun disk").[50] Pope ties this word to Akkadian *zateru* ("thyme") and assumes a denominative verb "to drop thyme."[51] W. F. Albright connects *ztr* and the word *zitr* of Amorite personal names, suggesting a relationship between *ztr* and the common verbal root √str ("to cover, veil").[52] We cannot resolve the issue. It suffices to judge as probable an interpretation of *ʿmy* as a preposition meaning "on my behalf."

The beginning of RS 24.272 (*Ugaritica* vol.5, text 6) reads:

kymġy adn
ilm rbm ʿm dtn
wyšal mṯpṭ yld

The text's editor Charles Virolleaud understood this to mean:

When the lord
of the great gods comes to *ʿm dtn* (the people of *dtn*),
then he asks the judgment of the infant.[53]

The majority of subsequent translators have seen in *ʿm* the preposition and not "people." This view may be correct, but it is difficult to suppress reservations about it. In Ugaritic there are no other instances of the construction *mġy ʿm*. When the verb signifies "to come to" it governs an accusative or the preposition *l*. Furthermore, there is a striking similarity between the phrase *ʿm dtn* and the personal name Ammiditana. Lipiński may have been right in translating the Amorite name "headman of Ditanu."[54] Would the lord of the great gods have gone to Ditanu? Not knowing the identity of the lord of the great gods makes it impossible to answer this question. There is much doubt about the significance of this text, and consequently much doubt about the meaning of *ʿm*. We suspect the word to be a noun, meaning either "people" or "head of the family," but the matter remains in doubt.

The one text in which we believe it most likely that the noun *ʿm* occurs is CTA 4.7.51-52:

ʿn gpn wugr
bn ġlmt ʿmmym
bn ẓlmt rmt prʿt

The text is reconstituted by comparing CTA 8.6-9. Stichometry and interpretation are obscure. The entire passage has been characterized as posing insurmountable problems of interpretation.[55] The meaning of the first line is clear: "Behold, Gapnu and Ugaru!" What follows offers endless possibilities of interpretation, but whatever the sense of the entire passage, the parallelism of *ʿmmym* (or perhaps *ʿmm ym*) and *prʿt* is noteworthy. *ʿam(m)* and *pĕrāʿôt* are a Biblical word pair, at Judg 5:2:

biprōăʿ pĕrāʿôt bĕyiśrāʾēl
bĕhitnaddēb ʿām
When captains come forth in Israel,
when the militia volunteers....[56]

On the basis of the Hebrew parallel, it appears likely that Ugaritic had a noun *ʿm* (plural *ʿmm* or plural nisba *ʿmmym*). The Hebrew parallel implies a meaning in the sphere of military affairs.

To summarize: Ugaritic seems to have had a singular noun *ʿamm* referring to a kinsman and a collective term.

* * * * *

Phoenician, Punic, and Neo-Punic

A noun *ʿm* occurs commonly in the Phoenician group. In personal names it designates a kinsman. Frank L. Benz has studied the onomastic evidence. Comparative Semitic data inspire his defining *ʿm* as "paternal uncle, kinsman, folk."[57] In the Phoenician group, "paternal uncle" has no support, and in personal names "kinsman" is to be preferred. Among previous studies of the Phoenician noun, the most extensive is that of M. Sznycer, who has restricted his essay to a quest for the meaning "popular assembly."[58] In large measure his study amplifies N. Sloush's earlier attempt to find in both Hebrew and Phoenician *ʿm* the *terminus technicus* for this institution.[59] There can be no a priori objection to the idea that *ʿm* has this meaning, but the proposal rests on slender evidence (see below, passim).

The word "people" best translates Phoenician *ʿm*. Consanguinity is not in view, unless much be read into the Mactar Inscription. A glance at proposed translations of this important Neo-Punic text reveals the degree of uncertainty plaguing the interpretation of its opening lines,[60] but there is general agreement that the pronominal referent of "*its* people inhabiting the land (*ʿmʾ yšb ʾdmt*)" is the *mzrḥ*-institution mentioned in line 1.[61] The text assigns the *mzrḥ* to *drt*, probably not meaning "families,"[62] but perhaps "cella."[63] To give *drt* the sense "families" would bring *ʿm* loosely into the domain of kinship terminology. Clermont-Ganneau's reconstruction of Neo-Punic society (*mzrḥ* as *ordo*, *ʿm* as *populus*) in connection with this inscription has not attracted support. A bilingual inscription from Leptis Magna equates *ʿm* and *populus*, *ʾdrʾ* and *ordo* (KAI 126:7; cf. 119:4),[64] but from this it is safe to infer only the use of *ʿm* for the population of a city.

Phoenician *ʿm* often refers to the population of a city,[65] presumably because of the prominence of the city in Phoenician civilization. At Leptis Magna, Tiberius Claudius Quirina Sestius humbly styled himself *mḥb bnʾ ʿm*, "lover of the citizenry." This friend of the common man also called himself *mšlk bnʾ ʿm*, for which the conjectural rendering "savior of the populace" is plausible.[66] The word *ʿm* means "citizens" already in its earliest occurrence at Karatepe. Azitawadda's good will towards the citizens of Azitawaddiya is expressed in the wish, "May this *people* who dwell therein (i.e., in Azitawaddiya) possess herds and flocks, fullness and wine (KAI 26.A.3.7-9)." Here it is clear that an *ʿm* is not necessarily an urban group. By qualifying the people as living in Azitawaddiya the inscription implies that a "people" might be found in another setting. This, of course, could be another town. But Azitawadda's wish for the people is bucolic. We look to the country for herds and flocks, fullness (produce) and wine. The country (*ʾdmt*) shelters Mactar's "people," and it is the abode of that people whose favor the Byblian king Yeḥawmilk (fifth-fourth century) sought: "May the lady, Mistress of Byblos give him grace in the eyes of the people of this land (KAI 10:9-10)." In this inscription "people of the land" has no technical meaning.

Whether living in town or country, a people is capable of concerted effort. Sometimes its activity is religious. In Phoenician the phrase "the people of god x" does not occur, unless *kl ʿm šmš*[... in a fourth-third century papyrus means "all of Shamash's people."[67] This is unlikely. In another text Sznycer has corrected the reading *ʿm bt mlqrt* ("congregation of the Melqart temple") to read *ʿm rš mlqrt* ("population of Rosh Melqart"),[68] thereby eliminating an instance of the use of *ʿm* for a religious community. But it is possible that the noun *ʿmt* is so used: *ʾš bʿmt ʾš ʿštrt*, "a man from the congregation (?) of Astarte's men."[69] When a people restore and dedicate a temple, a popular votive act is more easily assumed than the enterprise of a political assembly.[70] The people of Cadiz *(ʿm ʾgdr)* styled themselves "slaves" of their god Molkastart:

lʾdn lʿzz mlkʿštrt wlʿbdm lʿm ʾgdr

For the almighty lord Molkastart, and for his (?) slaves, the people of Cadiz.[71]

Special importance attaches to a series of Carthaginian inscriptions recording dedications *lmyʿms ʿm qrtḥdšt*, for which the abbreviation *lmyʿms* occurs.[72] The editors of CIS rendered *lmyʿms "ex decreto,"* a meaning approved by M. Sznycer in his attempt to show that the formula reports an action of the city assembly. Février has taken the word *myʿms* as *"bons poids,"* the expression signifying "with full payment for the enfranchisement."[73] But the noun should be understood to represent Maioumas, the name of a religious festival.[74] The dedication formula means "for the Maioumas festival of the people of Carthage," and shows that a "people" may participate in a common cult.

A people can share a system of reckoning dates. Sznycer infers from the formula *bšt* x *lʿm* y, "in the year x of the era (literally, of the people) of y," a sense "assembly" for *ʿm*, arguing that the eras in question date to the beginning of local democratic institutions.[75] But the formula *št* x *lʾš* y ("year x of the men of y") must be compared.[76] In the second formula the word *ʾš* occupies the place of *ʿm* and this suggests that *ʿm* is used in the date formulae more as an incidental than as a technical term. The formulae probably indicate no more than that the local population follows its own system of reckoning dates.

Close inspection of the expression *ʾš bʿm* x ("a man from the people of x") leads to the same conclusion. Here Sznycer prefers the technical meaning "popular assembly"[77] for *ʿm*, but the expression *ʾš* x also occurs.[78] This shows the prepositional phrase *bʿm* to be dispensable.

A Carthaginian tetradrachma preserves a rare meaning of *ʿm* in the expression *ʿm mḥnt*. This is the complete legend of the coin, and as its editor observed, it must mean "army of the camp."[79]

* * * * *

Ammonite and Moabite

Apart from personal names, the word **ʿm* has yet to appear in the limited Ammonite literature. Fulco has shown the reading *bn ʿm*... in the Amman Theater Inscription to be incorrect. The correct reading is *bn ʿš*....[80] There is thus no basis in Ammonite for interpreting the evidence of personal names. The noun *ʿm* occurs in the Moabite stone, where it is used to denote the population of a city (KAI 181.11,24).[81] The important Deir ʿAlla plaster text has a word *ʿm*. First thought to mean "paternal uncle,"[82] it now seems in the light of Caquot and Lemaire's reconstruction of the fragments to be a preposition.[83]

* * * * *

Aramaic

The noun *ʿam(m)* occurs frequently in the dialects of Aramaic, as does the preposition *ʿam(m)/ʿim(m)*.[84] The noun rarely occurs in personal names.[85] In literary contexts it has both a singular and a collective referent.

The singular referent varies. Two Nabataean inscriptions document the sense "great grandfather." The texts merit citation:

dnʾ bytʾ dy bnh rwḥw br mlkw br ʾklbw br rwḥw lʾlt ʾlhthm dy bṣlḥd wdy nṣb rwḥw br qṣyw ʿm rwḥw etc. CIS 2:182.1-2

The editors of CIS originally understood the text to mean:

> This is the temple which Ruḥu, son of Maliku, son of Aklabu, son of Ruḥu erected for their goddess Allat, which is in Ṣalḥad, which Ruḥu the son of Qaṣiu set up *with* Ruḥu.[86]

Clermont-Ganneau quickly observed that the text can be compared with another Nabataean text for the purpose of defining *ʿm*. The second text comes from Petra and reads, according to CIS:

> *dnh ṣlmʾ dy ʿbdt ʾlhʾ dy ʿbdw bny ḥnynw br ḥtyšw br pṭmwn...*
> *d.lw.r wtrʾ ʾlh ḥtyšw dy bṣhwt pṭmwn ʿmhm* etc. CIS 2:354. 1-2

The crucial parts of these lines mean:

> This is the statue of the god Obodat which the sons of Ḥunaynu, son of Ḥaṭishu, son of Paṭmon erected...the god of Ḥaṭishu...of Paṭmon their *great grandfather*.

Clermont-Ganneau reconstructed family trees for both inscriptions to indicate that *ʿm* means "great grandfather":

Qaṣiu	X
Ruḥu — *ʿmh* ↓	Paṭmon — *ʿmhm* ↓
Aklabu	Ḥaṭishu
Maliku	Ḥunaynu
Ruḥu	sons of Ḥunaynu[87]

The definition "great grandfather" rightly gained rapid acceptance. It is unfortunate that Nabataean preserves no other occurrence of *ʿm* with a singular referent. Littmann believed to have found "paternal uncle in the short inscription *mʿnʾlhy wʿmh*, "Maʿanallāhī and his paternal uncle." But CIS and most recently Rainer Degen read *nʿmh* for *wʿmh*, thus "Maʿanallāhī (son of) Naʿamah."[88] The paucity of evidence makes it hard to affirm or deny that as a noun with a singular referent Nabataean *ʿm* means precisely and only "great grandfather." Nabataean diglossia poses a second problem. The possibility of contamination from an Arabic dialect cannot be excluded, and we shall see that one Arabic dialect may have used *ʿamm* for "grandfather."

There is indirect evidence of a second singular meaning of the noun. The word *ʿammĕtâ* occurs in Syriac with the meaning "paternal aunt." Th. Nöldeke and C. Brockelmann have provided textual references for the word. Jacob of Edessa (seventh century) used it in a list of female relatives - mother, daughter, sister, sister's daughter, brother's daughter, *ʿammĕtâ*, *ʿammĕtâ*'s daughter, maternal aunt *(ḥālĕtâ)*, maternal aunt's daughter, paternal uncle's daughter, maternal uncle's daughter.[89] From the final entries in the list it is clear that *ʿammĕtâ* is "paternal aunt." Syriac uses *dādâ* for "paternal uncle," but the existence of *ʿammĕtâ* may point to a time when *ʿam(m)* was used in the meaning later given to *dādâ*. *ʿammĕtâ* occurs already in a collection of Rabbula's directives (fifth century),[90] later in the biography of Simeon Stylites,[91] and in general often enough and, if the Rabbula text is authentic, early enough to dispel fears of Arabic influence. Medieval Syriac lexicography knew *ʿammĕtâ* to signify "paternal aunt,"[92] and one pre-modern lexicographer even knew of *ʿammâ* used for "paternal uncle."[93] But for the latter we know no textual proof, and the influence of Arabic must be suspected.[94]

The Syriac evidence clarifies the use of *ʿammĕtâ* as a personal name in Palmyrene.[95] "Paternal aunt" is a satisfactory rendering of the name. For the Nabataean personal name *ʿmw*,[96] "paternal uncle" is suitable, although in both cases Arabic forms may be preserved. Since Syriac gives the strongest evidence for "paternal uncle" in Aramaic, the Aramaic purity of these personal names and of the Arabic loanwords (*ʿamu* and *ʿama*) in Mandaic is not a vital concern.[97] What meaning to give the very early name *ʿmʾ* may be left undecided.[98]

It is possible that a third singular meaning of *ʿam(m)* is preserved in a Sefire inscription, KAI 224. We may compare two passages from the text:

> *whn mn ḥd ʾḥy ʾw mn ḥd by*[10]*t ʾby ʾw mn ḥd bny ʾw mn ḥd ngdy ʾw mn ḥd pqdy ʾw mn ḥd ʿmyʾ zy bydy ʾw mn ḥd šnʾy* etc. KAI 224.9-10
>
> And if anyone of my brothers, or anyone of my father's house, or anyone of my sons, or anyone of my commanders, or anyone of my officers, or anyone of *ʿmyʾ* in my control, or anyone of my enemies, etc.
>
> *whn ḥd ʾḥy hʾ ʾw ḥd ʿbdy ʾw ḥd pqdy ʾw ḥd ʿmʾ zy bydy* etc. KAI 224.13

> And if he is one of my brothers, or one of my servants, or one of my commanders, or one of *ʿmʾ* in my control, etc.[99]

A glance at the two passages reveals that *ʿmyʾ* and *ʿmʾ* have the same meaning. *ʿmyʾ* is a difficult form. The expected plural of *ʿam(m)* in Aramaic is *ʿamĕmîn*, etc. and so the plural of *ʿmʾ* should be written *ʿmmyʾ*.[100] We nevertheless concur in the verdict that Sefire *ʿmyʾ* is formally plural.[101] What does the word mean and how does it relate to its singular *ʿmʾ*? For the latter question a simple answer is at hand. We may take *ʿmʾ* as simultaneously a collective and a noun of unity. That is, *ʿmʾ* is both a group and an individual from the group. The plural *ʿmyʾ* denotes the individuals who together make up the collective. This is further evidence for the belief that a single noun *ʿam(m)* is to be postulated and not separate words with singular and collective referents. To determine the meaning of Sefire *ʿmʾ/ʿmyʾ* we must turn to the study of the Aramaic collective *ʿam(m)*.

As a collective, the noun ordinarily means "people." But the Sefire inscriptions tantalize the reader with the possibility of giving "people" a more precise interpretation. If the nouns *ngd* and *pqd* in the passage under discussion designate military officers, then a martial connotation might be inferred. A military sense cannot be proved for *ngd* and *pqd*, although for both nouns it seems likely.[102] But we may be able to distinguish the use of *ʿmʾ* here from a later occurrence of the noun in the same inscription. The phrasing "the 'people' in my control" contrasts noticeably with the simple expression "my people." The latter occurs in this context:

> *ltšlḥ lšn bbyty wbny bny wbny ʾḥy wbny ʿqry wbny ʿmy* KAI 224.21
>
> Do not publish sedition in my house, among my grandchildren, my nephews, my descendants, or the children of my "people."

The succession of degrees of relationship makes "my people" seem to be an ultimate kinship group, and we are tempted to translate "my tribe." The continuation of the passage supports this:

> *wtʾmr lhm qtlw mrʾ* [22] *km whwy ḥlph*
>
> ...saying, "Kill your lord and be his successor."

The previous list is evidently intended to embrace all who might aspire to the throne, and this probably indicates a royal house, family, and tribe. Be that as it may, it does not seem excessive to infer a difference in the meaning of *ʿam(m)* here when compared to the previous passage. How to define that difference is not certain. We might contrast "my tribe" with "the nation subject to me," but perhaps also "my tribe" with "my army."

Elsewhere in Sefire inscriptions the noun refers to the populations of Arpad and Bet Agusi; it designates the subject nation of Mati'el and his nobles.[103] The general concept "people" fits such occurrences. Other Old and Imperial Aramaic texts are not very informative. The size of the literature is small and the number of the noun's occurrences correspondingly slight. The plural *ʿmmʾ* occurs in the Elephantine fragments of the tale of Ahiqar; both occurrences mean "peoples," and neither permits a more nuanced appreciation. In the ancient inscription from Tell Halaf, no certain interpretation can be given to *bʿm*[.... (KAI 231).[104]

Frequently in the later dialects of Aramaic the noun means "nation." This meaning suits a number of Biblical Aramaic contexts (e.g., Dan 2:44). On one occasion *ʿam(m)* refers to the population of the province "Across the River (i.e., the Euphrates; Ezra 7:25)." Thereby is denoted a mixed group by no means identical with a single nation or ethnic population. The common phrase "all *peoples*, nations, and tongues" means "absolutely everyone" and reveals nothing important about the noun (Dan 3:7.31, etc.). The interesting noun phrase "the people of the holy ones of the Most High (*ʿam qaddîšê ʿelyônîn*; Dan 7:27)" appears to participate in late Hebrew traditions of the holy people.

The word occurs in a number of Nabataean royal epithets: "Philopatris" *(rḥm ʿmh)*; "he who gave life to and saved his people" *(dy ʾḥyy wšyzb ʿmh)*.[105] With Clermont-Ganneau we may compare a Palmyrene bilingual which equates *rḥymy mdythwn* and *philopatrides*.[106] The similarity between *rḥm ʿmh* and *rḥymy mdythwn* provides an indication of the political overtones of the former. Much later in Aramaic, Mandaic uses the expression *bit ama* to mean "synagogue," as though *ʿam(m)* had come to mean "congregation."[107]

A systematic survey of the later Aramaic dialects cannot be undertaken here. Translational literature beginning at Qumran uses the word with the general meaning "people," as do other Aramaic literatures. A close study of these texts might yield further insights, but here we must be content to register the meaning "people" without seeking special nuances.

* * * * *

Epigraphic South Arabian

A word written *ʿm* occurs often in Epigraphic South Arabian in a variety of meanings. The preposition *ʿm* (also *ʿmn* and in *bʿm*) is common, means "with, against, etc.," and witnesses a primitive noun signifying "group."[108] *bʿm* developed a wide range of meanings: along with; for; against; from; because of; under; on.[109] A verb *ʿmm* (h-stem) occurs and signifies "to cause to spread out."[110] It is used of water, and has the cognate *tʿmm* ("current"),[111] In the expression *tʿmm btʿbr*, "announcement of delimitation,"[112] this noun shows an underlying sense "to spread, make general." The concept "generality" seems therefore to be fundamental to the verb and its nominal congener. The evidence for such a fundamental meaning may be expanded by the inclusion of the noun *ʿmt*, which means "people" but may, like its Arabic cognate *ʿāmma*, derive directly from a verb "to be general."[113]

The noun *ʿm* occurs in South Arabian personal names.[114] Greek transcription establishes the vocalization *ʿamm*.[115] Its meaning in names is subject to a peculiar confusion caused by the existence of a Qatabanian god named ʿAmm; it is possible that the theophoric element *ʿamm* is a proper noun. The obvious criterion for deciding the signification of a particular personal name is geographic. Wherever ʿAmm was worshipped, *ʿamm*-compounded names may be assumed to carry the proper noun.

ʿAmm was a lunar god, as Fritz Hommel[116] and Hugo Winckler[117] argued at an early date. ʿAmm occupies in the pantheon of Qataban the position of the other South Arabian moon gods Wadd (Min.), Sin (Hadr.), and Ilmaqah (Sab.) in their respective pantheons. His epithets prove the lunar character:

ry'n / ry'm, "he who waxes"; *ry'n wšḥrm*, "he who waxes and rises." The Qatabanians are called the children of 'Amm.[118] It can only be assumed that the divine name originated in the use of kinship terminology for gods.

In ESA *'amm* commonly means "paternal uncle":

> *[m'd]krb.mlk.ḥḍrmt.sqny.'ṯtr.ḏqbḏn.mḫp²dhn ḫrp.mḫpd.bny.'ms.šhhrm.'ln* etc. RÉS 2775.1-2
>
> Ma'adkarib, king of Haḍramaut, dedicated to 'Athtar dhu Qabḍin this tower Kharf which his *paternal uncle* Shahharum 'Allan had built.

Its plural *''mm* must mean "paternal uncles" (RÉS 3017.2 [Min.]; RÉS 4018.2 [Sab.]), but is used with a wider meaning and seems sometimes to denote all agnates of the preceding generation except linear ascendants. The exception of linear ascendants is motivated by recurring lists of kinsmen in which "fathers" (or "forefathers") and "paternal uncles" are kept separate:

> *w'ḫhsm.wbhnsm.w'bhsm.w''mmsm* RÉS 2771.8 (Min.)
>
> and their brothers and their sons and their fathers and their *paternal uncles*....

The breadth of signification is indicated by the joining of "paternal uncles" to "fathers" when the latter includes several generations of predecessors (CIH 37.6). Rhodokanakis contrasts *''mm* and "sons" as the older and younger generations.[119]

In ESA *'amm* can also mean "people." A "people" evidently may be a sib. An inscription from Haḍramaut recording a building operation reports, "He obeyed *Hyš''l*, *Dws(m)*, and their *paternal family* among Haḍramaut's families."[120] Rhodokanakis' definition of *'amm* as *väterliche Verwandtschaft* suits the context. The same meaning suits the expression *'l'lt 'ms bmḥrmhs*, "his clan gods in his (Osarapis') sanctuary."[121] *Clan* may be inferred for *'amm* at RÉS 2980, where Thawab'il chronicles votive building for the god Nakraḥ[122] made possible by donations of Thawab'il's "people" *('amm)*:

> *bn.pr' ⁵ kwn.'m.ṯwb'l* RÉS 2980.4-5 (Min.)
>
> from the first fruits provided by the *clan* of Thawab'il....

To judge from RÉS 2814 (Min.), a "people" may also be larger in scope than a single family. This text reports an agricultural project of the "people" of Ma'in, by which is meant its population:

kbny.ṯʿdsm.ʿm.mʿn RÉS 2814.3 (Min.)

in order that the population of Maʿin build up their irrigation zone (?)....[123]

A Sabaean text from Bi'r Hima offers an instructive use of the word. Jamme has translated the relevant passage:

They went hand in hand with their king Yusuf 'As'ar Yaṯ'ar, when they conquered Qalisan and killed the Habašites in Zafar and overcame the fighters of 'Ašʿaran and of Rakban and of Farasan and of Muḫwan and also when they overcame the fighters and the military units of Nagran and strengthened the sand dunes Maddaban, and they gathered his [the king's] people [*wgmʿ.ʿmhw*]; and so, he could organize them into forces....[124]

The martial context suggests that "people" carries the signification "muster," as in other Semitic languages. We may note in this context a related text published earlier by G. Ryckmans, which reads:

kz'n.qrnm.kʿm.mlkn.bmḫwn.bn.ḥbšt

lorsque marcha une armée contre le roi à Muḫwan, d'Abyssins....[125]

Ryckmans noted that *kʿm* might be taken as a temporal particle and verb from the root √ʿwm, and Joan Kendrick has followed this idea, positing a verb "to march."[126] We may propose with all due caution finding instead a verb *ʿamma*, "to levy troops."

Briefly, in ESA *ʿamm* has both a singular and a collective referent. The collective can but need not have a connotation of kinship. It can also denote a militia.

* * * * *

North Arabic

Lihyanite, Thamudic, and Safaitic inscriptions make up the corpus of pre-Classical North Arabic. Thanks to the labors of A. van den Branden and, on behalf of the Académie des Inscriptions et Belles-Lettres, G. Ryckmans, convenient text editions for Thamudic and Safaitic now exist.[127] The character of all these inscriptions is such that precise, detailed interpretation of points of interest is difficult. In Thamudic inscriptions the word *ʿm* is common only in personal names. In Safaitic, it occurs fairly often both in personal names (*ʿmhm*, *ʿm*, *kʿmh, ʿmrm, ʾbʿm,* etc.) and as an independent noun. Its meaning is controversial. Littmann believed it to signify "grandfather," the noun *dd* to have the meaning "paternal uncle." This belief is founded on two inscriptions, L.P. 403 and L.P. 325. The former reads:

lġṯ bn ġṯ bn mṭr bn ʾnʿm wdmy lh ddh ʿm

We follow Ryckmans in understanding this to mean, "For Ġawth, son of Ġawth, son of Muṭar, son of Anʿam; and he sketched his *dd* ʿAmm." The second text presents:

lmṭr bn ʿm bn mṭr bn ʾnʿm bn qdm

For Muṭar, son of ʿAmm, son of Muṭar, son of Anʿam, son of Qadam.

Overlapping genealogies suggest this family tree:

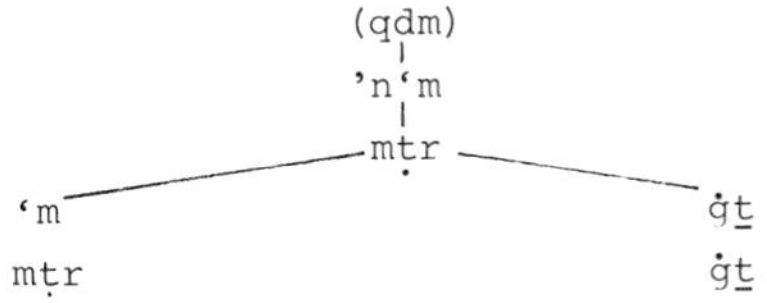

ʿAmm appears to be the paternal uncle of Ġawth, son of Ġawth, and he is called Ġawth's *dd*. *dd* therefore seems to mean "paternal uncle" and since the nouns *dd* and *ʿm* can occur together in a single inscripton designating degrees of kinship,[128] an alternate meaning for *ʿm* must be found, the most likely being "(paternal) grandfather."[129]

Ryckmans has opposed this analysis. He insists that *dd* means "maternal grandfather," and that in L.P. 403 it should be assumed that Ġawth son of Ġawth had not only a paternal uncle named ʿAmm, but also a maternal grandfather by that name. It is the latter to whom the inscription refers as *dd*. The argument is not compelling, even though Ryckmans has shown elsewhere that *ʿmt* cannot mean "(paternal) grandmother." A Safaitic inscription published by G. L. Harding reads, in part:

wʿl ms ʿmth wʿl ʿns ʿmth wʿl fḫmt ʿmth wʿl ʾsdt ʿmth[130]

The author of the inscription has listed four individuals *(ms, ʿns, fḫmt, ʾsdt)* as his *ʿmt*, and since a single person cannot have had four paternal grandmothers but can have had numerous paternal aunts, Ryckmans is probably correct in using this text to demonstrate that *ʿmt* means "paternal aunt" in Safaitic.[131] But the analogy of Syriac, where *ʿammĕtâ* means "paternal aunt," *dādâ* "paternal uncle" cautions against concluding that *ʿm* means "paternal uncle" in Safaitic. It seems best to assume a complex situation in which either *ʿm* or *dd* could be used with reference to "paternal uncle" or "paternal grandfather."

W. G. Oxtoby has published an inscription in which he believes *ʿm* to have a collective referent:

lʿdn bn znt bn ʿkk wġnm mʿm kbr

By ʿIddān b. Zīnat b. ʿAkkāk. And he took plunder from a large populace.[132]

By Oxtoby's reckoning, this would be the only Safaitic occurrence of the collective. In an isolated inscription of this length it is difficult to be certain of an interpretation.

It may be concluded that in pre-Classical North Arabic *ʿamm* was widely used to denote a degree of kinship. The noun's use as a collective remains insecurely attested.

*

* *

The richness of the Classical Arabic lexicon makes this body of material a burdensome as well as a potentially rewarding field for inquiry. For the early period the best sources of lexical information are Qur'an, Hadith, poetry, and the lexicographers. As it happens, the Qur'an gives little information about the meanings of *ʿamm*,[133] but elsewhere the root $\sqrt{\text{ʿmm}}$ is well attested. Indeed, it is so well attested that a representative survey of the cognates of *ʿamm* is not feasible here. Lane has gathered the lexical stock in a convenient form.[134] A perusal of the material leaves little doubt about the interrelation of words and their meanings. The verb *ʿamma* means "to encompass, be general, total," and ideas of completeness or perfection (including full growth) abound in this family of words. The *ʿimāma* is a turban, and a certain turban vocabulary can also be found. Rather than pursue the networks of related meanings, we wish simply to note that "to be general" is a sense tied to the collective noun *ʿamm*. The feminine active participle of the verb *ʿamma (ʿāmma)* means "generality of people," and thus is a synonym of *ʿamm*, "people." The independent existence of the idea of generality in both Arabic and Epigraphic South Arabian is a strong argument for the antiquity of the association of $\sqrt{\text{ʿmm}}$ and such ideas. Yet it seems unlikely that the noun *ʿamm* derives from a primitive verb "to be general." The reasons for this will be discussed in the conclusion of our study.

The Arabic noun *ʿamm* (pl. *ʾaʿmām, ʾaʿimma, ʾaʿumm, ʿumūm, ʿumūma, ʾaʿmumūna*) is ordinarily not a collective. It means "paternal uncle," used both for natural and adoptive paternal uncles.[135] Much has been said about the importance of the paternal uncle in Arab society, and the topic is too large to be investigated here.[136] Suffice it to remark that the bonds between and individual and his *ʿamm* have been among the strongest familial ties, and are reified in the uncle's place as both guardian and heir to the orphaned nephew or niece. In defense of the Qur'an's incorrect identification of Azar as Abraham's father (VI:74), it was reported at an early date that the beduin often use the word "father" when referring to the paternal uncle,[137] a fact which underscores the importance of the paternal roles played by the uncle. The favored position of the *ʿamm* must explain the word's later semantic developments yielding a term of respect and, in recent Arabic, the sense "father-in-law."[138]

A person's uncle or uncles are frequently invoked as the avatar of his genetic excellence. Ibn al-ʾAʿrābī recited this unattributed verse:

waman yaftaqir fī qawmihī yaḥmadu lġinā
waʾin kāna fīhim mājida lʿammi muḫwilā

A man poor among his people will praise wealth,
Even if among them his paternal and maternal uncle be honorable.[139]

Reference to a man's paternal and maternal uncles encompasses his entire genetic pool. Al-Jarīr praised the caliph Hishām ibn ʿAbd-al-Malik:

laka lmutaḫayyarāni ʾaban waḫālan
faʾakrim bilḫuʾūlati walʿumūmi

You have two that are choice - father and maternal uncle.
O what noble maternal and paternal uncles![140]

It is obvious that the literal referent of such a verse - the brothers of Hishām's father - is eclipsed by the figural sense, the entire agnatic stock. In effect, "paternal uncles" comprise everyone in the agnatic group in whom a defect would imply an inherited flaw in the caliph. So common was the use of paternal and maternal uncles as a sign of excellence that they could be used to betoken a particular, nongenetic quality. A poet said of the tongue-tied son of an eloquent preacher:

ʾabūka muʿimmun fī lkalāmi wamuḫwilun

Your father has noble paternal uncles and maternal uncles in speech.[141]

An important testimony, although difficult to evaluate, is brought by a verse attributed to an individual of the tribe Ḍabba ibn ’Udd:

ʾabanī tamīmin ʾinnanī ʾana ʿammukum
lā tuḥramunna naṣīḥata lʾaʿmāmi

O tribe Tamīm, I am certainly your "paternal uncle."
You will not be deprived of the counsel of uncles.[142]

The anonymous poet goes on to give his advice. The tribe Tamīm reckoned descent from Murr, son of ’Udd. The relationship between the poet and his audience may be represented in this fashion:

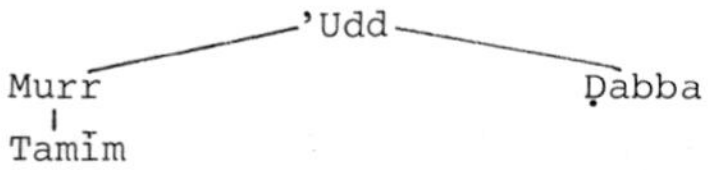

With respect to Tamīm, the *tribe* Ḍabba is a paternal uncle. But a descendant of Ḍabba cannot be said to be a paternal uncle of the sons of Tamīm except by way of metaphor. We thus encounter a dilemma. Is the poet's use of *ʿamm* to be discounted as a metaphor, or valorized as a witness to the rare meaning "tribesman, agnate"?

The former view is the more likely, but this does not resolve this issue, and we may refer to another verse, ascribed to a certain Ray‘an:

ʾiḏā kunta ʿammīyan fakun faqʿa qarqarin
waʾillā fakun ʾin šiʾta ʾayra ḥimāri
famā dāru ʿammīyin bidāri ḫufāratin
walā ʿaqdu ʿammīyin biʿaqdi jiwāri[143]

The poem seems to contrast the rival claims made on an individual by a client and a member of his own tribe. For this reason we prefer to translate *ʿammī* "tribesman" rather than "commoner" or "plebeian":

If you are a tribesman, then be a mushroom on soft dirt,
And if not, then be, if you wish, a donkey's penis.
A tribesman's house is not the same as that of a client,
Nor is a tribesman's bond the same as that of a guest.

At issue is whether to be related by *ʿamm-* bonds has the same force of obligation as to be a guest. The poet declares that it doesn't matter whether an individual is a tribesman or not, *nothing* matches the obligations of patronage. It would appear that *ʿammī* signifies "tribesman," one of the *banū ʿamm*. From this it may be deduced that *ʿamm* could signify "agnate, tribesman," or "agnatic group, tribe," or both.

Much attention has been given to the looseness with which *ibn ʿamm*, *bint ʿamm*, and *banū ʿamm* are used. These combinations mean respectively "male cousin," "female cousin," and "cousins," and given their restriction to agnatic relatives are used with the same range of meanings as the English terms. The poet al-Ḥuṣayn ibn al-Ḥumām is credited with these lines:

jazā llāhu ʾafnāʾa lʿašīrati kullahā
bidārati mawḍūʿin ʿuqūqan wamaʾṯamā
banī ʿamminā lʾadnayna minhum waraḥṭanā
fazārata ʾiḏ rāmat binā lḥarbu muʿẓamā[144]

May God recompense all the rabble of the tribe
In Darat Mawdu' for recalcitrance and sin,
Our cousins, our closest relatives among them, our band,
Fazāra, when fierce war rose against us.

Charles Lyall, the poem's editor, has reconstructed the genealogy linking al-Ḥuṣayn and Fazāra:

Dhubyan
Fazāra — Saʿd
'Auf
Murra
Sahm
Wāʾila
Ḥarām
Maṣāb
Rabīʿa
al-Ḥumām
al-Ḥuṣayn

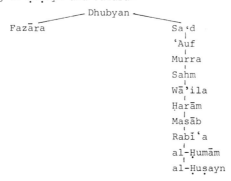

The relationship between Fazāra and the poet was hardly close, yet Fazāra's descendants are al-Ḥuṣayn's "cousins," a degree of relationship requiring concordant military activity.

The relationship between groups tends to eclipse the personal relationship in the combination *banū ʿamm*. A poet named al-Muthallam announced, concerning the group ʾAshjāʿ:

lafafnā lbuyūta bilbuyūti faʾaṣbaḥū
banī ʿamminā man yarmihim yarminā maʿā[145]

We enclosed their tents with ours so that they became
our cousins, whoever shoots at them shoots at us as well.

A poem of the Hudhali poet Maʿqil ibn Ḫuwaylid ibn Wathīla is to be compared. Speaking on behalf of the client group Liḥyān for his own group the Banū Sahm, the poet said:

faʾammā banū liḥyāna faʿlam biʾannahum
banū ʿamminā man yarmihim yarminā maʿā[146]

As for the Banū Liḥyān, know that they are
our cousins, whoever shoots at them shoots at us as well.

Cousins may be clients, and what is important is the extension of social obligations to encompass the potentially unrelated *banū ʿamm*.

It is tempting to assert that such a use of *banū ʿamm* arose from a confusion of "sons of the tribe." The correctness of such an idea cannot be proved, although it can be shown that "cousins" itself means "tribe." Al-Ḥuṭay'a makes this statement:

faqāla lʾajrabāni wanaḥnu ḥayyun
banū ʿammin tajammaʿnā ṣalāḥā[147]

And the "two scabs" (Dhubyān and ʿAbs) have said,
"And we are a tribe,
'cousins,' we join together for benefit."

Al-Farazdaq calls the Quraysh:

banī ʿammi rrasūli warahṭa ʿamrin[148]

Cousins of the Prophet and tribe of ʿAmr

Banū ʿamm are simply the tribe, an agnatic group for whom no particular paternal uncle can be identified.

"Cousins" are important in time of war. For *banū ʿamm* to fight among themselves is improper:

banī ʿamminā lā tabʿaṯū lḥarba baynanā
karaddi rajīʿi rrafḍi warmū ʾilā ssilmi[149]

O our cousins! Do not seek war between us
Like dung left by return (of flocks), aim (rather) at peace.

Among cousins, says Maymūn al-ʾAʿshā, war is an outrage. "Cousins" comes to signify those who fight together, as in the Hudhali poem:

wanaḥnu ladayhi naḍribu lqawma ʾinnanā
banū ʿammin ʾūlānā ʾiḏāmā nunākiru[150]

And we strike the (hostile) tribe before him, we are surely
"Cousins," the most forward of our troop, whenever we contend.

The theory, of course, is that martial obligations follow blood lines. In practice, blood ties can extend to replicate military alliances, as we saw in the case of the Banū Sahm and Banū Liḥyān.

A special problem not to be treated here is the preferential *bint ʿamm* marriage pattern. Ideally, a man enjoys a provileged right to the hand in marriage of his father's brother's daughter. The causes, extent, and significance of this marriage pattern are debated.[151]

There is evidence of an Arabic word *ʿamm* meaning "group, people" or the like. The preposition *maʿa* provides an indirect testimony, since it can be assumed a metathesis of the common Semitic preposition *ʿm*. A preposition *ʿm* is in fact attested in pre-Classical North Arabic.[152] The noun *ʿamam* gives evidence of a more direct sort. It means "gathering, group," and is cognate with *ʿamm*. A variant of *ʿamm* seems to stand behind *ʿimmīya*. This word occurs in several closely related traditions:

> In an incident which is *ʿimmīya* or which involves feelings of tribal solidarity (*ʿaṣabīya*), whoever kills another with a rock, a whip, or a stick is subject to the bloodwit appropriate to an accidental killing. But whoever kills with intention is subject to retaliation.[153]

> Anyone who fights beneath a banner which is *ʿimmīya* claiming membership in a group or being enraged for the cause

of the group and who is killed has died in the manner of the era of ignorance.[154]

Students of these and similar traditions were divided in their assessment of the meaning of *ʿimmīya*. Some thought the word to signify an *obscure* claim to relationship, thereby linking the word to the root √ʿmy from which words for obscurity derive.[155] The same root yields words for error, and so *ʿimmīya* was sometimes thought to mean errant action. The word was also, apparently correctly, taken to denote party feeling, partisanship. A verse ascribed to ar-Rāʿī contains the word:

kamā yaḏūdu ʾaḫū lʿimmīyati nnājidu

In the manner in which the brave partisan offers defense.[156]

The noun base of the word appears to be *ʿimm*, to which a feminine nisba suffix has been appended. It is likely that *ʿimm* refers to a group, whether or not it carried the connotation of kinship. It is unfortunate that we cannot determine whether the word bears military overtones.

The noun *ʿamm* itself occurs as a collective. The number of its occurrences with this meaning is restricted, and some of the evidence is disputed. Nöldeke cites a verse quoted in as-Suyūṭī's *Muzhir*:

ya ʿāmira bna mālikin yā ʿammā
ʾafnayta ʿamman wajabarta ʿammā[157]

The commentary to the verse indicates that the first *ʿamm* refers to the poet's paternal uncle, the second to a group. Ibn Durayd quotes the same verse (substituting *ʾaʿašta* for *jabarta*), ascribes it to the pre-Islamic/Islamic poet Labīd, and gives the same explanation of the two *ʿamm*s. In Labīd's diwan the further variant *ʾahlakta* for *ʾafnayta* occurs.[158] The variants do not affect the sense of the poem, which is:

O ʿĀmir ibn Mālik, O my paternal uncle!
You destroyed a paternal uncle but saved a tribe.

To this testimony Nöldeke adds the scholiast to ʿUrwa. ʿUrwa's poem reads:

jazā llāhu ḫayran kullamā ḏukira smuhū
ʾabā mālikin ʾin ḏālika lḥayyu ʾaṣʿadū
wazawwada ḫayran mālikan ʾinna mālikan
lahū riddatun fīnā ʾiḏi lqawmu zuhhadu[159]

May God recompense, whenever his name be mentioned, good
To Abū Mālik, when that tribe goes forward,
And may he provision Mālik with good. Mālik certainly has a refuge among us since the people are kind (?)

The scholiast noted a variant, reading *ʿamm* for *qawm*, and defining *ʿamm* as *banū ʿamm*. If the scholiast understood the word correctly, then his witness confirms what must be suspected, that *ʿamm* signified "tribe, cousins."

The collective seems to occur in another verse by Labīd:

lammā daʿānī ʿāmirun liʾasubbahum
ʾabaytu waʾin kāna bnu ʿaysāʾa ẓālimā
likaymā yakūna ssandarīyu nadīdatī
waʾajʿala ʾaqwāman ʿumūman ʿamāʿima[160]

When ʿĀmir bade me curse them
I declined, although ibn ʿAysāʾ is evil,
So that as-Sandarī might not be my equal,
And so that I not make peoples into tribes, scattered bands.

As-Sandarī, referred to as ibn ʿAysāʾ, was a rival poet. Two words merit comment. The term *ʿumūm* is the plural of *ʿamm* and probably means "tribes" in this context. More difficult to evaluate is the word *ʿamāʿim*, which medieval lexicographers understood to be another plural of *ʿamm*. Its form presupposes a singular noun with the consonantal structure *ʿmʿm*. Now two conclusions are invited by such a singular. First, it can safely be said that in the history of the word there once existed a biliteral *ʿm*. In our conclusion we shall return to the implications of this fact. The second inference is less secure but still plausible. A biliteral of the form *ʿmʿm* can be assumed to represent the derivative of an onomatopoetic verb. Analogies are provided by the Arabic verbs *ġamġama*, "to make the sound *ġam*," and *jamjama*, "to make the sound *jam*." *Ġam* is the noise made by cattle.[161] The difference in pronunciation between *ġam* and *ʿam* is not great, and if the latter is uttered with a full guttural ʿ, the sound of sheep or goats can be heard. It thus may be that **ʿamʿama* is to be reconstructed, from which a noun meaning "flock" is to be derived. That *ʿamāʿim* was held to stand in close relationship with *ʿamm* suggests what we believe to be true, that the flock gave its name to the human band.

Theoretically, primitive biliterals may leave traces distributed among different triliteral roots. An early biliteral word for flock, *ʿm*, seems to have done precisely this. A "choice" animal from the flock is an *ʿīma*.[162] A man deprived of flocks is called *ʿaymān (ʿaym + ān)*.[163] *ʿāmiya* is referred to an animal from the flock without milk, while the verb *ʿāma (yaʿīmu)* means "to thirst for milk," a situation which the lexica correctly noted results from the loss of flocks.[164] There is thus a small vocabulary preserved in Arabic which seems to harken to early developments of a primitive noun meaning "flock."

To summarize: Arabic uses *ʿamm* with both a singular and a collective referent. The singular referent is "paternal uncle," a meaning which shades into wider ideas - agnate, tribesman, etc. The collective sense is rare. "Tribe" or "sib" seems to capture the basic collective meaning. A special plural used of collective *ʿamm* probably reflects a primitive biliteral which may well have represented the sound of caprine beasts.

* * * * *

With the inclusion of the Arabic evidence the comparative Semitic data is completed. Before turning to *ʿam(m)* in the Bible, the implications of the Semitic materials must be briefly noted. The word appears to have had a rather complex prehistory, and when it emerges in the historical Semitic languages it seems to carry an elaborate range of connotations. The noun can, but need not, imply the bonds of kinship. It may carry a recollection of its pastoral origins. Particularly interesting is the extent to which the noun is linked to martial contexts. In virtually all of the Semitic languages in which the noun occurs it seems that it can designate a group with military obligations, whether those obligations be conceived as an encumbrance of kinship, as in Arabic, or whether the group itself is a militia, as in Phoenician. It is thus the case that the Hebrew noun may have inherited complex nuances, and therefore probably also the case that a facile key to understanding the Biblical idea of a people is not to be had.

Chapter III

BIBLICAL CONSPECTUS

Articles by Leonhard Rost and E. A. Speiser provide a background to the study of the Biblical word *ʿam(m)*. The place of their respective researches in the discussion of the noun's etymology has already been noted. Their contributions to the special problem of the Hebrew word may now be reviewed.

Both writers insist on a sharp differentiation of Hebrew *ʿam(m)* and *gôy*, Rost as a counterbalance to the Septuagint practice of promiscuously translating both words by *ethnos* and *laos*,[1] Speiser in opposition to Köhler-Baumgartner's notion that *ʿam(m)* and *gôy* are not to be strongly distinguished.[2] They are in substantial agreement that the root of the difference between the nouns is etymological. The word *ʿam(m)* derives from and retains the connotations of a kinship term, and consequently tends to denote a consanguineous human association. In contrast, the word *gôy* is preferentially employed with reference to a kingdom.

Rost and Speiser diverge in their methods of showing the difference between *ʿam(m)* and *gôy*. Rost parades texts in which he believes the plural *ʿammîm* means "relatives." These include, in addition to passages with the idioms *hēʾāsēp ʾel-ʿammāyw* and *hikkārēt mēʿammāyw*, Lev 21:1ff. and Lev 21:14. The former purposes a restriction on the range of decedent individuals for whom a priest may become defiled. Those for whom a priest may become defiled are various close relatives; those for whom he *might* become defiled are the larger group of his *ʿammîm*. Rost cannot imagine that a priest might participate in funerary acts for someone outside his clan, and so he insists that *ʿammîm* here must refer to the circle of paternal uncles. This is not a very compelling interpretation of the text, since the assumption that a priest would not participate in funerary rites for a mere friend or neighbor is unwarranted. An equally doubtful assumption supports Rost's interpretation of the later passage in Lev 21, a passage limiting those whom an anointed high priest may marry to persons from among his *ʿammîm*. Rost contends that this regulation was intended for the protection of priestly family purity, and hence *ʿammîm* are again the circle of paternal uncles. But Rost himself offers a telling objection to this assumption:

> Die spätere Entwicklung des jüdischen Rechts lässt freilich dem Hohenpriester gleich den andern Priestern die Möglichkeit, Frauen aus Levitenkreisen und der Zahl der vollbürtigen Israeliten zu wählen....[3]

It seems best in both places in Lev 21 to understand *ʿammîm* to denote members of the same cultic community *(ʿam[m])*.

Speiser's attempt to distinguish *ʿam(m)* from *gôy* begins with a denial of the pertinence of passages in which the nouns are interchangeably used. These, he writes, "...are relatively late and due in the main to stylistic variation or poetic parallelism."[4] One wonders how seriously these criteria are to be taken. That poetic parallelism can obscure differences between approximate synonyms is clear. By the criterion of poetic parallelism, the numbers seventy-seven and eighty-eight were "equal" at Ugarit:

> He lays with her seventy-seven times,
> She draws him up eighty-eight.[5]

Stylistic variation, however, ought not to be too readily dismissed. If a writer can freely exchange the nouns *ʿam(m)* and *gôy* without impairing his intended meaning, then what significance can be attached to the supposed difference between the words? This is a problem not to be isolated from the question of a text's date. The interchangeability of *ʿam(m)* and *gôy* tends to characterize later Israelite literature, but if "relatively late" is defined with some precision, then we are left with little to study. The nouns appear to be rather freely substituted for one another in Ezekiel (Ezek 21:17; 25:7) and Jeremiah (Jer 2:11; 6:22; 10:2-3; 12:16-17). Neither the Deuteronomistic Historian (Deut 4:6; Josh 3:16-17) nor the Priestly Writer (Gen 28:3; 35:11) differentiates the two clearly. If it is true that by the time of the Exile the differences between *ʿam(m)* and *gôy* had largely disappeared, then a great portion of the Biblical literature must be classified as irrelevant to Speiser's thesis. One consequence of taking the chronological question seriously will be a dismissal of Speiser's examples of the purposeful juxtaposition of *ʿam(m)* and *gôy*. The passages he offers to illustrate their nuanced use (Exod 33:13; Deut 4:6) come from writers whose lateness challenges the assumption that they appreciated the fine shades separating the two nouns. A second consequence of an earnest regard for a text's date will be a skeptical approach to those idioms in which Speiser (and Rost) finds traces of the original kindred connotation of *ʿam(m) (hēʾāsēp ʾel-ʿammāyw, hikkārēt mēʿammāyw)*. These are uniformly transmitted in P and Ezekiel. Yet here is an instance in which literary dating may be misleading. A late writer is capable of transmitting early material or of using idioms that fossilize early meanings. This consideration mandates an attentive treatment of stereotypical expressions housing the noun *ʿam(m)*, a task largely neglected by both Speiser and Rost.

Having set aside evidence which suggests the interchangeability of *ʿam(m)* and *gôy*, Speiser catalogues data indicating that which distinguishes the nouns. In broad terms, that association called *ʿam(m)* has a natural cohesiveness, while a *gôy* is held together from without, as for example by a political structure like the kingdom. Lying behind this difference is the kinship connotation of the noun *ʿam(m)*, a connotation attested in personal names, idiomatic uses of *ʿammîm*, and at Gen 34:16. "In contrast," he observes, "there is not the least hint of personal ties under the concept *gôy*."[6] This is an assertion which is subverted by the very example he cites as its proof - the Genesis table of nations. While it is true that the *gôyîm* of Gen 10 may be classified territorially and linguistically, it is nonetheless also true that the very structure of the table of *gôyîm* is genealogical and at a superficial level at least assumes that nations can be defined in terms of family trees. Conversely, there is ample evidence of a tendency to associate an *ʿam(m)* with a characteristic language and with a territory (Num 21:34; Isa 33:24; Ezek 36:20; Jonah 1:8).

In addition to their attempts to draw a clear distinction between the nouns *ʿam(m)* and *gôy*, both Speiser and Rost offer specialized insights into the noun *ʿam(m)*. Speiser contrasts

Eastern and Western Semitic social structures, a topic that raises questions too large to be considered here. Rost's special contribution is his insistence that in ancient Israel the noun *ʿam(m)* tends to denote only adult males exercising rights and performing duties of citizenship. This is an inference drawn on the one hand from Israel's patriarchal, genealogical organization - a structuring of society in which relationship is reckoned through male lines - and on the other hand from the frequent use of *ʿam(m)* to designate the Israelite militia. For Rost, the noun designates collectively those who function in the manly world of arts and affairs, and in ancient Israel that world encompassed social, political, and religious spheres. His rather precise definition of *ʿam(m)* merits reproduction:

> *ʿam* (bezeichnet) die Mannschaft eines Volkes als Zusammenfassung der verheirateten, auf eigener Scholle sitzenden Vollbürger mit dem Recht zur Dienstleistung im Heerbann, zur Teilnahme an der Rechtssprechung und zur Ausübung des Kultes.[7]

Rost's and Speiser's works have been widely influential,[8] although considerable controversy still surrounds Rost's restriction of *ʿam(m)* to the male members of society. Vogt has shown that for post-Exilic Israel the noun cannot be assumed to exclude women,[9] while A. R. Hulst balks at seeing even the meaning "militia" as an instance in which Biblical writers understood *ʿam(m)* to be restricted to men. For Hulst, the existence of the collocation *ʿam milḥāmâ* suffices to show that the noun was not self-evidently the designation of a population's male component; the necessity of qualifying the militia as the war *ʿam(m)* suggests to him that *ʿam(m)* did not imply a restriction to male individuals.[10] At the same time there have been writers who support Rost's thesis. In his study of the expression *ʿam hāʾāreṣ*, E. Würthwein affirmed the restriction,[11] while Gerhard Wallis' sensitive interpretation of Deut 27:15-26 has isolated at least one pericope in which it is appropriate to infer that the noun *ʿam(m)* designates men and not women.[12] But on balance, Rost's thesis seems doubtful. In the Bible, Kemosh's people are his sons and daughters (Num 21:29). Ruth can declare Naomi's people to be her own (Ruth 1:16), showing that both women considered themselves to be accounted within a people. The narrative of Judg 4 certifies that even warfare was not a sphere from which women were automatically excluded. To multiply examples will serve no purpose; in the end the meaning of *ʿam(m)* and the evaluation of the scope of individuals to whom it refers must be determined exegetically on a passage-by-passage basis. But a few examples suffice to warn against making any a priori assumption bearing on the gender of those to whom the noun refers. Apart from this point of controversy, it would be correct to state that the conclusions reached by Rost and Speiser represent the consensus of scholarly opinion on the meaning and nuances of Biblical *ʿam(m)*. It is widely held that the noun tends to denote a consanguineous human association.

No such consensus has greated the researches of Mitchell Dahood. Dahood postulates the existence of a verbal root √ʿmm etymologically related to the root √ʿmq and semantically its equivalent.[13] Both roots, he argues, mean "to be strong, wise." Upon this foundation are laid an assortment of personal names and occurrences of words formed from the root √ʿmm proposed - on one occasion with the disclaimer "not all the examples are fully convincing" - as the reflexes of the root.[14] Dahood's student H. J. van Dijk has joined Dahood in the hunt for evidence of the new √ʿmm. He derives the meaning "city" from the concept "strength" and thereby expands the list of occurrences of a noun *ʿam(m)* derived from the congener of √ʿmq.[15]

Whether it is appropriate to affirm the etymological connection between √ʿmm and √ʿmq is a question to itself. It should be remarked that considerable doubt has been cast on the theoretical justification for such a procedure.[16] The theoretical question has no decisive bearing on Dahood's suggestion, since Dahood's lexicographical method is primarily contextual rather than etymological: any contextually apposite meaning can be assigned to a word. The potential chaos engendered by such a method places a heavy burden on its practitioners to prove unequivocally the correctness of each lexical proposition. In the case of the new *ʿam(m)*, it cannot be said that Dahood and his students have satisfied this requirement. That the meaning "the Strong One" suits uses of the noun in personal names is hardly surprising since the word is a theophoric element in such names. The meaning "the Strong One" will also suit names compounded with *'āb* and *'āḥ*, but this is no argument for reappraising the meanings "father" and "brother." Van Dijk's discovery that *'am(m)* means "city" is made possible only by the fact that the noun can be referred to the population of a city. Among all the texts adduced by Dahood and van Dijk in support of their interpretation of *'am(m)*, only two merit serious attention. A verbal, apparent cognate of *'am(m)* occurs at Ezek 28:3:

hinnēh ḥākām 'attâ middāni'ēl
kol-sātûm lō' 'ămāmûkā

Text and translation are difficult. As it stands, MT construes *kol-sātûm* ("every secret") as a collective, grammatically plural. Dahood translates, "Look, you are wiser than Daniel, and no secret is too deep for you."[17] But it is preferable to associate the verb **'āmam* with the root √ ġmm (Arabic "to be obscure") and render "no secret is too obscure for you."[18] The second text is Job 12:2:

'omnām kî 'attem-'ām
we'immākem tāmût ḥokmâ
Truly you are a people,
and with you wisdom will die.

As J. A. Davies has noted, the troubles bedeviling this verse are not eased by Dahood's interpretation of *'am(m)* to mean "the Strong One." Davies has properly resisted this and other scholarly efforts to comprehend the logic of Job's retort.[19] In fact, the difficulty of Job 12:2 probably will not be solved by lexicographical or grammatical advance. It appears more likely that some familiarity with a lost popular saying is required for the understanding of the sense of Job's statement, a saying giving some meaning to the verse's image of a "people" with whom wisdom dies. In fine, neither here nor elsewhere does *'am(m)* mean "the Strong One, the Wise One."

Anyone seeking to understand the meaning of the noun *'am(m)* in the Israelite literature confronts complicated issues. It stands to reason that in the course of a millennium of use the noun's meanings and nuances were subject to change, but to sense and to document semantic developments is often quite difficult. Throughout the Biblical period Israel knew itself to be a "people," yet with the passing of time its social and political fabric evolved. Does this evolution trace the semantic evolution of the noun "people"? It is possible that it does, but equally possible that Israel's self-understanding as a people went unaffected by the course of its social history. To disentangle the evidence of substantive semantic changes in the noun from that of accidental shifts in its referent is an imposing task. In the past it has been customary to situate the Biblical evidence in a semantic continuum deduced from comparative Semitic data; "paternal uncle" or "kinsman" and "people" typically provided the poles of the axis, with the historical evolution of the noun's meaning being assumed to flow from one pole in the direction of the other. Attested meanings of *ʿam(m)* may then be plotted along the axis of historical development and classified as relatively primitive or advanced. Such a procedure must be eschewed altogether. There are in the first place meanings of Biblical *ʿam(m)* which cannot be fitted to an axis defined by the poles "kinsman" and "people." More importantly, there is no warrant in the Biblical evidence for regarding "kinsman" and "people" as polar opposites, separated by an historical development. In the Bible, "kinsman" and "people" exist side by side, from the beginning to the end of the Biblical period. This suggests what is in fact the case, that the singular and collective meanings expressed by the noun developed together. Our task is to recover that development.

There is no shortage of Biblical evidence bearing on the problem. Indeed, the noun occurs so frequently that procedural controls are needed to guide its study. An overview of the material is essential. Yet any overview is liable to the whim of the researcher, who may consciously or unconsciously select data for presentation in order to indicate a conclusion he has already reached. We hope to offset this danger by coupling our introductory overview with a close investigation of some of the characteristic formulae and noun phrases in which the word occurs. If our understanding of the noun's semantic development is correct, then the study of these formulae and expressions ought to reveal traces of the semantic evolution of *ʿam(m)* in the form of historical contextualization, the reinterpretation of traditional material in the light of changed historical or linguistic circumstances.

The noun *ʿam(m)* has two plural formations, *ʿammîm* and *ʿămāmîm*. In Biblical Hebrew the former is more common. The different forms are not semantically distinguished. Both are used with reference to individuals and collectives, viz. "tribesmen" (Gen 25:8; or "soldiers": Judg 5:14), "peoples" (Josh 4:24; Neh 9:22). The noun has no assured verbal cognates. However, the preposition *ʿim* ("with"),[20] the noun **ʿummâ* ("juxtaposition"), and the noun *ʿāmît* ("neighbor," see below) are etymologically and semantically related to the noun. The noun itself is used with both a singular and a collective sense. Temporal priority can be assigned to neither on the basis of the Biblical evidence alone.

The use of *ʿam(m)* to designate an individual is relatively restricted, being most common in the idioms *hēʾāsēp ʾel-ʿammāyw* and *hikkārēt mēʿammāyw*, to be studied separately. It has become fashionable to assume that the noun, predicated of an individual, means "kinsman." But it appears that the noun thus used refers to an individual of the collective *ʿam(m)*, the sense of the singular being dependent on the pertinent meaning of the collective (see below). To be sure, the meaning "kinsman" is sometimes the appropriate construction of *ʿam(m)*. This is best illustrated by the Yahwist's Ammonite name etiology (Gen 19:30-38). The story is well known. On successive nights, Lot's two daughters lay with their drunken father. They conceived and bore sons named Moab and Ben Ammi. The point of the story is that Israel's neighbors Moab and Ammon were the issue of incestuous relations and that their names signified as much. Moab is to be understood as *mēʾāb*, "from father," while Ammon is intended to evoke *ben ʿammî*, "son of my kinsman." The precise logic of the latter has proven elusive.[21] The etymological connection of *ben ʿammî* and Ammon must be sought in the ambiguity of the suffix *-î*, which can represent either a pronominal suffix or a nisba termination. Interpreted as the latter, *ʿammî* means approximately what Ammon must mean, *ʿamm*-ish. On this level, the connection between *ben ʿammî* and Ammon is straightforward. But the possibility of interpreting Ammon to mean *ʿammî* opens the door to Israel's satirical presentation of Ammon's genesis, for *ʿammî* can be made to signify "my kinsman," thus highlighting the "fact" that the Ammonites are the ultimate fruit of a shameful union. It is important to recognize that the interpretation of *ʿam(m)* in this passage to signify anything more precise than "kinsman" is unwarranted. The strength of the Ammonite name etiology is that it imposes on Ammon, "characterized by kindred relationship," the aspect of ironic understatement.

Here at least *ʿam(m)* can be construed to signify "kinsman," and it is possible to add to this example the evidence of Israelite personal names compounded with *ʿam(m)*.[22] In such names the noun often stands for a deity who, in all probability, was metaphorically conceived as a "kinsman" of the named individual. It is of course proper to inquire precisely what "kinsman" means, but the Biblical evidence falls short of supplying an answer to this question. There is no evidence to support the notion that the word means "paternal uncle." That it signifies "agnate" is a fair assumption, although "agnate" has special meaning only in opposition to "cognate," a word not attested in Biblical Hebrew. The sense "kinsman" is best understood by conceiving the kinsman as a member of a kinship group. By subordinating kinsman to kinship *group* it is possible to comprehend uses of the noun for which kinship ties are not much in evidence. Such uses may be attributed to the variable composition of the group.

This alternative use of *ʿam(m)* is illustrated in the Book of the Covenant, where Yahweh commands:

> If you lend money to my *ʿam(m)*, the poor person with you, do not be like a usurer to him. Do not reckon interest against him. Exod 22:24

That the referent of Yahweh's *ʿam(m)* is an individual appears to be correct.[23] The noun clearly does not mean "paternal uncle" or "ancestor." What it refers to is an individual from Yahweh's people, and as we shall see, the people of Yahweh tends not to be regarded as a collective tied by bonds of kinship to the deity.

The significance of "kinsman" is equally improper at Lev 19:15-18:

> Do not act wickedly in judgment. Do not prefer the lowly and do not honor the great. You will judge your neighbor *(ʿāmît)* in accordance with what is right. Do not carry gossip against your *ʿammîm*. Do not seek the life of your companion *(rēăʿ)*, I am Yahweh. Do not hate your brother in your heart. Correct your neighbor and forgive him. Do not seek vengeance from and do not target the sons of your people *(bĕnê ʿam)*. Love your companion as yourself, I am Yahweh.

The text strings together ordinances governing neighborly conduct. In so doing it multiplies synonyms for "neighbor" - *ʿāmît*, *ʿam(m)*, *rēăʿ*, *ʾāh*, *ben ʿam(m)*. It is correct to infer that *ʿam(m)* and *ben ʿam(m)* have the same meaning. A man's *ʿammîm* are his neighbors because his people are the population of the place where he lives.

Another occurrence of *ʿam(m)* where the kinship connotation recedes is to be found in the ancient poem of Judg 5. A recounting of the muster of *ʿam yhwh* reaches the tribe Benjamin with these words:

> *ʾaḥărêkā binyāmîn baʿămāmêkā*
>
> With you is Benjamin among your *ʿămāmîm*.[24]

Although it can be argued that *ʿămāmîm* here means "kinsmen," the context of this affirmation gives more support to interpreting the noun as "soldiers," subordinating *ʿămāmîm* to *ʿam(m)* with the sense "militia."

There are thus uses of the noun in which the kinship connotation is prominent and others in which it recedes. The fact that the meaning "kinsman" does not determine a specific degree of relationship suggests that in ancient Israel *ʿam(m)*-kinship is not to be distinguished from *ʿam(m)*-membership in a community.

When it has a collective referent, the noun is almost always translated "people." Often this meaning is contextually inappropriate, obscuring the subtlety of a text or imposing on it a false understanding.

It is of the foremost importance to dispel the idea that *ʿam(m)* always and originally was predicated of human associations. That such a use of the noun is predominant is clear, but there are passages in which the noun cannot be referred to men, and what is more important because more common, passages where the humanity of those designated shades into other categories of meaning. "Four of the world's smallest," a riddle begins,

> yet they are endowed with wisdom.
> Ants are an *ʿam(m)* not strong,
> yet in summer they prepare their bread.
> Hyraxes are an *ʿam(m)* not powerful,
> yet they make their house in rock. Prov 30:24-26

With these two paradoxes, the trick is to know that an *ʿam(m)* is not only a people, but also a colony of ants, a down of hyraxes. To insist that the meanings "colony" and "down" are metaphorical extensions of the sense "people" defeats the purpose of the riddle, which is to turn literal, animal *ʿammîm* into a figure of the human *ʿam(m)*, providing entertainment for the reader and inviting ironic comparison of animal and man. Thus, while ants and hyraxes are neither strong nor mighty, two characteristics of an important people, they are nonetheless *ʿammîm* boasting remarkable achievements.

It is incorrect to insist preemptively that the literal meaning of the noun is "people," its use for non-human groupings a metaphor. One psalmist offers this confession:

> *hûʾ ʿāśānû wĕlôʾ ʾănaḥnû ʿammô wĕṣōʾn marʿîtô*
> He made us and we are his, his *people* and the flock of his pasture. Ps 100:3

Another psalmist produces the same meaning but changes words in a suggestive manner:

> *kî hûʾ ʾĕlōhênû waʾănaḥnû ʿam marʿîtô weṣōʾn yādô*
> For he is our God and we are his pasture's *people* and the flock of his grazing plot. Ps 95:7[25]

The nouns *ʿam(m)* and *ṣōʾn* are used interchangeably, and this hints that to translate "people" for the former may miss the point. The noun seems to mean "flock." Zech 9:16 offers the same appearance:

> *wĕhôšîʿām yhwh ʾĕlōhêhem bayyôm hahûʾ kĕṣōʾn ʿammô*

The text seems to mean, "On that day Yahweh will save them like the sheep of his flock."

The possibility of confusing "flock" and "people" gives special life to a great many Biblical texts and makes many of them difficult to translate. Having defeated Amraphel's coalition, Abraham is said to have returned:

> all of the property. He also returned his kinsman Lot and his property, as also the women and the *ʿam(m)*. Gen 14:16

What does the noun mean here? Speiser may be correct in referring it to military personnel,[26] but the possibility of the noun denoting livestock cannot be eliminated on contextual grounds or on grounds of probability. "Pasture your *ʿam(m)* with your staff," writes the anonymous author of Mic 7:14, "the flock of your inheritance." Should the meaning "people" be introduced to the text? Another anonymous hand gives this prediction:

> The Sharon will become a flock's pasture, the Valley of Achor a cattle haunt, for my *ʿam(m)* who have sought me.
> Isa 65:10

Again the meanings "people" and "flock" are balanced. One may compare Nahum's taunt:

> Your shepherds are sleeping, O king of Assyria, your nobles are slumbering. Your *ʿam(m)* is scattered over the hills, and there is no one to bring them together.
> Nah 3:18

The balancing of "flock" and "people" is common in the ruling-shepherd typology. Where deity or king is shepherd, those ruled are naturally the flock.[27] Here is a point where Biblical materials participate in a ubiquitous Near Eastern pattern. It may be safely assumed that Israel's concept of the divine or royal shepherd developed in part under the direct or mediated influence of other Near Eastern ideologies. But Israel differs from other Near Eastern peoples at least in this, that it designates the human flock with the noun *ʿam(m)*, a word already ambiguous in its application to human associations.

We may note parenthetically that a corollary of the image of the ruling shepherd, the human herd, is the notion that a *people* may naturally have a king. A proverb reflects this idea, "A king's glory is a numerous *people*" (Prov 14:28). "People" may thus become a correlative of "kingdom":

> They travelled from nation to nation,
> from kingdom to other *people*. Ps 105:13

This may have been one of the factors contributing to the breakdown of distinctions between *ʿam(m)* and *gôy*.

The social matrix in which the similarity between a human association and an animal grouping is most plainly evident is the world of the pastoral nomad, where human and animal flocks live side by side, travel together, and share in the vicissitudes of non-sedentary life. Intuition suggests looking to the nomadic life setting for the roots of the ambiguity of the noun *ʿam(m)*, and to the extent that the Biblical literature addresses itself to the life of flock nomads, this intuition proves correct. The noun can designate a nomadic company (Gen 35:6). The term seems to include both people and flocks. That which initially defines such a group is its togetherness, one of the most common constructions in which the word occurs being "the *ʿam(m)* which was with him." Typologically, such an expression would seem to refer first to a pastoralist and his entourage, later to any individual and the group surrounding him. The noun may accordingly refer to a religious congregation (1 Kgs 8:66), a military band (Josh 8:1), a jural gathering (1 Kgs 21:9), and other groupings.

In the Biblical perspective, the human component of a pastoral group tends to be a kindred company. But the precise character of the ties of kinship uniting the group are not prominent. Indeed, the Biblical evidence resists any attempt to define the least common denominator of kinship in a pastoral setting. Abraham travelled with his nephew Lot (Gen 13:1). Jacob and his linear descendants formed a later group (Gen 35:6). But linear descent from a single ancestor seems not to have been the only concept of a people, as an episode assigned to the days of Jacob will illustrate. As part of a bloody ruse, Jacob's sons proposed to the town of Shechem:

> We shall give our daughters to you, and we shall take your daughters for ourselves, and we shall dwell with you and become a single people. Gen 34:16[28]

That by marriage and spatial association a single people could be forged shows the vagueness with which the kindred component of a people was understood. A people thus formed would have no single common ancestor, nor would agnatic bonds extend throughout the group, at least not initially. This vagueness corresponds nicely with the vagueness of the concept of the *ʿam(m)*-kinsman.

The word "tribe" may best capture the typologically primitive image of the pastoral people. The size of a tribe varied. Jacob's group is pictured as comprising a restricted number of individuals, but that roving tribe which, according to the Yahwist, attempted to build and settle Babylon (Gen 11:6) must have been imagined considerably larger. With respect to Israel as a settled tribe, it was the case that either all twelve tribes together constituted a single *ʿam(m)* (Judg 20:2), or that a single tribe of the twelve was an *ʿam(m)* (Judg 5:18). When a tribe is more than a nomadic group, the size of a people emerges as an important attribute. Jacob's promise that Ephraim would become a people (Gen 48:19) implies that a numerically significant group is in view. Heavy attrition could so reduce a group that it ceased to be a people (Isa 7:8).

In the history and literature of ancient Israel, pastoral nomadism belongs to a remote past. Regardless of when in time one locates the threshold of Israelite history, it is clear that all Israelite literature comes from a period characterized by town life or the transition to settlement. It is equally clear that the Israelite settlement of Palestine did not terminate the lifeways of pastoral nomads; town and country instead lived on in their age-old symbiosis. This situation bids interference for an attempt to recover the seriate meanings of *ʿam(m)*. Typologically, the use of the noun to designate the pastoral company appears most archaic, but empirically, the word's use to denote other groups rates equal antiquity. Indeed, were it the case that the dawn of Israel's literature lay in a period of pastoral nomadism, we should still expect to encounter early the use of the word to designate groupings other than the pastoral tribe, for the range of realities to which the noun might be applied, analogously or otherwise referred, was not altered by Israel's experience of settlement. Towns and nations preexisted Israel's transition to town and national life. Conversely, the continuation of pastoral lifeways provided a mechanism for the preservation of what we inferentially have called the typologically primitive sense "pastoral company." We thus expect and actually encounter an empirical jungle obscuring the semantic development of the noun.

There are nevertheless faint evidences indicating that the pastoral setting was a primitive context of the noun. The eclipsing of the noun's animal referent is suggestive. In the Biblical literature the use of the noun to designate animal groupings or mixed companies of man and beast is rare. If a purpose of Prov 30:24ff. was to inspire some mental gymnastic, then it could be inferred that a knowledge of the word's applicability to animal groupings was a matter of some erudition. Even the image of the human flock weathered with the passing of time, allowing a demotion of the tropological use of *ʿam(m)* to the level of a simile in which no recognition of the ambiguity of the noun is evident:

He drove his people like sheep,
he guided them on like a flock. Ps 78:52

Such a development may imply a gradual loss of the flock connotation, a loss which can be traced in the use of the rare Biblical cognate of *ʿam(m)*, *ʿāmît*. The original meaning of this noun has been preserved only by the writer of Zech 13:7:

Awake, sword, against my shepherd,
against the man of my *ʿāmît*.

Parallelism indicates that *ʿāmît* denotes an animal from the flock or, *pars pro toto*, the flock itself. But this original meaning was lost to the Priestly Writer and post-Biblical authors, for whom the noun meant simply "neighbor." The implication of these semantic developments is that, with the passing of nomadic lifeways, meanings of *ʿam(m)* pertinent to that setting were slowly surrendered.

Such data offer evidence that Israel's concept of a people may have been subject to semantic evolution paralleling the course of her social development. In Israel's literature, a people is not always a nomadic tribe, but often the population of a town (Judg 18:7; Amos 3:6). The origin of this use of the noun lies in the prehistory of the Hebrew language. It may reflect the common phenomenon that town life and affiliation supplant the life and ties of the tribe,[29] a process understood by the Yahwist, whose story of the tower of Babel reveals the changing referent of the noun (Gen 11:1ff.). An *ʿam(m)* became collectively the inhabitants of a town, individually a townsman.[30]

De Geus has argued that in ancient Israel town and clan were coextensive.[31] There is an element of theoretical truth to the argument. But in practice, the population of a town must have ordinarily exceeded the extent of a single clan. This was clearly the case for such major towns as Shechem (Judg 9), Hebron,[32] and Jerusalem (Judg 1:21), and probably the case generally. Speiser has rightly contrasted urban and non-sedentary social structures. Kinship ties are more significant in the latter.[33] This makes it difficult to assess the extent to which the noun *ʿam(m)*, applied to the population of a town, bears the connotation of kinship. It is tempting to infer that the transition from nomadic to settled lifeways brought not only an eclipse of the word's use for animal groupings, but also a lessening of its kinship connotations. Unfortunately, such an inference cannot be properly evaluated on the basis of the Biblical evidence. The composition of a people is too rarely indicated.

In view of the state of the evidence, caution should govern the noun's interpretation when it refers to the population of a town. Offered an influential voice at the royal court in Samaria, a Shunamite woman responds, "I live among my people" (2 Kgs 4:13ff.). John Gray finds in "people" a reference to the paternal clan and interprets the woman's response as an indication of the vitality of the Israelite family. So strong was the clan that the woman saw no need for protection against the authority of the central state.[34] Surely this interpretation goes beyond the evidence of the text, which is more naturally interpreted to intend by "people" the inhabitants of Shunem. What the woman means by her answer is not immediately evident. It may be that an offer of influence at the royal court implied moving to the capital to live at royal expense, and that the woman preferred to live in familiar surroundings.

In the book of Ruth, Boaz gathers the elders of his people to Bethlehem's gate to witness a legal transaction. The transaction is an act of redemption, an affair concerning the kinsmen of Naomi's deceased husband Elimelekh. But by Boaz's reckoning, Elimelekh had only two potential redeemers (Ruth

4:1ff.). This suggests first that the elders of Boaz's people stood in no closer relationship to Elimelekh than that of cousins, since cousins appear to have been potential redeemers in ancient Israel.[35] A corollary of this observation is the inference that Boaz himself stood in no close kinship relation to the elders of his people. Boaz's people must be seen as nothing more than the population of his town. Kindred relationship is not in the picture.

In addition to designating the population of a town, *ʿam(m)* may designate that part of a town which functions on the town's behalf, the town council (1 Kgs 21:13). These gather to hear jural disputes (1 Kgs 21:8ff.), to witness legal transactions (Ruth 4:9; Gen 23:11), to execute judgments rendered against an individual (1 Kgs 21:13), and correspond in large measure to the *Vollbürger* envisioned by Rost as the fundamental referent of the noun. From the fact that "people" can refer to the collective council might be inferred a use of *ʿam(m)* to designate the singular councillor. Goldman's effort to derive the meaning "councillor" from "paternal uncle" (Arabic *ʿamm*, one whose voice merited hearing) cannot be supported.[36] In point of fact, the possibility of a singular sense "councillor" is only theoretical. That text in which this meaning has sometimes been found is misinterpreted when *ʿammîm* is defined as councillors. Micaiah's call "listen *ʿammîm*, all of them" (1 Kgs 22:28) is the incipit of the book of Micah and means "listen peoples, all of them." Now it is to be expected that the town council was composed of men of some rank, and this expectation leads naturally to the inference that *ʿam(m)* can mean "gentry." This inference is not to be buttressed by reference to "the people of the land,"[37] an expression which 2 Kgs 24:14 shows to have borne no necessary connotation of social status. It is, however, supported by textual evidence:

He pays no respect to princes,
Nor favors rich over poor.
They are all the work of his hands.
In a moment they die, at midnight;
Gentry are shaken and pass away,
The mighty are removed without hand.   Job 34:19-20[38]

Whether or how to relate the use of *ʿam(m)* for "council" and its use for "militia" poses a special problem. The noun can designate virtually any military company, be it the town muster (Josh 8:14) or an irregular gathering (Judg 9:34-36). With this meaning the solitary noun *ʿam(m)* alternates with the expression *ʿam milḥāmâ* (Josh 8:1), but there are enough occurrences of the solitary noun with this sense to justify assigning "army" to a list of *ʿam(m)*'s meanings. It is possible that a people is a militia because the politically competent citizenry of a town or district was liable to military obligations.[39] Such a conception suits the framework of settled peoples. But that the military use of the noun originated from such beginnings seems doubtful. Malamat has suggested that the kinship connotation of the noun harmonizes with a military organization based on kith and kin fighting units.[40] Against this view must be reckoned the fact that the noun refers not to fighting units, but rather entire armies. De Vaux's observation that among Arab tribes the fighting force is accounted to be the entire tribe commends itself as an explanation of the noun's military use.[41] His view may be supplemented by noting that an army resembles a mobile tribe by virtue of its travelling and camping together. If *ʿam(m)*'s military sense is to be elevated to a primary position in an etymological scheme, then a proper analogy is not to be found in German *Volk* deriving from **Pulk ("Heerlaufe")*,[42] but rather in a comparison of French *troupe* and *troupeau*.

The noun *ʿam(m)* designates not only the collective militia, but apparently also the individual militiaman:

ʾap ḥōbēb ʿammîm kol-qĕdōšāyw bĕyādekā

He has mustered the troops,

all his holy ones are at your side. Deut 33:3[43]

This meaning may lie behind the enigmatic Amminadib of Cant 6:12:

lōʾ yādaʿtî napšî śāmatnî markĕbôt ʿammî-nādîb

Unknowing, my soul set me amid the chariots of a noble warrior.

The suffix -î of *ʿammî* may be explained as a residual genitive case ending.

Settlement was not restricted to towns, and the word *ʿam(m)* is used of the population of other geographic entities - districts (Gen 23:12), wider regions (Judg 12:2). Although the population of a district sometimes shows no trace whatever of kindred relationship (Num 13:28), there are other times when the population of an area may be a consanguineous group. In such cases the clan seems to have been rather vaguely conceived as the outermost circle of individuals with whom a feeling of solidarity was shared. Distressed at Samson's intention of taking a Philistine bride, his parents asked him:

> Is it because there is no woman among my nieces or throughout my entire people that you are going to take a bride from among the uncircumcised Philistines? Judg 14:3

Two circles are in view - nieces and *people*. Ps 45:11 can be compared. Here is the psalmist's advice to a comely royal bride:

> Listen, daughter, and behold; and give ear,
> and forget your people and your father's house.

Here the paternal family and *people* define inner and outer spheres of relationship. In the case of the story from the book of Judges, it should be noted that while blood relationship can easily be inferred for *ʿam(m)*, such ties are not prominent. Samson's people constitute the limits within which a desirable marriage can be arranged, a district population considered to be vaguely related to Samson and his family. That which distinguishes this population is not its blood line, but the fact that it practices circumcision.

There are other texts in which the noun *ʿam(m)* is said to mean "clan."[44] During an abatement of a Babylonian siege of Jerusalem, Jeremiah tried to travel to the district of Benjamin to receive a tract among its *ʿam(m)* (Jer 37:12). A strong basis for making the word signify clan is not evident here. Isaiah's gloomy forecast seems at first unambiguously to intend "clan" by *ʿam(m)*:

> A man will seize his brother in the house of his father.
> "You have a cloak. You will be our prince, and this ruin beneath your hand."
> On that day he will raise (his voice) saying,

> "I won't be a healer; there is neither bread nor cloak in my house. You won't make me prince of an *ʿam(m)*."
>
> Isa 3:6-7

But the correspondence between father's house and *ʿam(m)* is more apparent than real. The reluctant individual seeks to avoid becoming a public official, not a family lord.

The noun *ʿam(m)* is used not only of the collective population of a district, but also of an inhabitant of the district. In post-Biblical Hebrew *ʿam-hāʾāreṣ*, used to deprecate one ignorant of the Torah, can refer to an individual inhabitant of the land.

The Bible and post-Biblical literature witness the word's use in ever widening spheres of meaning. An *ʿam(m)* may be the population of a country (2 Kgs 14:21), of the entire world (Ps 22:7),[45] or of the netherworld (Isa 44:7[?]; Ezek 26:20).[46] The word's use for a nation's population is common. Such a people tends to belong to a defined territory (Num 13:18; Isa 33:24; Jonah 1:8), and the name of the territory and that of the people may be the same. Such a people speaks a common language (Isa 28:11; Esth 1:22), participates in a common cult (see below, chapter 4), and shares a common fate. In short, it is that entity Buccellati calls a national state.[47] But a people may also be a territorial state (Amos 1:5), and this cautions against assuming that a national people is inherently a consanguineous reality. Thus, whereas Israel's theory of descent from a single ancestor is relevant to defining the nation Israel as an ethnic association, this theory is not directly relevant to the meaning of the noun *ʿam(m)*. Rather than assert that the noun carries overtones of ethnicity, it is more proper to recognize that at the national level kinship bonds are not prominent in the use of *ʿam(m)*. A people may think itself, as Israel did, an ethnic federation, but at the same time, a people can be a federation without ethnic identity.

We have suggested that an *ʿam(m)* was at first a nomadic group comprising men and all that was in their company, later the population of a fixed locale. We shall test this idea to a certain extent in the following chapters where an attempt at diachronic analysis is made. We must first call attention to a salient feature of the Biblical evidence emerging from an overview of the material. There is a close relationship between the singular and collective meanings of the noun. An *ʿam(m)* can be a tribe or a tribesman, a clan or a kinsman, a town or a townsman, a militia or a militiaman, the population of a region or an inhabitant of a region. A kinship connotation affects only one of these pairings. The overall pattern of the Hebrew evidence is not easily accommodated to the notion that a term of kinship is the foundation of the noun's semantic history.

Chapter IV

BIBLICAL FORMULAE

The word "people" occurs in a number of Biblical formulae and noun phrases the study of which may illuminate the semantic history of the noun. These formulae and expressions provide an opportunity to investigate the term in a controlled environment. In this chapter and in that which follows we shall attempt to learn what may be inferred about changes through time in the use and understanding of the noun *ʿam(m)*. We begin with a small number of formulae; in chapter V we turn to shorter noun phrases.

* * * * *

The Covenant Formula

The terms "Covenant Formula" and "Bundesformel" are conventionally used to designate recurring variations of the compound sentence:

wĕhāyîtî lākem lēʾlōhîm wĕʾattem tihyû lî lĕʿām

Lev 26:12

The full formula is widely attested in Exilic and post-Exilic literature (Jer 7:23; 11:4; 24:7; 31:1; 32:38; Ezek 11:20; 14:11; 36:28; 37:23.27; Exod 6:7 [P]; Lev 26:12; Zech 8:8; Deut 29:12). Its literarily earliest occurrences may be Jer 30:22 and Deut 26:16-19, but the dates of both texts are uncertain. Given the breadth of its literary attestations, the formula probably originated before the Exile.[1] Although it is used in promises of restoration (e.g., Ezek 11:20), it is also used as a formulation of Exodus beginnings (Exod 6:7), and the latter does not presuppose the Babylonian captivity.

Problems beset the Covenant Formula. Deviations in wording from the pattern of Lev 26:12 abound, and this makes it difficult to describe the formula's basic word structure. The order of the two clauses may be reversed (Zech 8:8). Either clause may appear in isolation from the other (Zech 2:15; Gen 17:8). Either clause may be converted to an infinitive phrase

(Deut 26:17-19). For the verb *hāyâ* of the *ʿam(m)*-clause may be substituted the verbs *hēqîm* (Deut 28:9), *ʿāśâ* (1 Sam 12:22), *pādâ* (2 Sam 7:23), *lāqaḥ* (Exod 6:7), *hibdîl* (1 Kgs 8:53), or *kônēn* (2 Sam 7:24). The noun *ʿam(m)* may be qualified by its inclusion in the noun phrases *ʿam naḥălâ* (Deut 4:20), *ʿam sĕgullâ* (Deut 7:6; 14:2), or *ʿam(m)* may be suppressed in favor of the noun *naḥălâ* (1 Kgs 8:53). The I-thou pattern of Lev 26:12 alternates with the pattern I-they (Jer 24:7). Only two features of the formula are encountered with some consistency, the noun pair *ʿam(m)/ʾĕlōhîm* and the double occurrence of the preposition *lĕ-* in each clause. Using the double preposition to define the corpus of texts in which all or half of the formula appears, there are thirty-six passages germane to the formula's study (those already listed and Ex 29:45; Lev 11:45; 22:33; 25:38; Num 15:41; Deut 27:9; 2 Kgs 11:17; Jer 13:11; 31:33; Ezek 34:24). Yet the diagnostic use of this trait encounters a problem. A structural correspondence between the Covenant Formula and the royal adoption formula of 2 Sam 7:14 is commonly assumed. The verbal structure of the latter certainly replicates that of the Bundesformel:

> *ʾănî ʾehyeh lô lĕʾāb wĕhûʾ yihyeh lî lĕbēn*
>
> I shall become his father and he will become my son.

The balanced halves of this compound sentence display the structure of the Covenant Formula. Outside of the Bible a similar construction is known in the Nuzi adoption formula *ana PN ana marūti nadānu.*[2] But a comparison of 2 Sam 7:14 with another Biblical royal adoption formulation, *ʾāmar ʾēlay bĕnî ʾattâ* (Ps 2:7), reveals that the idiom *hāyâ lĕ- lĕ-* inadequately defines the genre "adoption texts" and excludes relevant material. The pertinence of this for the study of the Covenant Formula is seen at Hos 2:25:

> *wĕʾāmartî lĕlōʾ-ʿammî ʿammî ʾattâ wĕhûʾ yōʾmar ʾĕlōhāy*
>
> And I shall say to Not-my-people, "You are my people," and he will say "my god."

Here we find one of the characteristics of the Covenant Formula - the balanced distribution of the nouns "people" and "god" - but not the other. The double preposition is missing. Such a text may be relevant to an understanding of the Covenant Formula.

Difficulties confront translating the formula into English. Norbert Lohfink[3] and A. R. Hulst[4] have disputed whether *hāyâ lĕ-* should be rendered "to be" or "to become." Lohfink's preference for the latter seems to be justified. But another issue must be pondered. Although the customary English equivalents of *ʿam(m)* and *ʾĕlōhîm* are respectively "people" and "god," it is sometimes the case that these renderings obscure rather than elucidate the meaning of the formula. In ancient Israel there were at least two different understandings of the Covenant Formula conditioning two subtly different meanings of these nouns.

One understanding has been transmitted by priestly circles. At Exod 29:44-46 the Priestly Writer records Yahweh's statement:

> I shall sanctify the tent of meeting and the altar. I shall sanctify Aaron and his sons to serve me as priest. I shall tabernacle in the midst of Israel and *I shall become their god*. They will know that I am Yahweh their god who brought them out of Egypt in order to tabernacle in their midst. I am Yahweh their god.[5]

The trailing reminder "I am Yahweh their god" is curious. It lends authority to what precedes,[6] but how is it possible to declare "I am their god" immediately after promising "I shall become their god"? The answer is provided by the text. The Priestly Writer intends the latter to signify no more than the establishment of a cultic presence. With tent, altar, and priests, Yahweh becomes a "god" for Israel, but beyond this restricted frame of reference stands the unrestricted reality which gives Yahweh his authority: he is the god of Israel.

This understanding of the Covenant Formula implies a complementary restriction on the meaning of "people." As Yahweh's people, Israel ought to be the community in which the deity is cultically present, a congregation. This was manifestly Zechariah's understanding:

> Jubilate and rejoice, daughter Zion, for I am about to come, and I shall tabernacle in your midst, says Yahweh. On that day many nations *(gôyîm)* will be united to Yahweh, and *they will become my people*, and I shall tabernacle in your midst.... Zech 2:14-15

That many nations will become Yahweh's people shows that the latter is being construed to signify neither an ethnic nor a geo-political people; it is the community gathered to the temple. That this was also the Priestly Writer's understanding can perhaps be inferred from a peculiarity of Priestly use of the Bundesformel. P sometimes cites the full formula, but when abbreviating it always omits the *ʿam(m)*-clause. To denote "congregation" with the noun *ʿam(m)* is a usage foreign to P, where *ʿēdâ* carries this sense. The Priestly Writer may consequently have been disinclined to cite in isolation the *ʿam(m)*-clause of the formula, for its diction was not his own. It is implied that in his use of the Covenant Formula the Priestly Writer transmitted material of which he was not the creator.

The priestly understanding of the Covenant Formula may be contrasted with that of various Deuteronomistic texts. At Deut 14:2 it is clear that the noun *ʿam(m)* has not been interpreted to mean "congregation":

> For you are a holy people to Yahweh your god. Yahweh has chosen you *to become a treasure-people for him* from among all the peoples who are on the face of the earth.

The implicit comparison of Israel and the world's other peoples shows that this use of the Covenant Formula construes *ʿam(m)* simply to mean "people." Unlike the Priestly Writer, Deuteronomistic authors abbreviate the formula by omitting the *ʾĕlōhîm*-clause. The reason for this is that such writers could speak of Yahweh becoming Israel's god only with reference to a unique moment when this transition was accomplished by covenant; the full formula is used only with reference to that covenant. At the same time, Deuteronomistic texts conceive Israel's status as Yahweh's people as a dynamic situation, one which involves each generation by imposing on it an obligation to obey Yahweh. Through obedience, Israel can continually become Yahweh's people, and hence the *ʿam(m)*-clause of the formula may be used more freely than that clause which addresses only the outset of Yahweh's relationship to Israel.[7] That Yahweh is Israel's god, then, means everything that being a god implies, and not just a cultic presence. Deuteronomistic texts construe the nouns "people" and "god" in their usual, full senses.

There were thus variant understandings of the Covenant Formula in ancient Israel which resulted in or from a shading of the meanings of *ʿam(m)* and *ʾĕlōhîm*. To account for the rise of these understandings necessitates a careful investigation of the relevant texts and a probing for the formula's life setting.

The Covenant Formula is so called because of the assumption that its balanced halves represent the covenant posture of Israel and her god. The occasional occurrence of the formula in direct or indirect association with the noun "covenant" has encouraged the nomenclature (Gen 17:7; Exod 6:4-7; Lev 26:45; 2 Kgs 11:17; Jer 11:3-4; 31:33; Exek 37:24ff.), although here a caveat must be issued. Whereas one may expect a coherent profile of the covenant to which the formula is related to emerge from the texts, there is in fact no single covenant to which the formula is consistently applied. The Priestly Writer has attached the formula to Yahweh's "eternal covenant," his promise of land and progeny to Abraham (Gen 17:7ff., etc.). Ezekiel, too, knows an association of formula and "eternal covenant" (Ezek 34:24ff.), but Ezekiel also speaks of a "covenant of peace" (Ezek 34:24ff.) which bears a striking similarity to the covenant imagined at Hos 2:20ff. Ezekiel writes further of a future covenant of which the Bundesformel is an expression (Ezek 37:26ff.). The book of Jeremiah relates the Covenant Formula to both a future covenant (Jer 31:32ff.) and a foundation covenant at the time of the Exodus (Jer 11:4). Deuteronomy and Deuteronomistic texts attach the formula to foundation covenants at Sinai and in the land of Moab (Deut 29:11-12; 26:17-19), and on one occasion to a covenant compacted in the reign of Jehoash (2 Kgs 11:17).

The uncertainty of the Biblical data over the covenantal setting of the Covenant Formula has been matched by disagreements among modern writers over the exact relationship between formula and Israelite covenant. For G. von Rad the Bundesformel is the formula of the covenant made at Sinai, transmitted in the covenant festival at Shechem.[8] Rudolf Smend situates the formula in the covenant made by Josiah and narrated at 2 Kgs 23.[9] Norbert Lohfink has suggested locating it in a Judaean enthronement festival.[10] Some have resisted the covenant association altogether. Alfred Jepsen offers the alternative hypothesis that the Covenant Formula originated in priestly or prophetic speech,[11] while Lothar Perlitt denies that any discrete *Sitz im Leben* is evident for the formula.[12] Few if any would deny that the formula is sometimes presented as though it were a covenant formulation. Our task is therefore to seek the origin of this use of the Covenant Formula and determine whether the association of covenant and formula is primary or secondary. We begin with a number of Deuteronomistic texts.

2 Kgs 11 narrates a temple and palace revolution in which the Omrid queen Athaliah was deposed and killed. Jehoiada, priest of Yahweh's Jerusalem temple, sought the replacement of the deposed queen by David's sole remaining scion Jehoash. In order to secure this succession,

> Jehoiada made a covenant among Yahweh, the king (Jehoash), and the people *to become Yahweh's people*. Then all the people of the land went to the Baal temple, tore down its altars, and rightly destroyed its images. They killed Mattan the priest of Baal in front of the altars.
>
> 2 Kgs 11:17-18

Despite Lohfink's contrary opinion,[13] the text gives ample evidence of belonging to a Deuteronomistic hand. Its writer has imposed a telltale positive evaluation of the destruction of the pagan images and paraphernalia of the Baal temple. The verbal and ideological relationship of the passage to Deut 7:5-6 is clear. The latter enjoins Israel's eradication of pagan cults with these words:

> You shall tear down their altars, and you shall destroy their *maṣṣebôth*, you shall pull down their Asherahs, and you shall burn their images in fire. For you are a holy people to Yahweh your god. Yahweh your god chose you *to become his treasure-people* from among all the peoples on the face of the earth.

It is hardly coincidental that this text invokes the Covenant Formula to motivate the obliteration of foreign cults. The formula is used congruently at 2 Kgs 11 where, having compacted to become Yahweh's people, all the people of the land actually do eradicate Baal worship. 2 Kgs 11:17-18 must be reckoned Deuteronomistic in its use of the Bundesformel; it cannot be interpreted to record an early covenantal setting of that formula.[14]

The motivation for retrojecting the formula at this place in the Deuteronomistic History is not clear, but it is clear that Deuteronomistic circles understood the formula to belong in some way to a covenant. This fact provides a badly needed background against which to set the controverted text Deut 26:17-19, whose covenant situation has been both affirmed and denied.[15] The passage is notoriously problematic. Its infinitive syntax is difficult to render in European languages, and it offers two occurrences of an otherwise unexampled hiphil of the verb *'āmar* ("to say"). The meaning of *he'ĕmîr* has been debated without the emergence of a consensus.[16] Consensus is impossible because there is insufficient evidence for deciding the verb's signification. There is a certain a priori likelihood that it is the causative of its qal and means "to cause someone to say." But the suitability of this rendering is open to question on theological grounds. Would a Deuteronomistic writer have declared, "You have caused Yahweh to say that he will become your god"? Such a breach of the deity's freedom of activity seems unlikely. Smend has preferred to adopt Ben Yehuda's estimation that *he'ĕmîr* means "to proclaim solemnly," and this view is perhaps correct but is not demonstrable. Joüon's derivation of the verb from the noun *'ōmer*, "word," hence *he'ĕmîr*, "to give one's word,"[17] is also attractive. Textual emendation is not to be preferred. For the sake of convenience we follow Joüon's proposal to translate:

> This very day Yahweh your god commands you to perform these statutes and the judgments. You will watchfully perform them with all your heart and with all your soul. Today you have given your word to Yahweh that *he will become your god*, that you will walk in his ways, keep his statutes, commandments and judgments, and heed his voice. Today Yahweh has given his word to you that *you will become his treasure-people*, just as he said to you, and that you will keep his commandments, that he will give you supremacy over all the nations whom he has made for praise, name, and glory, and that you will be a holy people to Yahweh your god just as he said. Deut 26:16-19

The Covenant Formula is embedded within the passage, sundered and made the gist of mutual proclamations of Israel and Yahweh.

Lohfink has shown that these verses are literarily an accretion to an early text of Deuteronomy, which he identifies as approximately chapters 5-26. The noun series statutes-commandments-judgments is un-Deuteronomic. Deuteronomic usage pairs statutes and judgments without intervening term.[18] Lohfink may be partly correct in his estimation that the intervention of the term "commandments" anticipates the joining of the laws of Deut 12-26 and the blessings and curses of Deut 28 where the determinant rubric is "commandments." But the situation is more complicated than he imagined; these verses from Deut 26 link not only blocks of material in Deuteronomy, but also couple Deuteronomy to the epic traditions. According to v. 19, "Yahweh has given his word to you that you will become his treasure-people, *just as he said*," and, moments later, "...that you will be a holy people to Yahweh your god *just as he said*." There are two eventualities which will occur in accordance with previous declarations of the deity. At these two points, the text of Deuteronomy has been subordinated to another text or tradition where Israel is promised that it will become a treasure-people and a holy people.

The tradition referred to is manifestly that recorded at Exod 19:3-6:

> Moses went up to God and Yahweh called to him from the mountain saying,
>
> "Thus you shall say to the House of Jacob
> And inform the sons of Israel,
>
> 'You have seen what I did to Egypt, and I have carried you on eagles' wings and brought you to myself. Now if you will heed my voice and observe my covenant, *then you will be a treasure for me* from among all the peoples, for the entire earth is mine, and *you will be* a kingdom of priests and *a holy nation*.' These are the words which you shall speak to the sons of Israel."

The text has frequently been discussed.[19] It is not easily assigned to any of the Pentateuchal sources. According to its linguistic affinities, it should be aligned with Deuteronomy. The noun "treasure" *(sĕgullâ)* is attested nowhere in the Tetrateuch apart from this passage, but occurs several times in Deuteronomy.[20] The expression "I carried you on eagles' wings" is reminiscent of a poetic description of Yahweh found at Deut 32:11:

> Like an eagle watchful over his nest, sweeping above his brood,
> he spread his wings, he seized you, he carried you on his pinions.

Yet like this poem, the Exodus text seems to be older than the promulgation of Deuteronomy. The poetic remnants of Exod 19:3 give the passage an aura of antiquity,[21] and at certain key points the diction of the passage is at variance with Deuteronomic usage. Whereas Deuteronomy speaks only of a holy people (*ʿām qādôš*), the Exodus text refers to a holy nation (*gôy qādôš*). Perlitt has disputed the significance of this variance, righly noting the emergence in Deuteronomistic usage of the use of the noun *gôy* for Israel.[22] But the shift in usage accompanying the temporal progression from "Deuteronomic" to "Deuteronomistic" literature was not so radical as to yield collocations such as *gôy qādôš*, *gôy naḥălâ*, *gôy sĕgullâ*. The balance of probability tilts in favor of an earlier date for the Exodus passage than its Deuteronomic or Deuteronomistic relatives. Such a relative dating is at all events mandated by the professed dependence of Deut 26:16-19 on the Exodus tradition. Whether the latter belongs to E (as seems likely) or whether it is at home in the limbo to which Wildberger has assigned it need not be determined.[23]

Exod 19:3-6 presents a Sinai covenant tradition, and because Deut 26:16-19 issues from it, the assumption that the Deuteronomy text participates in a covenant tradition can be confirmed. Deuteronomy's dependence on Exodus at this point makes of the covenant underlying Deut 26:16-19 either a renewal of or a fulfillment of that which was begun at Sinai. Now Deuteronomy's heritage from the Exodus text consists of two important features. It has interpreted the mutual proclamations of Yahweh and Israel to signify an obligation against Israel to obey her god. This is accomplished in an awkward manner. The two halves of the Bundesformel which are set forth as Yahweh's and Israel's solemn declarations have been encrusted with explicative infinitive clauses which have as their goal an imposition of the obligation to obey Yahweh. But the application of these phrases to both halves of the Covenant Formula results in syntactic disruptions. The subject of each successive infinitive is determined by the need to oblige Israel to obedience and not by the natural flow of the sentence. The resultant awkwardness has led von Rad and others to assume that the build-up of infinitive clauses represents a literary expansion of a purer core.[24] For von Rad and Smend the core is represented by the sundered Bundesformel unencumbered by obedience-bidding infinitives. This core represents Yahweh's and Israel's mutual, ceremonial proclamations. Yet if one asks why Deuteronomy insists on making the Covenant Formula betoken obedience, one finds the first important feature shared by Deuteronomy and Exodus. Von Rad's analysis runs afoul the fact that the obligation to obey Yahweh is a theme which Deuteronomy has inherited from Exodus. The elimination of the awkward infinitive phrases in Deut 26:16-19 eliminates simultaneously an important link to the antecedent Exodus tradition. Ironically, the reason for the awkwardness in Deut 26 can be found only by inverting von Rad's analysis. The syntactical strain stems from an unnatural partitioning of the Covenant Formula into covenant proclamations and not from a secondary introduction of the theme of obedience. Obedience is primary to the tradition, but the mutuality of the Bundesformel as presented in Deut 26 is not, as a glance at Exod 19:3-6 will show.

The Bundesformel seems to be out of place in Deuteronomy's covenant tradition. This is confirmed by a consideration of the second important link between the Exodus and Deuteronomy texts: their common vocabulary. In Exodus, obedience will result in Israel being *(hāyâ)* a treasure *(segullâ)* and a holy nation *(gôy qādôš)*. None of these terms belongs to the Covenant Formula, yet in Deut 26 they suddenly appear in Covenant Formula guise: *being (hāyâ)* has been made *becoming (hāyâ lĕ-)*; *treasure (segullâ)* has become *treasure-people (ʿam sĕgullâ)*; *holy nation (gôy qādôš)* has emerged as *holy people (ʿām qādôš)*. The changes are subtle, but their implication is definitive. At Deut 26, the location of the Covenant Formula in a covenant setting is tradition-historically an innovation. There is no warrant for seeing in the Bundesformel an original formulation of the Sinai covenant.

What is true for Deut 26 appears to be true for all other Biblical texts associating the Covenant Formula with a covenant. Arranged hierarchically, many of these texts are simple derivatives of Deut 26 itself. This is most evident in two Deuteronomistic texts from the book of Jeremiah:

> Thus says Yahweh of Hosts, god of Israel: Add your holocaust offerings to your sacrifices and eat flesh. For I did not speak to your fathers nor did I command them concerning holocaust and sacrifice on the day I brought them out of the land of Egypt. Rather, this is what I commanded them: Obey me and *I shall become your god and you will become my people.* Jer 7:21-23

> The word which came to Jeremiah from Yahweh, saying: Hear the words of this covenant, and declare them to the man of Judah and the inhabitants of Jerusalem. Tell them: thus says Yahweh the god of Israel: Cursed be the man who does not heed the words of this covenant which I commanded your fathers on the day I brought them forth from the land of Egypt, from the iron furnace saying, "Obey me and perform everything I command you, and *you will become my people and I shall become your god.* Jer 11:1-4

Both texts presuppose a foundation covenant calling for obedience. In formulating the call for obedience, these texts use language common to Exod 19 and Deut 26, but they part company from the tradition of Exod 19 and align with Deuteronomy in making the issue of the covenant the terms of the Bundesformel. Such associations of the Covenant Formula and covenant presuppose the transformation of the tradition of Exod 19, and thus prove to be secondary.

The secondary linking of Covenant Formula and covenant is also evident from Deuteronomistic texts in the book of Deuteronomy. Nowhere is the presupposition of a covenant setting of the formula more clearly expressed than at Deut 29:9-12:

> All of you are standing today before Yahweh your god - your heads, your tribes, your elders, your officers, every Israelite, your children, your wives, he who is a client in the midst of your camp, everyone from wood gatherer to drawer of water - to pass through the covenant of Yahweh your god and through his oath *(ʾālâ)*, which today Yahweh

> your god is making with you, in order to *establish you as his people and he will become your god*, just as he told you and just as he promised your fathers Abraham, Isaac, and Jacob.

Presupposed is the link between the Covenant Formula and the curses of Deut 28, and if Lohfink is correct in seeing Deut 26:16-19 as a filigree binding law and curses, then this passage depends on Deut 26. Linkage of the Bundesformel and Yahweh's promises to the patriarchs probably relies on the idea of the Priestly Writer, known directly or indirectly, that the Covenant Formula expresses a promise made to Abraham and repeated later (see below).

There are thus a number of texts associating the Bundesformel and covenant where that association is to be judged secondary, relying on the innovative use of the Covenant Formula attested for the first time in Deut 26. The innovation's effects were widely felt and extend to a second generation of Covenant Formula-covenant texts where the covenant expressed by the Bundesformel is a "new" covenant.

At Jeremiah 31:31-33 this new covenant is set forth:

> Behold, days are coming, says Yahweh, and I shall make a new covenant with the House of Israel and with the House of Judah - not like the covenant I made with their fathers on the day I seized their hand to bring them out of the land of Egypt, for they violated my covenant even though I had been a husband to them, says Yahweh. Rather, this is the covenant which I shall make with the House of Israel after those days, says Yahweh: I shall set my torah in their midst, upon their hearts I shall write it. *I shall become their god and they will become my people.*

The authorship of the text has been disputed.[25] Because the passage is in prose and not poetry it has been denied that Jeremiah was its writer. The advantage gained by such a denial is scarcely evident. To attribute the text to one of Jeremiah's disciples is to displace the burden of expressing Jeremiah's thoughts. To attribute the text to a Deuteronomistic author is incorrect, as R. Martin-Achard has shown. His assessment of the historical and theological situation of the passage is impressive. For Martin-Achard, the text expresses a response to the failure of the reforms of Deutenonomy. Having witnessed the inability of his contemporaries to implement the Deuteronomic covenant, to fulfill its laws and purposes, the prophet announces a new covenant the success of which is to be assured by Yahweh. Yahweh himself will inscribe the law on the hearts of men, who are thus not abandoned to an independent accomplishment of this aim (cf. Deut 11:18).[26] The new covenant is thus modelled on the old, and the basis for using the Covenant Formula to describe the new covenant is to be found in its formulation of the old. In texts which announce the new covenant (Jer 24:7; 30:22; 31:1; 32:28; all occurrences in Ezek) we encounter the Bundesformel because it had already found a position in the Deuteronomic covenant which forms the background against which the "new" is defined.

A survey of the covenants to which the Covenant Formula is attached concludes with a consideration of a number of texts from the Priestly Writer and Ezekiel. P attaches the Bundesformel to the eternal covenant narrated at Gen 17. The covenant of Gen 17 is in fact not a mutual compact but rather a self-binding promise on the part of the deity, and the Deuteronomistic writer of Deut 29:12 did well to refer to the tradition as an oath. In Genesis, the formula is not in an original setting.[27] When one pursues the Priestly tradition of the Covenant Formula into Exod 6 and 29 it becomes clear that the promise to become a god to Abraham's descendants means, for the Priestly Writer, a promise to set the deity's tabernacle amidst Israel. Using the Covenant Formula, P ascribes to Yahweh these words: "I am Yahweh your god who brought you out of Egypt *in order to become your god*" (Lev 11:45). But the purpose of the Exodus can be expressed in another way: "I am Yahweh their god who brought them out of Egypt *in order for me to tabernacle in their midst*" (Exod 29:46). For P, to become a god means to tabernacle among. Yahweh's promise to Abraham is thus fulfilled when the tabernacle is established. This is an event which concerns only generations beginning with the Exodus; the patriarch's participation in the tradition should be seen as secondary. This is already clear at Gen 17:8, where it is evident that Abraham himself does not really share in the Covenant Formula promise:

> I shall give to you and to your seed after you the land of your sojourning, the whole land of Canaan, as an eternal possession, and I shall become *their* god.

Plainly, the Covenant Formula is pledged to Abraham's descendants and not the patriarch. The attachment of the Covenant Formula to the eternal covenant of Gen 17 is another secondary use of the formula.

This is a conclusion which is not changed by the fact that Ezekiel, too, speaks of an eternal covenant and associates the Bundesformel with it. The relevant text is Ezek 37:23-27:

> They (Israel) will never again be defiled by their idols and their detestable things and all their rebellious acts. I shall rescue them from their recalcitrant acts by which they have sinned and purify them. *They will become my people and I shall become their god.* My servant David will be king over them, they will all have one shepherd. They will behave according to my judgments, and they will watchfully perform my statutes. They will inhabit the land I gave Jacob my servant, a land in which your fathers dwelt. They will inhabit it, their children, and their grandchildren forever, with my servant David their prince. I shall make a covenant of peace, they will have an eternal covenant. I shall multiply them and put my sanctuary in their midst forever. My tabernacle will be among them, and I shall become their god and they will become my people.

Ezekiel's dependence on the traditions of P, be it direct or indirect, is clear. The literary environment of the Covenant Formula is filled with images of the first covenant - the promise of land and progeny. This is the eternal covenant of Gen 17.

Ezekiel also speaks of a covenant of peace, and this final covenant must be elucidated by citing Ezek 34:24-30:

> *I Yahweh shall become their god*, my servant David a prince in their midst. I Yahweh have spoken. And I shall make a covenant of peace for them and obliterate the savage animal of the land. They will dwell safely in the desert and grow old in the forests. With them and round about my hill I shall establish a blessing. I shall cause rain to

> fall in its time, and there will be abundantly fertile rains. The tree of the field will give its fruit, the land will yield its produce. They will be safely in their land and know that I am Yahweh when I break the bars of their yoke and rescue them from those whom they serve as slaves. They will no longer be a spoil to the nations, and the land's wild animal will no longer eat them. They will dwell safely without being terrified. I shall give them a noble plantation, and they will no longer be harvested by famine in the land, nor will they bear the reproach of the nations. They will know that I Yahweh their god am with them. They are my people, the House of Israel, says my lord Yahweh.

The covenant of peace evidently concerns the realm of nature. Wild animals will be subdued, fertility of the land assured, Israel's safe dwelling arranged. The text ends with the declaration *ʿammî hēmâ*, "they are my people." This is reminiscent of Hos 2:25, *ʿammî ʾattâ*, "you are my people." It is probably not a coincidence that this statement from Hosea is preceded by the promise,

> On that day I shall make a covenant for them with the wild animal of the field, with the birds of the sky, with that which creeps on the land. Bow, sword, and war I shall destroy from the land, and I shall cause them to lie down in peace.

There follows a description of the renewal of fertilily in the land of Israel. In general, the concerns of Ezekiel replicate those of Hos 2: security against wild animals; dwelling safely in the land; fertility of the earth. This suggests that the pattern of Ezekiel's covenant of peace is modelled on that of the text of Hosea. It is possible that the inspiration for linking the Bundesformel to the covenant of peace was provided by the similarity of Hos 2:25 and the formula. But Ezekiel has not inherited the Covenant Formula with its characteristic double *lĕ*-from the text of Hosea. He has rather applied the formula known from elsewhere to a covenant of peace transmitted by the earlier prophet. This indicates that in Ezekiel the connection between the covenant of peace and the Covenant Formula is secondary, not a primary encumbrance of the formula.

To summarize: an investigation of the relationship between the Covenant Formula and covenant shows that in none of the manifold covenants to which the formula is applied is the formula in a primary setting.

We have repeatedly seen that the Bundesformel attached to Yahweh's tabernacle. This association is preeminently characteristic of the Priestly Writer's use of the formula, but is by no means restricted to P. The same association is presupposed in previously quoted texts from Zechariah (Zech 2:14-15) and Ezekiel (Ezek 37:23-27). The connection between tabernacle and Bundesformel is striking. It is expressed most clearly at Lev 26:11-12:

> I shall set my tabernacle in your midst and my soul will not despise you. I shall travel in your midst, and *I shall become your god and you will become my people.*

These verses fall amidst an inventory of blessings to result from obedience to Yahweh. The list is by no means a creation of the Priestly Writer. It is rather a compilation of individual blessings which may be isolated for study, Lev 26:11-12 comprising one discrete block which may perhaps be restored to a more pristine form by eliminating the remark "my soul will not despise you," a remark participating in a redactional leitmotiv of the chapter.

There is nothing to indicate that the passage originated as a blessing formula. Its inclusion in a list of blessings can be ascribed to the influence of Deuteronomic use of the Covenant Formula. For Deuteronomy, the Covenant Formula expresses not only the terms of a covenant, but also and simultaneously a desirable outcome of obedience to Yahweh, a sort of blessing. But taken by itself, the passage from Leviticus conveys quite a different picture of the formula. The balanced clauses "I shall become your god and you will become my people" are presented as a tabernacle saying. Furthermore, it is presupposed that the tabernacle is a mobile sanctuary: "I shall travel in your midst" is Yahweh's promise.

These inferences resonate correctly with the pattern of use associating tabernacle and Bundesformel. To judge from the literary settings of this association (in P, Ezekiel, Zechariah), the Covenant Formula circulated as a tabernacle saying at Yahweh's Jerusalem temple. But the Jerusalem temple was not a mobile sanctuary, and the original home of the Bundesformel as tabernacle saying therefore cannot have been the house of cedar built by Solomon. The question must therefore be put: is the association of the Covenant Formula and the tabernacle, like that of formula and covenant, to be seen as secondary? There are indications that it is not. The diction of the Bundesformel was foreign to P. By construing the Covenant Formula as a tabernacle saying, the Priestly Writer made the noun *ʿam(m)* a designation of the congregation. This understanding of the Covenant Formula seems therefore to have been inherited and not created by P.

This inference may be coupled with a form-critical observation. The Covenant Formula has the formal character of an adoption. This has been recognized by most writers. But this formal insight has not been successfully exploited in seeking the formula's life setting. Some writers have been satisfied to speak of a vague borrowing of the legal form of marriage and adoption.[28] Lohfink has pressed the matter further by insisting that the Bundesformel occurs in passages where the thought world of marriage and adoption are in evidence, yet his evidence is not fully compelling. At Deut 7:6 the Covenant Formula is cited in the vicinity of a word meaning "love." At Jer 7:23 it falls close to the word "instruction," a term which Lohfink argues belongs to the economy of father-son relations. In 2 Sam 7 it occurs in the same chapter as an adoption formula. The remainder of Lohfink's evidence is more impressive, but still unconvincing. At Deut 14:1-2 we read:

> You are sons to Yahweh your god. Do not gash yourselves and do not make a baldness between your eyes for the dead. For you are a holy people to Yahweh your god. Yahweh has chosen you *to become his treasure-people* from among all the peoples on the face of the earth.

The passage gives the impression of joining Covenant Formula to an assertion of Yahweh's fatherhood to Israel. But the appearance is deceptive. The declaration "you are sons to Yahweh your god" motivates the following prohibition. The acts forbidden belong to the realm of the cult of family ancestors. As Yahweh's sons, Israel is not to revere in mourning their mortal fathers. The verse which follows this prohibition contains the Covenant Formula. It has been added secondarily to what precedes, as the shift from second person plural to singular pronouns accompanying it reveals. In Jer 31 the Bundesformel occurs before a block of material which includes Yahweh's declaration "I have become a father to Israel" (v. 9). But this block of material is literarily distinct from the citation of the Covenant Formula (v. 1), being separated from it by the introductory phrase "thus says Yahweh" (31:2). Later in the same chapter Jeremiah attaches the Covenant Formula to an affirmation of Yahweh's role as husband to Israel (vv 31ff.). The connection is original. The image comes from Hosea, who played with the themes of marriage and adoption and used the nouns "people" and "god" in his oracles (Hos 2:20ff.). These are the only texts which might corroborate the notion that the Covenant Formula and the field of marriage and adoption ideas circulated together. We must reckon with the possibility that this confluence resulted primarily from Hosea's creative use of materials and not from a traditional appreciation of the Bundesformel.

The structure of the Covenant Formula seems nevertheless to be that of an adoption. The failure of researchers to account adequately for this fact stems from the limitations imposed by the analogy of marriage and father-son adoption. It should be immediately evident that the Covenant Formula records neither the taking of a bride nor the adoption of a son. It lacks the words "husband" and "wife," "father" and "son." The terms it does offer are *ʿam(m)* and "god," as though to portray the adoption of a tribe by a deity. But a formula for such an occasion hardly existed for routine use in the Ancient Near East. At least it is fair to say that such a formula must be patterned after a more usual formula, the adoption of a tribe by an individual, a "client" formula.

The concerns of such a formula are easily imagined. A potential client may be expected to affirm solemnly that the tribe he would join is his own tribe, and furthermore that the gods of that tribe are his own. This is the stuff out of which the Covenant Formula has been fashioned. When allowance is made for the unique situation of a god joining a tribe, then the Bundesformel presents precisely what would be expected of a client formula. Yahweh proclaims that Israel is his own tribe *(ʿam[m])*, and instead of the normal correlative declaration of allegiance to the tribe's gods, he declares himself to be that god. Now when the tribe to which a client attaches himself is mobile, the token of the addition of the client to the tribe will be the addition of the client's tent to those of the group he joins. In ancient times among the Arabs the rule of clientship was expressed by the phrase *aṭ-ṭunub biṭ-ṭunub*, "tent rope touching tent rope."[29] The joining of tents establishes a client relationship. This is made clear by a poem quoted in chapter two:

> We encompassed their tents with our tents,
> and they became our "cousins" *(banu ʿamm)*.

The same ideology is reflected at Gen 34:16, where the proposal of Jacob's sons to Shechem is "we shall dwell with you and become a single *ʿam(m)*." Here, of course, there is more to becoming a single tribe than just living together. But to become a client of a mobile tribe will certainly have involved joining tent to tents and travelling together.

It would be possible to reconstruct the client formula on the basis of the Covenant Formula alone. Yet we are not without additional evidence to secure the picture emerging from the Covenant Formula. A version of the client formula has been preserved in the book of Ruth. Asked to abandon her mother-in-law Naomi, the Moabitess Ruth makes this declaration:

> To the place where you go I shall go;
> where you pass the night I shall pass the night.
> *Your tribe is my tribe,*
> *your god is my god.*
> Where you die I shall die and there be buried.
> Thus and more may Yahweh do to me if death separates us.
>
> Ruth 1:16-17

The rhythmic pattern of Ruth's words set them apart from their context. They have all the appearance of formulaic sayings. The life situation they imagine is that of a roving tribe, which travels and spends the night together. At the heart of Ruth's statement is the client formula "your tribe is my tribe, your god is my god."

The implication of identifying the Bundesformel as a client formula should be clear. Yahweh's tabernacle is his tent; at Exod 29:44-45 the formula is explicitly linked to the "tent of meeting." That a client formula should circulate with a tent is entirely appropriate. The joining of Yahweh's tent to Israel accomplishes exactly what the Covenant Formula expresses: the adoption of a tribe by its new deity. The association of formula and tabernacle thus appears to be primary.

This conclusion may imply that the Covenant Formula originated at a remote time in the history of Israel. Its survival is to be credited to the Jerusalem temple, which perpetuated, it seems, the ideology of an early tent shrine. The manner in which the formula was preserved cannot be known directly, but can perhaps be inferred from indirect data. The secondary association of formula and covenant is striking. So, too, is the Priestly Writer's idea that the formula found its fulfillment in the erection of the wilderness tabernacle. If it can be assumed that this foundation event was recalled in conjunction with the celebration of the Jerusalem temple dedication (the Deuteronomistic narration of which includes at 2 Kgs 8:53 a citation of the formula), then a moment is at hand in ancient Israel's festival calendar when themes linked to the Bundesformel converged: the festival of Booths. This festival provided the occasion for dedicating the Jerusalem temple. According to the dictates of Deut 31:10, it was also the time for celebrating covenant law. And Sukkoth was regarded as a reenactment of Israel's Exodus living conditions in booths (tents), a situation resembling the life setting imagined for the Covenant Formula. The transmission of the Covenant Formula at the festival of Booths can thus be thought to account for the secondary linking of covenant and obedience themes to a tabernacle saying. Because of the intimate association of the House of David in the affairs of the Jerusalem temple, the location of the Covenant Formula in the festival of Booths may also account for the occasional attachment of Davidic interests to the citation of the Bundesformel (2 Sam 7; Ezek 37:23ff.).

We come at last to a consideration of the history of the use of *ʿam(m)* in the formula. At the outset, the noun appears to have intended the itinerant tribe for which the bonds of tenting together were significant. At the Jerusalem temple which acceded to the place of the tabernacle, the meaning of the formula gradually broke down. Those who gathered to Yahweh's temple were no longer a tenting federation, but rather a religious assembly, and in the Biblical literature the formula often requires the interpretation of *ʿam(m)* to signify congregation. Attracted into the orbit of covenant ideas, the Bundesformel began to address Israel in the large and general sense of a people. Here the noun seems to have no special nuance and refers to national Israel. The broad course of the formula's history, if correctly interpreted, conforms to what would be expected if, as we have argued, the noun *ʿam(m)* has a primitive referent in the pastoral, nomadic company.

* * * * *

Kareth

The idiom *nikrĕtâ hannepeš hahîʾ mēʿammêhā* and its variants are referred to as the *kareth* penalty. The nature of the penalty is disputed. Pre-modern Jewish exegesis explained it as childlessness, premature death, exclusion from the afterlife, or destruction of the family.[30] E. Fink has given an excellent review of early modern understandings of the punishment, which has often been thought a death penalty.[31]

In his systematic investigation of the penalty, David Daube rejects the idea that it is a death sentence. He argues that while offenses governing *kareth* are by their nature acts of an individual, the verb *kārat* (hiphil) means "kill" only when its object is plural. If *kareth* seems to be a death penalty, it is because it has entered Biblical legal traditions as a modification of an earlier, explicit judgment of death. Lev 20:10ff. is crucial to the idiom's interpretation. Here a series of penalties (to be cut off in view of the children of one's people, to die without children, to go through life childless) point to a deterrent public spectacle - castration. Castration was not necessarily practiced in ancient Israel; castrati are excluded from the cult of Israel's god, and so the punishment may be intended metaphorically.[32]

W. Zimmerli has twice studied the *kareth* formula, isolating two legal clauses with separate histories. One of these is the *kareth* penalty, the other is the expression *ʾîš ʾîš mibbêt yiśrāʾēl*. Both originated before the Exile, as the use of the plural noun *ʿammîm* shows in the case of the penalty. Although Lev 20:2ff. implies that *kareth* is a death penalty, its completion is an act of God. Even where men are the putative subject of the verb *hikrît* (Num 4:18; 2 Sam 6:6ff.), the true agent is God. Man's role in *kareth* is to expel the offender from the cult.[33]

The most recent and also the most extensive treatment of the *kareth* formula is given in Donald Wold's unpublished dissertation "The Meaning of the Biblical Penalty *Kareth*." Wold attempts to situate the formula in the *Gattung* "conditional divine curse formulae." He compares the verb *kārat* with a collection of Akkadian and Northwest Semitic verbs meaning approximately "extirpate." Since the verbs he chooses for comparison occur in curses and sometimes have as their object both the cursed individual and his descendants, Wold concludes that *kārat* is also a divine curse formulation and also intends the extermination of an individual together with his seed. He supports this conclusion by arguing its compatibility with the use of the *kareth* penalty in the Bible.[34]

To identify the fundamental verbal structure of the formula is vital. The expression occurs with both the niphal and the hiphil of the verb *kārat*. The former is generally and correctly regarded as primary. Were the hiphil primary we would expect as its passive not the niphal but the hophal; the hiphil seems to derive from the niphal and means "to cause someone to be cut off." The priority of the passive form is an obstacle to Wold's thesis, for the passive construction accords poorly with the genre "divine curse," where active verbal forms with the deity as explicit subject are found.

To indicate the extent of relevant evidence is equally vital. Despite the exegetical tradition joining material like Lev 20:20 to the *kareth* corpus, it must be insisted that only those texts which invoke the *kareth* are suitable for inquiry into the formula. Zimmerli has indicated the extent of the material (Gen 17:14; Exod 12:15.19; 30:33.38; 31:14; Lev 7:20.21.25.27; 17:4.9.10.14; 18:29; 19:8; 20:2.5.6.17.18; 23:29.30; Num 9:13; 15:30.31; 19:13.20; Ezek 14:8.9).

Both Zimmerli and Wold have given adequate overviews of the use of the *kareth* penalty. Its basic form is *nikrĕtâ hannepeš hahî' mē'ammêhā*. It is invoked as the apodosis to legal protases governing a variety of sacral offenses subsumed by Wold under the rubric holiness. Although the formula occurs only in literature of the Exile, it was not a creation of that period. The reasons Zimmerli sets forth in support of this conclusion are suggestive but not conclusive. The word *'am(m)* can occur at a late date with a singular referent. But the antiquity of the *kareth* formula seems to be assured. The Priestly Writer made subtle changes in its wording, substituting for *'ammîm/'am* the nouns *qāhāl, 'ēdâ, yiśrā'ēl*, indicating a process of interpretation and of shaping the formula to his own vocabulary (Num 19:20; Exod 12:19; Exod 12:15). He has made the penalty pertain to Israel as a cultic establishment, but beyond the Priestly horizon there seems to lie a more neutral sense to the idiom.

It is clear that the Priestly Writer intended *'ammîm/'am* to signify "fellow Israelites" in some cultically circumscribed way. Just what he intended or understood the penalty as a whole to mean has been disputed. The fact that offenders can be cut off in plain view of the community (Lev 20:17) implies that the punishment was not entirely metaphysical. In this particular case, both male and female sex offenders are made subject to the *kareth*, and the penalty therefore cannot be castration. Exod 31:14 seems to show what the penalty actually was:

> Keep the Sabbath because it is holy for you. Those who defile it shall be put to death, because each person who does work on it, that soul shall be cut off from the midst of his *'ammîm*.

The execution of Sabbath violators is justified by citing a legal formula whose apodosis is the *kareth*. This unavoidably shows that Priestly circles took *kareth* to be a call for execution. The assumption of historical layering, that execution and *kareth* represent different stages in the treatment of Sabbath violation, cannot alter the fact that in the Priestly stratum the two are reconciled. "To be cut off from one's *'ammîm*" means, for P, to be executed.

Lev 20:2ff. does not contradict this view:

> Any Israelite or client sojourning in Israel who gives his seed to Molekh shall be put to death. The people of the land will stone him with stones. I will set my face against that man and cut him off from the midst of his people, for he gave his seed to Molekh, polluting my sanctuary and defiling my holy name.

The meaning of this disputed text is not that the people of the land will execute the offender and that the deity will bring about another, subsequent and different penalty. It is rather that the actions of the community express the will of God and are therefore appropriated by him as though his own. The text can therefore continue:

> If the people of the land cover their eyes from that man when he gives his seed to Molekh in order not to kill him, then I shall set my face against him and his family and everyone whoring with him by whoring with Molekh and cut him off from the midst of their people.

The evident meaning of the passage is that Yahweh himself will execute the offender in the event of noncompliance of the community. Punishment by death is P's interpretation of the *kareth* penalty.

Having expressed this view, we must add that *kareth* is more than just a death sentence. The frequency with which the penalty is supplemented by a declaration that the offender will carry his sin (or similar remarks) hints that for Biblical writers the *kareth* death sentence brings to its victims misfortunes beyond death (Lev 20:17; Ezek 14:8.9, etc.). What these misfortunes might be is not made clear.

We noted that the Priestly Writer inherited and gave an interpretation to the formula. A determination of its earlier meaning(s) is important, but a way clear to prior settings is not easily found. The study of the laws to which the idiom attaches has not illuminated its origin. One sometimes suspects that the Priestly Writer has used the formula freely and not in reliance on a complex legal tradition. At other times he seems to have received the *kareth* penalty with its protasis. Zimmerli has shown, however, that legal protases and the *kareth* apodosis ultimately have a separate history. Form criticism offers small prospect for advance. Formally, the *kareth* penalty is already in an appropriate setting in its legal use. The passive form of the verb *nikrat* corresponds to the passive forms of Israel's *môt-yûmāt* death verdict as well as the use of the n-stem of *dāku* in Babylonian law. But it is unlikely that the *kareth* formula originated as a law code formulation. It is absent from Israel's earliest legal literature and without cognate in the Semitic languages. In manner of expression it is an unusual way of saying "put to death."

The only data at hand for the recovery of an early use of the idiom are its diction and the fact that the Priestly Writer understood it to signify death and continuing misfortune.

We can perhaps understand the continuing misfortune by reference to a tribal ethos. The tribal adoption formula from Ruth concludes with the remark, "Where you die I will die and be buried. Thus and more may Yahweh do to me if death separates me from you." As we observed, the text embodies the ideal of a mobile tribe. Unity in the band implies communion in death and burial. Separation from one's *tribesmen* (*ʿammîm*) includes isolation in death and burial, condemnation to being absented from one's proper repose among the related dead. Such an idea may lie in the distant past behind the Priestly sense that *kareth* carries misfortunes beyond death.

It is probably unnecessary to invoke a tribal ethos to account for the fact that *kareth* denotes death. Following what has been said, the literal sense of the formula is "to be cut off from one's *tribesmen*." Of course the fatal severance might have been expulsion from a group whose physical survival depends on collective activity, perhaps a pastoral tribe. Or being cut off from one's tribesmen may have amounted to a loss of legal status and the forfeit of that protection afforded by blood retaliation.[35] But it seems most likely that in origin the formula exploited a metaphorical substitution of *hewing* for *killing* (cf. Jer 11:19). An individual cut off from his tribesmen is like a tree cut down and removed from the living.

If we have correctly understood the *kareth* penalty, then the noun *ʿam(m)* can show changes of meaning through time. It may first have designated "tribesman." Because in later Israel an *ʿam(m)* was a cultic community, it was natural for the idiom to be attracted to the formulation of cultic law, where it has survived. Used as a penalty clause, it retained the figural sense "to be put to death" while conveying a new literal meaning - to be eradicated from the community of Yahweh's worshippers.

* * * * *

neʾĕsap ʾel-ʿammāyw

The expression *neʾĕsap ʾel-ʿammāyw* occurs nine times in the Old Testament (Gen 25:8.17; 35:29; 49:33; Num 20:24; 27:13; 31:2; and twice Deut 32:50). Most reckon with a tenth occurrence which is created by emending *ʿammî* to *ʿammay* at Gen 49:29. But since all occurrences are in P[36] and since the Priestly Writer can vary his style by substituting *ʿam* for *ʿammîm* (compare *nikrat hāʾîš hahûʾ miqqereb ʿammô*, Lev 17:4, and *nikrĕtâ hannepeš hahîʾ mēʿammāyw*), the emendation should not be made. With singular or plural noun, the expression has the same meaning; the problem is to identify that meaning and explain its origin.

The literal sense of the idiom is "to be gathered to one's *ʿammîm*." It signifies death, and so *ʿammîm* is regularly understood as "forebears." To be gathered to one's forebears can mean either to be buried in the family tomb or to join the souls of the departed in the netherworld.[37] For P such literal significations are probably excluded. He reports the gathering of individuals not buried with their ancestors (Abraham, Moses, Aaron) and gives no indication of an immaterial reunion of the gathered, whatever his beliefs in this regard. It has therefore been necessary to assume that his use of the expression preserves an archaic idiom and that he knew only its figural sense.

There are two sources of doubt about this assumption. The fact that P alone uses the idiom does not require its lateness, but one may ask how P came to preserve it. He uses it on the whole in framework narratives which probably do not derive from independent, ancient traditions. It could be assumed that some priestly knowledge of mortuary ritual authorizes trust in the Priestly expression, but mortuary activity cannot have been the exclusive domain of P circles, and no one else employed the expression. Instead, other writers used variations of the idiom from which the noun *ʿammîm* is absent, and this is the second source of doubt. If it can be shown that the idiom originated without the noun *ʿammîm* or if the Priestly introduction of that noun can be motivated, then it must be concluded that *neʾĕsap ʾel-ʿammāyw* is not the home of a rare and ancient sense of *ʿam(m)*.

There is confusion in the use of *neʾĕsap* in biblical death euphemisms, but an Ugaritic text brings some order to the chaos. In a recitation of human loss suffered by Keret, we read

mḫmšt yitsp ršp

Reshef harvested a fifth CTA 14.1.18[38]

The grim reaper brings death; to be harvested is to expire. The pertinent verb is *ʾsp* (Gt) without prepositional augment. Biblical Hebrew has similar constructions. Ezekiel conveys the promise "no more will men be *harvested* by starvation" (*ʾăsûpê rāʿāb*; Ezek 34:29). An end to starvation is meant. The niphal *neʾĕsap* can be used in place of the passive participle *ʾāsûp*: "Faithful men *are removed* but no one notices" (Isa 57:1). The antiquity of the Ugaritic text argues for the originality of the use of the simple verb to mean to die. The addition of prepositional phrases (*ʾel-qibĕrōtêkā* "to your tombs" at 2 Kgs 22:20; *ʾel-ʾăbôtāyw* "to its ancestors" at Judg 2:10) is easily explained as the effect of popular etymologizing. That is, *neʾĕsap* was understood to mean "to be brought (to the grave)" or "to be reunited (with one's ancestors)." The Priestly Writer's "to be gathered to one's *ʿammîm*" belongs to this stage of development.

Why did Priestly circles associate *ʿammîm* with this idiom? It could be argued that they knew the word to be a synonym of *ʾābôt*, "ancestors." Although this idea cannot be disproved, it has no support from Priestly use of *ʿammîm* and in fact no support from Hebrew use in general. While a people sometimes has a vertical component, a person's *ʿammîm* are never the union of his departed relatives to the exclusion of the living. An alternative to the idea that *ʿammîm* are ancestors is at hand in Wold's observation that the expressions *nikrĕtâ hannepeš hahîʾ mēʿammāyw* and *hēʾāsēp ʾel-ʿammāyw* are phrased as antonyms.[39]

We have already seen that for P the former signified death with guilt. We suspect that the latter has been shaped after the pattern of the former in order to signify death without guilt. The meaning is suitable, for P uses the phrase only to record the passing of revered forefathers - Abraham, Ishmael, Isaac, Jacob, Moses, and Aaron. In Priestly theology only Moses and Aaron died after the institution of a system for expiating guilt, and both died condemned for the sin at Meriba. It is at least possible that the Priestly use of *neʾĕsap ʾel-ʿammāyw* qualifies the passing of forefathers as guiltless, although the motivation of Ishmael's inclusion is not transparent.

For our purpose it matters that the antiquity of the idiom is in doubt. Its preservation of a rare meaning of *ʿam(m)* is far from assured.

Chapter V

BIBLICAL NOUN PHRASES

A study of Biblical formulae has offered some confirmation to the idea that an *ʿam(m)* was at one time a pastoral band. In the Covenant Formula at least there appears to be a level of primary meaning in which this is a "people's" identity. In this chapter we shall attempt to augment the picture through an investigation of a number of Biblical noun phrases.

* * * * *

Stiff-Necked People

The expression *ʿam-qĕšēh-ʿōrep* occurs six times in the Old Testament (Exod 32:9; 33:3.5; 34:9; Deut 9:6.13). An understanding of these occurrences is impossible apart from a careful investigation of the related construction *hiqšâ ʿōrep*, "to stiffen the neck." The latter signifies "to be obstinate" and is confined to literature beginning in the late pre-Exilic period.[1] Because the literarily earliest occurrences of this idiom fall in the Deuteronomic corpus and those portions of Jeremiah with strong affinities to Deuteronomy, the collocation "to stiffen the neck" has often been regarded as characteristically Deuteronomic.[2] Such an evaluation is misleading. The expression occurs in a variety of literary forms differing from the essentially parenetic contexts which house the construction in Deuteronomic texts. It is found in a proverb (Prov 29:1), a public prayer of confession (Neh 9:29), and, if allowance be made for the "break-up of stereotypical phrases," its nominal reflex is found in poetic prophetic discourse (Isa 48:4). At the same time, the manner in which Deuteronomic texts employ *hiqšâ ʿōrep* gives evidence of the expression's appropriation from other circles. Within the Deuteronomic corpus (including Jeremianic prose), neck-stiffening obstinacy is often related to a refusal to receive direction of one sort or another - prophetic word, commandment, torah, or simply instruction (*mûsār*;

Jer 7:26-28; 17:23; 2 Kgs 17:13-14). This is wisdom terminology, a fact which combines nicely with the proverb "a man of reproofs who stiffens the neck is suddenly, irreparably ruined" (Prov 29:1) to indicate that neck-stiffening obstinacy belongs to the economy of instruction. To assume that Deuteronomic circles borrowed wisdom vocabulary causes no difficulty.[3]

"To stiffen the neck" is at home in didactic settings, and this harmonizes well with the commonly held view that the expression derives its meaning "to be obstinate" from the observation of animal behavior. Endorsing an older opinion, Franz Hesse has suggested that the metaphor imagines the yoked beast of burden which stiffens its neck to express resistance to its directed course.[4] He has been followed by A. S. van der Woude in adverting to Jer 5:5 and Hos 4:16 for a suitable textual indication that this was the case. The former recounts Jeremiah's false hope that wrongdoing was confined to Israel's lower classes:

> I shall go to the great men and speak to them, for they know Yahweh's way, the wont of their god. Yet they together have broken yoke, they have cast off fetters.

The latter records the complaint,

> How like a rebellious heifer has Israel rebelled! Will Yahweh now pasture them like a lamb in broad meadow?

Both texts show that obstinacy and rebellion could be illustrated by animal behavior. The former presupposes that the yoked beast of burden was a fit subject for comparison in this regard. Now the study of the animal world was sometimes a wisdom enterprise, and this alone might suffice to account for the didactic rooting of an animal metaphor for obstinacy. As it happens, it may be possible to clarify the genesis of "neck-stiffening" as a metaphor for resistance to education with some specificity. In Hebrew, the term used to designate "trained (to plough)" is *mĕlummād*. The literal meaning of *mĕlummād* seems to be "educated," and this coincidence makes the trained beast of burden a particularly fit subject for a metaphor of education. Jeremiah used the trope in this fashion:

> I have heard Ephraim lamenting,
> "You corrected me and I took instruction,
> as a calf not yet *trained*." Jer 31:18

Educational correction is likened to the training of a calf to plough. Here as elsewhere, Jeremiah may have drawn his inspiration from Hosea. We may compare the difficult text of Hos 10:11:

Ephraim is a *trained* heifer, one that loves to thresh.
I shall pass a yoke upon her fair neck.

To these Biblical texts may be added Sira 51:17, which M. H. Goshen-Gottstein has translated:

Her yoke was an honor to me and I praise my *teacher (mlmdy)*[5]

It is clear that *mĕlummād* was taken to mean "educated" and that the educated beast of burden was used as a figure of human instruction. That this understanding of *mĕlummād* was etymologically correct, however, is not clear. Goshen-Gottstein's comparison of *mĕlummād* with Ugaritic *mdl* is apposite. The Ugaritic verb denotes the fixture on a donkey of some apparatus required by a donkey's rider. It occurs in a typical context at CTA 4.4.9:

mdl ʿr
ṣmd pḥl
He fixed a *mdl* to a donkey,
he harnessed a stallion.

The etymology of Ugaritic *mdl* is problematic, and hence its translation uncertain. An appropriate Semitic root $\sqrt{\text{mdl}}$ is lacking. Jonas Greenfield's attempt to identify the Ugaritic verb with an Aramaic verb *lmd* meaning "to attach" represents the best effort to solve the problem.[6] Yet it seems more likely that Ugaritic *mdl* is a denominative verb whose initial consonant was not originally a root consonant but rather a nominal prefix, the preformative of a noun of instrument. The verb should mean "he fixed a **mdl*." The noun **mdl* is probably to be derived from the consonantal root $\sqrt{\text{dll}}$ which in both Aramaic and Arabic can convey the meanings "to point out,"[7] originally "to guide." A **mdl* is thus a guiding apparatus, and this meaning suits both the Ugaritic and Hebrew evidence. A formal analogy to this development is provided by Hebrew *māgēn*, "shield" ($\sqrt{\text{gnn}}$) and the verb *miggēn*, "to shield."

As an apparatus for guiding an animal, **mdl* may be rendered "tether"; the verb *mdl* means "to tether." In Hebrew the metathesized form of this verb *(limmēd)* means "to guide, to train an animal to accept guidance," senses easily confused with the etymologically distinct *limmēd* "to teach." The confusion is evident in two passages adduced by Goshen-Gottstein in search of the nexus between Ugaritic *mdl* and Hebrew *limmēd*:

With whom has he consulted? Who gives him understanding?
Who *guides* him in the way of judgment? Isa 40:14

I shall *guide* offenders in your paths,
sinners shall return to you. Ps 51:15

To distinguish "to guide" from "to teach" in such contexts is virtually impossible.

That Hebrew *limmēd* means both "to educate" and "to train an animal (to plough)" may be a coincidence arising from the metathesis of an earlier **middēl* having the latter meaning. This coincidence contributed to the analogy of training a beast and educating an individual. The existence of this analogy increases the likelihood that "to stiffen the neck" is correctly understood to be an image of the beast of burden resisting guidance; so, too, an individual who refuses education may be said to stiffen the neck. This is a logical use of *hiqšâ ʿōrep*. But to observe this use and to account for it do not exhaustively explain the Biblical use of the metaphor, for it remains to note and interpret the strong attraction of "the fathers" for this image.

The attraction between "the fathers" and the metaphor "to stiffen the neck" may be formulated in this fashion: There is an observable tendency in the Biblical literature to associate neck-stiffening directly or indirectly with Israel's "fathers." The fathers, as we shall see, are the wilderness generation. This tendency affects both Deuteronomic and non-Deuteronomic literature and provides a link between the expression *hiqšâ ʿōrep* and the noun phrase *ʿam-qĕšēh-ʿōrep*.

An exposition of the relevant texts makes this clear. A prose section of the book of Jeremiah records Yahweh's complaint against Israel that:

they would not listen, nor would they open their ears.
They evilly *hardened their necks* more than their *fathers*.
Jer 7:26

Again in the prose of Jeremiah, we read the divine imperative and complaint:

> Sanctify the Sabbath just as I commanded your *fathers*. But they would not listen nor would they open their ears. They *hardened their neck* more than their *fathers* in order not to hear and in order not to accept instruction.[8]
>
> Jer 17:22-23

Those commanded to sanctify the Sabbath were the wilderness generation to whom the law was given. That these were the fathers appears also from the Deuteronomistic summary of the wrongs of the northern kingdom of Israel:

> Yahweh bore witness concerning Israel and concerning Judah by means of every prophet and seer, saying, "Turn back from your wicked paths and keep my commandments and my statutes, according to all the torah which I commanded your *fathers* and which I committed to you by means of my servants and prophets." But they would not listen; they *hardened their neck* like their *fathers'* neck, those who did not trust Yahweh their god. 2 Kgs 17:13-14

Here the fathers are clearly the men coming out of Egypt, the wilderness generation to whom the law was entrusted. The Chronicler offers a message from Hezekiah to all Israel, delivered by palace guards and royal officials:

> Sons of Israel, return to Yahweh, the god of Abraham, Isaac, and Israel in order that he may remove from the dominion of the kings of Assyria your remaining fugitives. Be not like your *fathers* and brothers who rebelled against Yahweh the god of your fathers, whom he gave over to destruction just as you see. Now, do not *harden your neck* as your *fathers*. 2 Chr 30:6-7

The context does not clarify what is meant by "fathers," but in the public prayer of confession recorded at Neh 9, it is again clear that "fathers" represents the wilderness community:

> You came down from Mount Sinai and spoke to them from heaven, and you gave them right judgments, true torahs, and good statutes and commandments....But they our *fathers* presumptuously *hardened their neck* and refused to hear your commandments. They loathed obedience and would not remember the wonders you had performed among them. They *hardened their neck* and chose a leader to return to their bondage in Egypt. Neh 9:13-17

To this register of texts in which neck-stiffening is attributed to the fathers must be added certain passages from the book of Deuteronomy. Near the end of his ministry, Moses charged the Levites:

> Take this book of the torah and place it beside the ark of the covenant of Yahweh your god, and let it be a testimony against you there. For I know your rebelliousness and your *stiff neck*. Even now as I still live among you, you have been rebellious against Yahweh, and what about after my death? Deut 31:26-27

The fathers are not mentioned by name because the literary setting presupposes that the wilderness generation is being addressed. Admittedly, the introduction to the book of Deuteronomy embraces the view that part of the wilderness generation has died prior to Moses' speeches on the brink of the promised land. But this view has not been systematically nor thoroughly incorporated into the perspective of Moses' addresses, which regularly presuppose that those addressed have witnessed the wonders of Yahweh and participated in the rebellions of Israel. Here it is therefore the wilderness generation who have a stiff neck, who are obstinate. Moses' hortatory remark:

> Yet Yahweh delighted to love your fathers, and chose you, their seed, after them from among all the peoples as on this day. So circumcise the foreskins of your hearts and do not again *harden your neck*. Deut 10:15-16

belongs to the same category of phenomena. (The "fathers" here are Abraham, Isaac, and Jacob.) Those addressed must not stiffen the neck *again*. Their previous neck-stiffening is recounted at Deut 9:6ff. in a passage to which we shall turn our attention shortly. Suffice it here to indicate that the previous incidents of neck-stiffening belong to the wilderness generation and that it may reasonably be inferred that this same community is the model audience for Moses' addresses.

A passage such as this last does not function in its imagined context. The place of the wilderness fathers is in fact occupied by a much later generation of Israel whose own "fathers" form a vertical chain leading back to the wilderness era. For such a real audience there is a potential source of confusion, since to later generations "fathers" may refer to any or all of the preceding communities. Thus, the referent of "fathers" in Hezekiah's message is ambiguous, and the public confession of Neh 9 pursues the theme of Israelite rebellion after the wilderness period and complains of later generations that they, too, hardened the neck. Yet this confusion must not obscure the peculiar affinity of the wilderness era for "to stiffen the neck." That earliest generation of rebellious fathers exemplified neck-stiffening, and therefore became a recurring term of comparison for later generations, a touchstone of wrongdoing. This touchstone was in active use at the close of the first temple period and in the following years in an era and in circles in which the exposition of Israelite error flourished. To use the wilderness fathers as a model of obstinacy presupposes an evaluation of that generation as stiff-necked. Since this pattern of use emerges in the Deuteronomic literature, a search for an explanation of the attraction between *hiqšâ ʿōrep* and the wilderness fathers must begin in Deuteronomy's presentation of wilderness materials.

We noted with respect to Deuteronomy 10:15-16 that Moses' request of Israel not to stiffen the neck again is rooted in the exposition of prior instances of neck-hardening. The relevant incidents are narrated at Deut 9:7-19 and consist of, in order, the golden calf apostasy, provocations at Taberah, Massah, Kibrot-hattaavah, and Israel's refusal to take possession of the promised land from Kadesh-barnea. The list is a catalogue of wilderness rebellion tales borrowed from the Tetrateuch,[9] but is little more than a catalogue. Only the golden calf apostasy is narrated; other incidents exist in name only, with Israel's timorous failure to possess the land from Kadesh-barnea expanded by the theological interpretation of that failure as refractory and faithless. Immediately after this itinerary of rebellion, the text (Deut 9:25ff.) recounts Moses' intercession for Israel in which Moses requested that Yahweh pay no heed to Israel's stiffness *(qĕšî)*. We must understand "of neck" to be elliptically suppressed; the request ties the wilderness inventory to neck-stiffening. The two are more solidly linked by the introduction to the entire passage. Addressing Israel, Moses declares:

> You know that it is not because of your righteousness that Yahweh your god is about to cause you to inherit this good land, for you are a *stiff-necked people* (*ʿam-qĕšēh-ʿōrep*).
>
> Deut 9:6

Furthermore, the entire section ultimately issues in Moses' hortatory commandment, "Do not again *stiffen your neck*" (Deut 10:16). For the redacted form of the text, neck-stiffening is associated with an itinerary of specific wilderness events.

But the redacted form of this material seems to obscure a layering in the text which is significant to the understanding of the metaphor *hiqšâ ʿōrep*. In its present form, Deut 9:1ff. represents a mixture of materials of which the earlier (called here for convenience "Deuteronomic") core may be identified as 9:1-7a,26-29; 10:12-15. This nucleus presents a coherent, self-contained narrative and, in addition, is generally set apart by its grammatically singular forms of address. The expression *hiqšâ ʿōrep* is foreign to the Deuteronomic core, which uses only the noun phrase *ʿam-qĕšēh-ʿōrep* and the elliptical noun *qĕšî*. The Deuteronomic writer did not relate these terms to any specific event from Israel's traditions, but rather knew them to describe generally the character of wilderness Israel. It was a Deuteronomistic writer who linked the noun phrase "stiff-necked people" and the idiom "to stiffen the neck" and who anchored both in concrete events from Israel's traditions. A way clear to historicizing these terms was partially prepared for the Deuteronomistic author by Israel's epic traditions, which had already located the expression *ʿam-qĕšēh-ʿōrep* in the story of the golden calf (see below). It is therefore neither surprising nor coincidental that of the wilderness happenings chronicled by the Deuteronomistic writer only the story of the golden calf is offered in detail.

A Deuteronomistic writer tied the idiom *hiqšâ ʿōrep* to the wilderness generation in dependence on an earlier tradition labeling the wilderness generation *ʿam-qĕšēh-ʿōrep*. This indicates that the earlier material underlies the attraction of "to stiffen the neck" and the fathers. The Deuteronomic understanding of this tradition tied it to no specific event and gives no evidence of dependence on material in the book of Exodus. Apart from Deuteronomy, only Exod 32-34 witnesses the expression "stiff-necked people" and the tradition that wilderness Israel was *ʿam-qĕšēh-ʿōrep*. These chapters form an independent block of material moulded into a pattern of sin and forgiveness by a redactor.[10] The expression *ʿam-qĕšēh-ʿōrep* occurs four times in this block of material and functions as a redactional leitmotiv making the connection between larger units explicit. Thus, Israel's sin in Exod 32 leads to the characterization of the people as *ʿam-qĕšēh-ʿōrep* (v. 9). The consequences of this sin are resumed at 33:1-6 in connection with the same expression (vv.3,5). Finally, the consequences detailed at 33:1-6 are mitigated in chapter 34, again with explicit reference to Israel as a stiff-necked *ʿam* (v. 9). It remains to determine in each case whether the phrase occurs as the work of a redactor or whether it is rooted in older material.

This alternative is easily resolved for Exod 34:9. The verse breaks its context and has no function apart from the overarching redactional purpose of portraying in Exod 32-34 a pattern of sin and forgiveness. Beyerlin has given the problem a convincing exposition and it requires no further comment.[11] The verse depends on Exod 33:1-6, where *ʿam-qĕšēh-ʿōrep* is first related to the divine presence in Israel.

The situation is more complicated for the remaining occurrences of the expression. We begin with Exod 32:9. Most recent commentators have regarded vv. 7/9-14 as a Deuteronomistic intervention into the story of the golden calf. At vv. 11-14 Moses' function is that of the Deuteronomistic intercessor, and the entire section is thought saturated with Deuteronomistic language.[12] It is conventionally argued that the intervention offers an explanation for why Yahweh did not immediately destroy Israel in the wake of her apostasy: Moses successfully, immediately interceded on Israel's behalf. Yet the necessity of immediately placating Yahweh is an issue raised for the first time at v. 10, thus within the supposed Deuteronomistic intervention itself. Moreover, a comparison of Exod 32:7-14 with the parallel account in Deut 9:8ff. reveals a seam within the former. Deut 9 replicates material found at Exod 32:7-10, but omits any mention of events recounted in vv. 11-14 of Exodus' version of the incident. Deuteronomy postpones

Moses' intercession for Israel and is untrammeled by the question why Yahweh did not immediately destroy the people. The dominant seam in the Exodus material therefore appears to lie between vv. 10 and 11; the heart of the expansion of Exod 32 must be restricted to vv. 11-14. These verses were added to the story of the golden calf in response to v. 10, which was recognized to imply that Moses' descent from the mountain should have led to the destruction of Israel. That vv. 7-10 belong to an earlier core of the chapter is indicated, an indication supported by Deuteronomy's replication of this material in dependence on the epic traditions.

The expression "stiff-necked people" occurs at Exod 32:9, thus in an early text of the chapter. Its occurrence seems also to antedate the redaction of chapters 32-34. Yahweh's declaration:

rāʾîtî ʾet-hāʿām hazzeh wehinnēh ʿam-qĕšēh-ʿōrep hûʾ

I have seen this people, that it is a stiff-necked people,

attaches to a word play developed later in the chapter. Hugo Gressman detected the paronomasia of vv. 22b and 25:

yādaʿtā ʾet-hāʿām kî bĕrāʿ hûʾ

you know the people, that they are inclined to evil,

wayyarʾ mōšeh ʾet-hāʿām kî pārūăʿ hûʾ kî-pĕrāʿōh ʾahărōn

Moses saw the people that they were wild, for Aaron had driven them wild.[13]

Neither sentence is easily translated, and Albright has characterized both as "almost hopelessly obscure."[14] Along with Mitchell Dahood,[15] he is inclined to disregard the Masoretic vocalization of *bĕrāʿ* (v. 22b) and attach the consonants *brʿ* to a root √brʿ (=√prʿ). Such an analysis does not contribute to the interpretation of the text. The writer of these passages certainly intended *bĕrāʿ* to evoke *pārūăʿ*, but it is unnecessary to contrive a triliteral root equation to account for this word play, as Exod 32:17a shows:

wayyišmaʿ yĕhôsūăʿ ʾet-qôl hāʿām bĕrēʿōh

Joshua heard the sound of the people as they shouted.

The collocation *bĕ-rēʿōh* belongs to the continuing word play of the chapter. It is thus proper to interpret *bĕrāʿ* as a combination of preposition and substantive. A close inspection of the word play in Exod 32 reveals that it involves combinations of the noun *ʿam(m)* and words or collocations whose skeletons are the consonants b/p,r, and ʿ: *ʿam bĕrēʿōh; ʿam bĕrāʿ; ʿam pārūăʿ*. The expression *ʿam-qĕšēh-ʿōrep* attaches to this series. The noun *ʿōrep* contains the consonants p, r, and ʿ. We may define the function of this elaborate paronomasia negatively: it has nothing to do with the pattern of sin and forgiveness dominating the redaction of Exod 32-34. The expression "stiff-necked people" must therefore have lain within the text of the story of the golden calf of which the compiler of Exod 32-34 made use.

The remaining occurrences of the noun phrase are found in Exod 33 at vv. 3 and 5. Probably neither instance is to be reckoned the work of a redactor. A comparison of 3b-4 with 5-6 shows that a single tradition with slight variations has been preserved in 33:1-6. That tradition links the characterization of Israel as a stiff-necked people to Israel's removal of jewelry. The extent to which the presentation of this tradition has been influenced by redactional interests is difficult to judge, but not vital to the understanding of the expression *ʿam-qĕšēh-ʿōrep*.

Certainty in allocating Exod 32; 33:1-6 to Pentateuchal sources is probably unattainable. Source divisions between J and E within Exod 32 have met with little success, and it has become common to assume that one or the other of these strata alone dominates the chapter.[16] The assumption that J dates to the reign of Solomon has led Cross to conclude the story of the golden calf under E, but Noth prefers J even at the cost of assuming the chapter's knowledge of post-Solomonic events (compare 32:4 and 1 Kgs 12:28) is attributable to a J supplement. Exod 33:1-6 seems to represent at least two sources. If 33:5-6 are a unitary fragment, then the use of the proper noun Horeb (v. 6) suggests its alignment with E. Vv. 1-4 probably are not a single, coherent literary fragment. In their redacted position these verses launch the transition from Sinai to the wilderness. This function is premature in relationship to a Pentateuch including Priestly writings, since an enormous block of Priestly material intervenes between Exod 34 and the activity anticipated by 33:1-4. Noth has suspected 33:1-6 in its entirety of being Deuteronomistic.[17] Suspicion that the expression "stiff-necked people" is Deuteronomistic is allayed by its occurrence in Exod 32. The search for Deuteronomistic touches may therefore be confined to 33:1-3a, where one encounters Yahweh's oath to the patriarchs, the "Deuteronomistic nation list," and the expression "a land flowing with milk and honey." That these elements are known to Deuteronomic literature is certain, but that they are characteristically or originally Deuteronomic is far from clear. All three elements occur elsewhere in the Tetrateuch (Exod 13:5) and are best regarded as well-known formulae available to writers in circles wider than what is defined by Deuteronomistic. That which raises difficulties in reckoning 1-3a Deuteronomistic is the angel mentioned at 2a. An angel is not expected in a Deuteronomistic context,[18] still less one which is regarded as an inferior replacement for Yahweh. Where a Deuteronomistic reworking of non-Deuteronomic materials is found (Exod 23: 20ff.)[19] it is insisted that Yahweh's name abides within his angel. It therefore seems likely that vv. 1-4 carry an amalgamation of a stiff-necked people tradition (vv. 3b-4) with a formulaic, transitional narrative. It is possible that the transitional narrative and the amalgamation are both the work of the crepuscular figure Rje (or, if E is an annotator, E). His source for the tradition at 3b-4 cannot be determined.

To summarize: the expression *ʿam-qĕšēh-ʿōrep* was known both to Deuteronomy and the epic sources of the Tetrateuch. That Deuteronomy understood the phrase to describe wilderness Israel has already been seen; how the expression was understood in the traditions of Exodus must now be investigated.

The principal narrator of the story of the golden calf reported that Yahweh labeled Israel a stiff-necked *ʿam*. The immediate contextual motivation for this is Yahweh's complaint that Israel has "departed quickly from the road I commanded them (v. 8)." Israel has gone astray, and this has a dual significance, for whereas "to leave the road" may figuratively designate error, it literally defines misdirected movement. This duality generates a congruent duality in the meaning of *ʿam-qĕšēh-ʿōrep*, which offers the same tropological-literal ambiguity. But for the latter, the literal sense applies primarily to flocks or other animals; a man or men are stiff-necked only in the figural sense "intractable." That which literally stiffens the neck in order to go astray is the beast of burden. Thematically, it is the literal problem of direction which informs the story of the golden calf. Israel demands a calf in order to have a god to go before her, i.e., to guide her (v 1). When Yahweh therefore utters his complaint (vv. 8-9), his words create a figural interpretation of the action in Israel's camp by pursuing the literal issue involved: guidance and direction. When we consider that Israel's golden *Führergott*[20] is in the form of a calf (*ʿēgel*), the beast of burden *par excellence* which stiffens its neck to move in the wrong course, we are led to suspect that the narrator intended in his use of *ʿam-qĕšēh-ʿōrep* to balance a literal and a figural signification. As an *ʿam(m)*, Israel seems simultaneously to be both a herd and a human company.

To discern within the story of the golden calf an earlier context than this for the expression *ʿam-qĕšēh-ʿōrep* is difficult. Yet there is an interesting similarity between elements of this tale and the tradition doublet at Exod 33:3b-6. The latter ties the label "stiff-necked *ʿam*" to a removal of jewelry. In Exod 32, it is a removal of rings and the fashioning of a golden idol which leads to the application of the noun phrase to Israel. In effect, it seems possible that a tradition akin to that preserved in Exod 33 lies somewhere in the background of the story of the golden calf. But such a tradition is no longer retrievable from Exod 32.

The compiler of Exod 33:1-4 seems to have understood "stiff-necked people" as a designation of wilderness Israel. This is implied at least by his build-up of the great themes of the Pentateuch/Hexateuch. V. 1a alludes to the theme "Exodus"; v. 1b to "Promise to the Patriarchs"; v. 2 to "Conquest of Canaan." In its present setting v. 3a is syntactically and contextually difficult; it may have been dislocated in the transmission of the text. Given the build-up of themes in vv. 1-2, it may be that v. 3b (including "stiff-necked people") represents the topic "Wilderness Wanderings." The only great theme not explicitly invoked in vv. 1-4 would therefore be "Sinai Revelation." Sinai is, however, the presupposed setting of the discourse making up this block of material. Such a use of 3b is not self-evidently motivated by the complex 3b-4. If the shape of 1-4 is correctly attributed to Rje (E), and if he is to be located in an early Deuteronomic sphere,[21] then this understanding of "stiff-necked-people" and that of Deuteronomy are probably to be related. Any nuances of the expression are lost in this redactional use of vv. 3b-4.

The jewelry removal tradition can be examined independently. There are perhaps three witnesses to it, that found within the story of the golden calf (Exod 32), Exod 33:3b-4, and Exod 33:5-6. The tradition is thoroughly obscured in the first, but rather clearly seen in the latter two. Yahweh declares that he will not ascend in the midst of Israel because Israel is a stiff-necked *ʿam*, and hence if Yahweh were to ascend in her midst he would necessarily destroy her. The tradition is rooted at Horeb (v. 6), and hence the ascent anticipates Israel's journey through the wilderness to the promised land. The tradition has no bearing on the issue of Yahweh's presence in a stationary Israel. This is an issue raised only by the redactional use of this material to lead into narratives concerned with theophany (Exod 33:7ff.). Rather, Yahweh will not travel in Israel's midst lest he destroy her *in the path.* Plainly, Israel as a stiff-necked *ʿam* will tend to leave the path. To force it into the correct path would destroy it. Israel's response to the knowledge that Yahweh cannot travel in her midst is to remove jewelry either as a sign of mourning (v. 4) or in response to a commandment (v. 5).

The Elohist's version of this tradition (vv. 5-6) has the character of an etiology. It concludes with the remark, "So the sons of Israel removed their jewelry beginning at Mount Horeb." The etiology itself attempts to explain the nature of the connection between Israel's label *ʿam-qĕšēh-ʿōrep* and the fact that Israel removed jewelry beginning at Horeb. That the etiology is not uniquely concerned with the removal of jewelry is indicated by the recurring association of the epithet *ʿam-qĕšēh-ʿōrep* with a removal of jewelry.

Neither Exod 33:3b-4 nor vv. 5-6 clarifies the logic connecting the epithet and the removal of *ʿădî*. If it is true that *ʿam-qĕšēh-ʿōrep* imagines a herd prone to errant movement, then an early connection may be sought in the meaning of *ʿădî*, "jewelry." Among the varieties of ornament it may designate is a horse or mule trapping, part of the apparatus required for leading the animal. This rare meaning is found at Ps 32:9:

> Be not like a horse or mule, without understanding, curbed with bridle and his *trapping*'s halter.

That Israel removes her *ʿădî* is an appropriate response to the proposition that she is a stiff-necked herd, for the noun *ʿădî* suggests a guiding device while designating "jewelry." It is possible that this *double entente* was still known to the Elohist. His version of the etiology makes no attempt to account rationally for Yahweh's commandment to remove "jewelry" as a sequence to the characterization of Israel as *ʿam-qĕšēh-ʿōrep*. The tradition preserved at Exod 33:3b-4, however, is no longer sensitive to the appropriateness of stripping *ʿădî*, and has fashioned an explanation for this activity by imposing on it the interpretation, "When the people heard this evil word, *they began to mourn*." Israel's refusal to wear ornamentation is thereby made an act of contrition.

The stiff-necked *ʿam* traditions belong to the theme of guidance. This is evident at every level of tradition, in every literary setting in which *ʿam-qĕšēh-ʿōrep* occurs. A stiff-necked people are not easily led. But whether the expression was from the outset intended *sensu malo* to be applied to an Israel conceived as a flock in need of guidance in the wilderness is not certain. In the traditions of Exod 33, the fact that Israel is a stiff-necked people is not contextually motivated. In the larger context of a redacted block of materials setting the story of the golden calf immediately before the fragmentary notices of Exod 33:1-6, the label fits. But apart from this redactional placement, it is difficult to understand why Yahweh calls Israel *ʿam-qĕšēh-ʿōrep*. One gains the impression that this phrase existed independently as an epithet of all or part of what became Israel, an epithet which has been incorporated into the historical traditions of the people, interpreted, and made a feature of the theme of guidance. The expression was put to suitable use, but it is not improper to inquire whether at some remote period it signified something quite different from a people who resist guidance.

A number of considerations suggest (without proving) that it did. The odious appearance of the epithet may be deceptive. Rather than implying resistance to guidance, the sobriquet may have intended military resoluteness. Warfare is a particularly attractive sphere for such an expression, as appears from the use of both the noun *ʿam(m)* and *ʿōrep* in military contexts:

> I shall send my terror before you and rout every *army* (*ʿam*) to whom you come, and I shall hand you your enemies by the neck (*ʿōrep*). Exod 23:27

> I pray, lord, what can I say after Israel has turned her *neck* before her enemies? Josh 7:8

Having a firm neck may imply not turning the neck in flight from adversaries. That the neck was the seat of militant character and that the noun *ʿam(m)* can denote an army is suggestive. A reconsideration of the relationship between *ʿam-qĕšēh-ʿōrep* and the removal of ornaments is thereby invited. This association is reminiscent of an ornament-stripping custom occasionally attested in the cuneiform literature. The removal of a soldier's *irtu*, either a chest ornament or a pectoral, is sometimes portrayed as a token of ferocity, as in the Tukulti Ninurta Epic:

> *[kâ]d-ru ez-zi-iš a-na te-še-e ba-lu tah-li-pe/i*
> *[i]l-⌜tah⌝-ṭu i-ra-a-ti ut-⌜tâk⌝-ki-ru lu-bu-ši*
> They (go) fiercely and ferociously into the fray, without armor.
> They had st⌜ripp⌝ed off their chest ornaments (and) changed their clothing.[22]

The linking of ferocity with a removal of chest ornaments is a potentially instructive parallel to the Biblical connection between the epithet "stiff-necked *ʿam*" and the stripping of *ʿădî*.

In the expression *ʿam-qĕšēh-ʿōrep* the noun *ʿam(m)* reveals itself to have passed through many understandings. It must be entertained as a possibility that it originally signified a fighting force and that the expression complimented the belligerent resolve of those to whom it referred. At a very early date the phrase was related to wilderness Israel, which was conceived as a herd prone to wander. The noun's animal referent was probably known to the earliest narrator of golden calf events and (if different) the Elohist. But already the composer of Exod 33:1-4 shows no sensitivity to this nuance, and Deuteronomy's seemingly independent use of the expression knows no more than that it pertains to the obdurate generation coming out of Egypt. This conforms to what was indicated in the introduction to the Biblical evidence. With the passing of time, meanings strongly rooted in a nomadic matrix vanished.

* * * * *

The People of the Land

To interpret the expression *ʿam hāʾāreṣ* has been a persistent problem of twentieth century Biblical scholarship. The collocation occurs approximately fifty times in locations scattered throughout the Old Testament, although most occurrences fall within the books of Jeremiah, Ezekiel, and Kings (Gen 23:7; 42:6; Lev 4:27; 20:2.4; Num 14:9; 2 Kgs 11:14.18.19. 20 [= 2 Chr 23:13.20.21]; 15:5 [= 2 Chr 26:21]; 16:15; 21:24 [= 2 Chr 33:25]; 23:30.35 [= 2 Chr 36:1]; 24:14; 25:3.19 (twice) [= Jer 52:6.26 (twice)]; Isa 24:4; Jer 1:18; 34:19; 37:2; 44:21; Ezek 7:27; 12:19; 22:29; 33:2; 39:13; 45:22; 46:3.9; Dan 9:6; Hag 2:4; Job 12:24; Zech 7:5). The number of occurrences must be raised if account be taken of variations of the noun phrase in which either *regens* or *regens* and *rectum* occur in the plural: *ʿammê hāʾāreṣ* or *ʿammê hāʾărāṣôt* (Deut 28:10; Josh 4:24; 1 Kgs 8:43.53.60 [= 2 Chr 6:33]; Ezek 31:12; Zeph 3:20; Ezra 3:3; 9:1.2.11; 10:2.11; Neh 9:24.30; 10:29.31. 32; 1 Chr 5:25; 2 Chr 32:13.19; Esth 8:17). These variations are largely confined to post-Exilic texts and have usually been regarded as unrelated to the problem of the meaning of "the people of the land." Outside of the Old Testament, an expression similar to *ʿam hāʾāreṣ* is known from a Phoenician inscription (KAI 10:11-12; *ʿm ʾrṣ z*). A Punic text associates *ʿam* and *ʾădāmâ* (KAI 145:3; *ʿmʾ yšb ʾdmt*), and a resemblance between the Hebrew noun phrase and Akkadian *nišē māti* has been proposed.[23] In post-canonical Jewish literature *ʿam hāʾāreṣ* came to mean "one ignorant of the law," but this semantic evolution and the texts relevant to its study lie beyond our inquiry.

A responsible survey of the literature generated by the expression "the people of the land" would require a separate monograph.[24] Here it is possible to indicate only the broad outlines of scholarly research into the topic. Perhaps the most famous treatment of the problem is Judge M. Sulzberger's 1909 monograph, *ʿAm ha-aretz - The Ancient Hebrew Parliament.* Sulzberger's title conveys his thesis - "the people of the land" designates Israel's parliament, an institution complete with upper and lower houses, thus reflecting the wilderness *ʿēdâ* whose "Lords" were twelve *nĕśîʾîm* and whose "Commons" seventy *zĕqēnîm*. Sulzberger recognized a looseness in Biblical terminology, as the parliament could be denoted by various congeners of "the people of the land" - *ʿam*, *ʿam yĕhûdâ*, etc.[25] He was not alone in perceiving a parliamentary institution behind *ʿam hāʾāreṣ*. N. Sloush followed Sulzberger's volume with a sketch of Israel's democratic institutions made in the light of both Phoenician and Hebrew use of the noun *ʿam(m)*,[26] while E. Auerbach arrived independently in 1947 at a conclusion similar to Sulzberger's.[27] Echoes of this institutional understanding have persisted in the subsequent literature, although in keeping with the evidence the anatomy of the institution has been portrayed with decreasing definition.[28]

The institutional interpretation of *ʿam hāʾāreṣ* has never wanted opponents or rival theories. Robert Gordis severely criticized Sulzberger's thesis in 1934-1935 and substituted for it his own view that the meaning of the expression proceeds from the differentiation of urban (Jerusalemite) and rural life. "The people of the land" speaks of the latter.[29] Albrecht Alt held a similar view. He insisted that Jerusalem's status as a royal city was the fount of this differentiation.[30] This hypothesis has been controversial. Moshe Weinfeld has criticized it, insisting that the distinction between Jerusalem and the rest of Judah represents a stratification along the line Jerusalemite officialdom:Judaean citizenry. The latter are to be identified as the Biblical "people of the land."[31] Such a refined appreciation of the urban-rural dichotomy still retains the presumption that the meaning of *ʿam hāʾāreṣ* is to be sought by opposing "land" and "city."

Sociological interpretations of the expression have been proposed. Kurt Galling conceived the phrase as a designation for the Israelite proletariat,[32] while E. Klamroth believed the expression to denote the exploited masses.[33] Max Weber offered early objections to Klamroth's views, preferring to think of *ʿam hāʾāreṣ* as a sort of landed aristocracy which, separate from the personnel of cult and kingdom, played an important role in Judaean politics. Weber suspected the expression to be closely related to the unmodified term *ʿam(m)* in its meaning "militia," but he insisted that the evidence on the entire problem was too ambiguous to permit the proving of even his own thesis.[34] Eva Gillischewski gave a similar treatment to the topic in 1922. She interpreted the term *ʾereṣ* to mean "district" and the entire phrase as the free citizens of various city districts who, as free citizens, constituted both a cultic and a political community.[35] An essentially similar view was defended by E. Würthwein, whose monograph on the topic has been widely influential. According to Würthwein, *ʿam hāʾāreṣ* designates Israel's full citizens *(Vollbürger)*.[36] Within the same tradition stands Père Roland de Vaux, whose summary of the matter perhaps best represents a current *communis opinio*:

> (*ʿam hāʾāreṣ*) représente tous les hommes libres qui jouissent de leur plens droits civiques, les "Vollbürger," ce qui suppose, au moins à l'origine, qu'ils possèdent une terre et qu'ils sont soumis aux prestations en nature et au service militaire....[37]

The *ʾereṣ* of *ʿam hāʾāreṣ* is thus the land of landed freemen.

The acknowledgment of a military aspect to the problem of "the people of the land" led to the development of the thesis that *ʿam hāʾāreṣ* constituted the early, inner Deuteronomic circle. Already in 1928 A. Menes discerned a possible connection between *ʿam hāʾāreṣ* and Deuteronomy. That connection lies in the similarity between the activity of the people of the land in the reign of Jehoash (2 Kgs 11) and Josiah (2 Kgs 21:24). The discovery of the book of Deuteronomy in Josiah's reign and its covenantal legitimization finds a counterpart in the reign of Johoash when the people of the land compact to become the people of Yahweh. The participation of the people of the land in the former is to be inferred from the fact that they had been those to proclaim Josiah king.[38] The proposed tie between *ʿam hāʾāreṣ* and Deuteronomy was expanded by von Rad. Von Rad accepted the thesis of a decimation of Judah's professional army at the end of the eighth century and subsequent revitalization of the old Israelite militia. For von Rad, such an amphictyonic militia would be an ideal audience for Deuteronomic preaching, particularly for preaching on the well-represented topic of holy war.[39] J. A. Soggin has criticized this view and rejects the thesis of a decimation of the professional army. For Soggin, there is sufficient evidence in the books of Chronicles to demonstrate that the Israelite militia never fell into disuse. Soggin nevertheless acknowledges the connection between Deuteronomy and *ʿam hāʾāreṣ*, a faction which, in his opinion, is additionally represented in the Biblical literature by terms other than *ʿam hāʾāreṣ*.[40] S. Talmon rejects the connection between Deuteronomy and the people of the land because early portions of the Deuteronomistic History do not mention *ʿam hāʾāreṣ*.[41]

The episodes narrated at 2 Kgs 11 and 21 occupy two points in a three-point chain of references to the political activity of *ʿam hāʾāreṣ*, and this chain has exercised a fascination for students of both the political history of Israel and the expression itself. The common denominator of the activity ascribed to the people of the land appears to be loyalty to David's throne. They expel the Omrid queen Athaliah and replace her with the Davidid Jehoash (2 Kgs 11). They execute regicides and proclaim Josiah king (2 Kgs 21). Following Josiah's untimely death they proclaim Jehoahaz his successor (2 Kgs 23:30). In each case the Davidid accession is secured by *ʿam hāʾāreṣ*. The full significance of this has been thoroughly studied,[42] yielding the most recent identification of Judah's *ʿam hāʾāreṣ*. Talmon argues that they are the descendants of an elite faction of David's supporters, drawn from Hebron and settled in Jerusalem by David. For Talmon, *ʿam hāʾāreṣ* is an abbreviation of the full expression *ʿam hāʾāreṣ libnê yĕhûdâ* (an expression nowhere attested), and so terms other than *ʿam hāʾāreṣ* may be used to denote the same faction: *ʿam yĕhûdâ; kōl ʿam yĕhûdâ*.[43]

Over against the many scholars who have attempted to define *ʿam hāʾāreṣ* with some specificity stand a number of writers who deny the expression any special significance. Writers for theological dictionaries and encyclopediae have approached the problem with great caution and, occasionally, skepticism of nuanced understandings of the noun phrase.[44] To these should be added E. Nicholson, whose detailed exegetical treatment of the problem, often interacting with interpretive views of earlier writers, has led him to the conclusion that the expression means precisely "the people of the land," and that it takes on any special shades only by virtue of the context in which it appears.[45] Whereas most writers have blurred the distinctiveness of the noun phrase, either by limiting their investigations to a selection of the expression's occurrences or by coupling the expression with other phrases designating the same phenomenon, Nicholson has scrupulously attended to the expression.

To summarize: the significance of the expression *ʿam hāʾāreṣ* has been sought in institutional, sociological, and political terms. At the same time, a number of writers have denied the expression any special signification. A fresh appraisal of the material is in order.

The first step towards understanding the expression *ʿam hāʾāreṣ* is to decide which of its occurrences and variations fall together as a unified subject for inquiry. Two data should govern this decision. The first has been underscored by S. Talmon. Whenever the people of the land are an Israelite body, its composition is Judaean.[46] The second has been consistently overlooked, even though it explains the first. All references to the Judaean *ʿam hāʾāreṣ* come from literary sources composed after the first Judaean deportation (598), thus from a time when Israel's national horizons were effectively limited to Judaea. The importance of this chronological fact cannot be overestimated. Those who have sought to interpret the expression *ʿam hāʾāreṣ* by reference to the institutions, sociology, or politics of the Judaean kingdom have never confronted the dissonant fact that the expression is absent from the writings of that kingdom. It is hard to imagine how any fundamental sociological, political, or institutional "people of the land" managed to elude the notice or comment of Isaiah, Micah, or Zephaniah. How, then, can one account for the lack of even a single mention of Judah's *ʿam hāʾāreṣ* in writings predating the first deportation? It may be that this singular state of affairs is a literary accident, or it may be that the absence of contemporary documentation of the kingdom's "people of the land" is to be offset by the expression's transmission in early materials used by later writers. The former possibility cannot be tested, but to a limited extent the latter can, and we shall subsequently probe this potentiality. But a starting point of the investigation of *ʿam hāʾāreṣ* must maintain an earnest regard for temporal issues. Such an attitude carries with it an answer to the question how to delimit the material germane to a proper appraisal of the noun phrase. The criterion of literary dating must be allowed to canopy the relevant corpus. This criterion mandates including all instances of the plural variants of *ʿam hāʾāreṣ* and requires excluding only one occurrence of its more common, singular form. Such a result fully warrants the use of literary chronology in the analysis of *ʿam hāʾāreṣ*, for not only do references to the Judaean people of the land cluster after the first deportation, but so also do references to non-Israelite peoples of the land(s).[47]

The observation that the noun phrase materialized in Israelite literature commencing with the sixth century should be coupled with a second observation. Despite its relatively sudden appearance, the expression is widely distributed in the literature of this period: in P; Ezek; Jer; Dtn; Ezra-Neh; Chr; Isa apocalypse; Hag; Zech; Zeph supplement; Esth; Dan; Job. The signal breadth of the expression's distribution highlights the importance of resolving the problem of its prior use. If *ʿam hāʾāreṣ* was current before the sixth century, then its extensive dispersal in that century and the following period merits no surprise. Yet if the literary appearance of the noun phrase coincides with its entry into common parlance, then its wide distribution has a special moment. It must immediately be noted that there can never have been a time when the collocation did not occur by haphazard juncture. What must be sought is evidence of a special use or meaning of *ʿam hāʾāreṣ* which would account for the expression's blossoming after the first deportation. Such evidence is potentially to be found in those literary works which sometimes transmit earlier material, P and Dtn. Here we may encounter the vocabulary of a period earlier than the sixth century date of the compilation or final edition of the literary work.

The Priestly Writer used the noun phrase *'am hā'āreṣ* several times in two sorts of context, narrative and legal. That the diction of Priestly narrative is not that of the Priestly Writer cannot be assumed, and so the former may not be summoned to witness the language of an earlier era. But legal complexes may at least be suspected of preserving the language of an earlier time, and the occurrences of *'am hā'āreṣ* in Priestly law deserve examination.

At Lev 4:27, the Priestly Writer records:

> If a soul from among *the people of the land* sins unwittingly by doing something which, according to the commandments of Yahweh, is not to be done, and is guilty, and he is informed of the sin he committed....

Regulations for a sin offering follow. The case of an inadvertent offender from the people of the land is one of four categories of offense treated in Lev 4, the other categories being the unwitting offenses of the anointed high priest, of the entire congregation, and of a prince *(nāśî')*. The society defined by this catalogue is not that of the period of the monarchy. There is no mention of the Judaean monarch or his princes *(śārîm)*. The anointed high priest is a figure unknown to pre-Exilic Israel.[48] In contrast, every figure of the list is known to the literature of the Exile and/or to post-Exilic writings. The Exilic emergence of the people of the land as a cultic category is witnessed by Ezek 45:22, Ezek 46:3.9. The language of Lev 4 is thus that of a late period, and the preservation of *'am hā'āreṣ* as a term from pre-Exilic Judaea is to be excluded.

Elsewhere, Priestly law refers to the people of the land only at Lev 20:1-5:

> Yahweh spoke to Moses saying: You shall tell the sons of Israel, "Any Israelite or client sojourning in Israel who gives his seed to Molekh shall be put to death. *The people of the land* will stone him with stones. I will set my face against that man and cut him off from the midst of his people, for he gave his seed to Molekh, polluting my sanctuary and defiling my holy name. If *the people of the*

> *land* cover their eyes from that man when he gives his seed to Molekh in order not to kill him, then I shall set my face against him and his family and everyone whoring with him by whoring with Molekh and cut him off from the midst of their people."

An old kernel of Israelite law is certainly preserved in the *môt-yûmat* series of which this ordinance is a part,[49] but that kernel appears to be represented only by v. 2. The casuistic style of vv. 3ff., in which the noun phrase *ʿam hāʾāreṣ* occurs, sets this material apart as an addition to the older core. Although the addition's date cannot be fixed, these occurrences of "the people of the land" may not safely be assigned to the legal vocabulary of any early period. Such an assignment is opposed by the very real possibility that the expansion of the *môt-yûmat* kernel comes from and is in the language of the Priestly Writer himself.

P thus preserves no occurrence of *ʿam hāʾāreṣ* which may be inferentially assigned to the vocabulary of the era of the Israelite monarchy. What may be said of the Deuteronomistic History? That its compiler used earlier narratives in his presentation of Israel's history is reasonably certain. These fall in the early portions of the history, and it is therefore noteworthy that in the Deuteronomistic History, *ʿam hāʾāreṣ* is nowhere to be found prior to 2 Kgs 11. The expression "the peoples of the earth" occurs at Josh 4:24 and three times in 1 Kgs 8, but these passages are both probably late. Now Deuteronomistic authors may have used the noun phrase with reference to relatively recent events in Israel's history because their sources for those events already used it. But this does not appear likely. The extent to which occurrences of the expression bunch together at the end of the Deuteronomistic History is striking. Of thirteen occurrences of the expression, seven are to be found in narratives pertaining to events within a mere eighty years of the final, Exilic edition of the tome (2 Kgs 21:24; 23:30.35; 24:14; 25:3.19 twice), and four of these seven belong to narratives of incidents subsequent to the fall of Jerusalem in 598. Two of the remaining six occurrences of *ʿam hāʾāreṣ* are text-critically doubtful (2 Kgs 15:5; 16:15), and four are contained within a single narrative (2 Kgs 11:14. 18.19.20). That narrative requires special attention.

The four occurrences of *ʿam hāʾāreṣ* lie in the text of 2 Kgs 11, a text riddled with difficulties.[50] In addition to problematic readings, a problem of sources besets the chapter. The text initially recounts Athaliah's interruption of the Davidid succession to Judah's throne (vv. 1-4) and her near extermination of the royal line. The scene then shifts forward seven years to an account of a conspiracy directed by the priest Jehoiada to restore the crown to David's line. He enters into a covenant with the Carites and the captains of the palace guard and causes them to swear loyalty, it seems, to the young Davidid Jehoash. Jehoiada then arranges the stationing of the Carites and palace guards in preparation for the crowning of Jehoash. The actual crowning is now narrated in terms which presuppose a public ceremony from which Athaliah is remarkably absent. Jehoash is invested with royal insignia, whereupon "...they made him king, anointed him, clapped hands, and said 'Long live the king!'" (v. 12). The subject of the action is unspecified, but in the following narrative Athaliah enters the action and upon her arrival at the Yahweh temple discovers an assembly *(ʿam)*. These are evidently those who made Jehoash king. Suddenly the assembly becomes "all the people of the land" rejoicing and playing trumpets. The drama closes when the guards remove Athaliah toward the Horse Gate and execute her "there" (v. 16).

A new thread begins at v. 17, for now we hear of a covenant among Yahweh, king, and people *(ʿam)* "to become Yahweh's people." The expression *ʿam hāʾāreṣ* occurs three times in what follows, designating those who eradicate the signs of Baal worship, who accompany the new king from temple to palace, and who, at the narrative's conclusion, are reported to be rejoicing while the city is quiet. A statement is appended according to which "...they killed Athaliah with sword at the palace" (v. 20).

There is an apparent discrepancy between this final note and the earlier declaration that the palace guards took Athaliah towards the Horse Gate and killed her "there." If "there" refers to the Horse Gate, then the chapter provides two different versions of the death of Athaliah. B. Stade has proposed to divide the chapter into two distinct sources (1-12, 18b-20; 13-18a).[51] More recently, W. Rudolph has insisted that the referent of "there" in v. 16 is an undisclosed location along the way to the Horse Gate, hence conceivably the palace.[52] He denies the existence of two different sources within the chapter, and after making major adjustments in its text produces a unified, coherent account of the conspiratorial rise of Jehoash. Of the two approaches to the chapter, Stade's is the more persuasive. The tensions in the chapter are real, and yet they seem not to have resulted from a juxtaposition of the sources he imagined. Rather, the chapter seems to have blended an account of the palace conspiracy to oust Athaliah and elevate Jehoash to the throne with material concerning the Yahwistic piety of "all the people of the land." The point of contact between these two perspectives lies in vv. 13-14, where the conspiracy is augmented to a popular action by the introduction of an assembly *(ʿam)* and its transformation to "all the people of the land" *(kol-ʿam hāʾāreṣ)*. The awkwardness of this transition was recognized by the Chronicler, and his harmonization of the material is instructive. The Chronicler's account of these events introduces the conspiracy of Jehoiada and the captains, but then immediately tells of the dispatching of the captains throughout Judaea to gather the Levites and the heads of fathers' houses. The latter, of course, represent "all the people of the land" from the account of 2 Kgs. Levites and heads of fathers' houses now join the conspiracy, pledging by covenant loyalty to David's rightful heir Jehoash, and the problematic transition has been smoothed over (2 Chr 23). But the tension remains in the account of 2 Kgs. Now it is possible that Jehoiada's conspiracy utilized some routine temple assembly for the manifestation of the new king. The Baal-worshipper Athaliah's absence from such a Yahwistic gathering might occasion no surprise. But the transformation of an assembly into a gathering of "all the people of the land" introduces severe historical improbabilities. Athaliah's supine disregard for an affair of such potential importance, her absence from an assembly of Judah's notables (or whatever else *ʿam hāʾāreṣ* might denote), is out of place in the career of a regent with sufficient survival instinct to attempt to extinguish the line of David. The introduction of "the people of the land" at v. 14 must be explained on the basis of its occurrence in vv. 17-20. That is, an *ʿam* has been utilized to bind two different blocks of material; the term *ʿam hāʾāreṣ* belongs to the second block (vv. 17-20) and was introduced at v. 14 to fashion a link between the two.

We have already seen that the second block, centering as it does in the Covenant Formula, must be reckoned Deuteronomistic in its language. It appears therefore that *ʿam hāʾāreṣ* in this chapter belongs to a late linguistic horizon.

In neither P nor in the Deuteronomistic History are there occurrences of the expression "the people of the land" which may be judged to represent the vocabulary of Israel before the sixth century. This observation returns us to our starting point. An understanding of the noun phrase must situate it in the life of Judaea after the first deportation.

At the commencement of this period, two circumstances affected Israelite attitudes towards people and land: the division of the Judaean population and its partial separation from the land of Judaea. An emergent concern with these features of life reveals itself in Ezekiel's proclamation:

> The word of Yahweh came unto me saying: Son of man, your brethren, your brethren are the men of the Exile and the entire house of Israel, of whom Israel's inhabitants have said, "They are far away from Yahweh. The *land* has been given to us as an inheritance." Therefore say: Thus says my lord Yahweh, "Although I have sent them away among the nations and although I have scattered them among the *lands*, yet shall I be a sanctuary for them for a little while in the lands to which they have come." Therefore say: Thus says my lord Yahweh, "I shall gather you from the *peoples* and collect you from the *lands* in which you have scattered, and I shall give you Israel's soil." Ezek 11:14-17

Contrary to the conviction of Jews remaining in Judaea after the first deportation, Yahweh intended to exclude Judaea's deportees neither from his own worship nor from possession of the land. Ezekiel clearly implies that those living in the territory of Judaea comprised comething less than the total population of Judaea. Beginning with the first deportation, Judaea was no longer perfectly defined as "Judaea." Rather, its population was "the people of the land," an expression which at first must have implied a contrast with the people not of the land, Judaea's exiles. For their part, these people in exile now stood in new relationship to the other peoples of the world, the peoples of the lands, those among whom and in whose territories the exiles were scattered.

This is the background against which Ezekiel's use of *ʿam hāʾāreṣ* should be set. Ezekiel always uses the expression to designate the Israelite community which retained or would regain possession of its land. This generalization applies even to the one apparent exception, where a hypothetical people and land transparently refer to Judaeans and Judaea:

> The word of Yahweh came unto me saying: Son of man, tell the sons of your people and say to them, "If I bring sword against a land, and *the people of the land* choose one man from their midst and make him their lookout, and he sees sword coming against the land, sounds trumpet and warns the people, and if someone hears the trumpet without taking warning, sword comes and claims him, then his blood is on his own head. He heard the trumpet but did not take warning. His blood is on his own head - had he taken warning he would have saved himself. But if the lookout sees sword coming and does not sound the trumpet, the people are not warned, sword comes and claims one of them, then the victim will be claimed because of his own guilt, but I shall require his blood from the hand of the look-out." Son of man, I have made you lookout for the House of Israel. Ezek 33:1-7

The collocation *ʿam hāʾāreṣ* as a designation of landed Judaeans occurs in Ezekiel because the relationship between people and land is no longer taken for granted.

Now concerning the people of the land Ezekiel has much to say that is critical (Ezek 7:23-27; 12:17-19; 22:29), and it is not difficult to imagine that those not subjected to exile were the object of jealous accusations from those not in the land. This may account for the Deuteronomistic Historian's use of the noun phrase. If one examine's the presentation in the Deuteronomistic History of "the people of the land," one gains the impression that *ʿam hāʾāreṣ* were the guiltless victims of the course of events. At 2 Kgs 11 they are zealous Yahwists. At 2 Kgs 21:24 they faithfully execute regicides and proclaim as king the righteous man Josiah. When Judah began to suffer reverses, they suffered fully, being taxed (2 Kgs 23:35), starved (2 Kgs 25:3), executed (2 Kgs 29:19-21). They are the *poor* of the land (2 Kgs 24:14). The Deuteronomistic Historian, living after the exile still in the land, has portrayed the people of the land in terms which invite sympathy and a judgment that they had been faithful to Yahweh. His use of the noun phrase seems to presuppose the dichotomy people of the land, people not of the land.

What is true of the Deuteronomistic Historian and Ezekiel is true for other writers of their era. Their use of *ʿam hāʾāreṣ* mirrors a linguistic ebullition with a recognizable historical catalyst. It was the new perspective imposed by deportation which appears to have given rise to the frequent use of the expression and its plural variants. The perspective from which the expression emerged and not its referent is to be highlighted. When the Deuteronomistic Historian mentions the people of the land, he speaks from no arcane knowledge of an ancient Israelite institution or faction. Rather, he denotes the population of Judah using the vocabulary of his own time.

Such a conclusion is not intended as a renunciation of efforts to locate special institutions and factions in the life of the Judaean monarchy. But from a methodological standpoint, these efforts should not proceed from the assumption that the noun phrase *ʿam hāʾāreṣ* is a *terminus technicus* lingering from the period to be illuminated. It is not.

Whether the occurrence of *ʿm ʾrṣ* in a Phoenician inscription is relevant to the understanding of Biblical *ʿam hāʾāreṣ* cannot be decided. The relevant text dates to the fifth century, thus to a time when *ʿam hāʾāreṣ* had emerged as a popular Hebrew expression. Unfortunately, the corpus of Phoenician texts is so limited that it is impossible to know whether this temporal coincidence is anything more than a coincidence.

For the purpose of our investigation of the noun *ʿam(m)* we reach the sufficient conclusion that the word simply means "population" in the expression *ʿam hāʾāreṣ* and that the expression is not archaic.

* * * * *

Holy People and Treasure-People

Although the expression *ʿam qādôš* occurs only a handful of times (Deut 7:6; 14:2.21; 26:19; 28:9), it has frequently been studied. Its association with singular forms of address in Deuteronomy has led G. von Rad to account it an element of the so-called *Urdeuteronomium*. Von Rad believes the expression to have arisen already in the period of the judges in the practice of holy war,[53] but Lothar Perlitt rejects this idea because the sources for that period lack the collocation.[54] Kraus highlights Deut 14:21 in his study of the expression:

> Eat no carrion. Give it to the client at your gates and he may eat it, or sell it to a stranger, for you are a *holy people* to Yahweh your god.

Exod. 22:30 must be compared:

> You (pl.) shall be holy men *(ʾanšê-qōdeš)* to me. Flesh in the field, torn flesh, you shall not eat. You shall throw it to the dog.

It is clear that the two verses are similar. The latter has the expression "holy men" where the former speaks of a "holy people." "Holy people" occurs in Deuteronomy, the laws of which can ordinarily be assigned to a secondary phase of development *vis-à-vis* those of the Book of the Covenant. But Kraus doubts the priority of Exod 22:30. He thinks its plural "you" is ill-suited to the linguistic horizons of the Book of the Covenant and suggests that Deut 14:21 is an earlier witness to this regulation.[55] Lohfink is satisfied to assume the Exodus text's priority and describes Deuteronomy's use of *ʿam* as a modification *(Abwandlung)* of earlier *ʾanšê*.[56] This seems to be correct, and it appears that Lohfink was equally correct in joining the remaining uses of *ʿam qādôš* to the Covenant Formula.[57] Now we saw in the Covenant Formula that in picking up the tradition of Exod 19:3-6, Deuteronomy transformed the noun phrase *gôy qādôš* into *ʿam qādôš* in order to make it fit the language of the Covenant Formula, where the noun *ʿam(m)* is at home. We therefore cannot find an ancient noun phrase *ʿam qādôš* among its occurrences, either because that expression arose from earlier *ʾanšê-qōdeš* or because it comes from a transformation of *gôy qādoš*.

What has been said about *ʿam qādôš* applies equally to *ʿam sĕgullâ*. That *sĕgullâ* may have originally meant "herd" is interesting,[58] but there does not seem to have been an ancient expression *ʿam sĕgullâ*. Deuteronomy uses this noun phrase only in the Covenant Formula (Deut 7:6; 14:2; 26:18), and if we are correct in tying Deuteronomy's use of the formula to Exod 19, then the noun phrase arose from the juncture of covenant traditions in which Israel is said to be simply a *sĕgullâ* with the Covenant Formula in which Israel is an *ʿam(m)*. In Deuteronomy the noun phrase seems to mean "treasure people" and carry no pastoral connotation.

* * * * *

Yahweh's People

The expression *ʿam yhwh* is the subject of a recent article by Norbert Lohfink. Lohfink's essay is fundamental to the study of the collocation and masterfully achieves its stated purpose - a preliminary appraisal of the history of the expression's use. It provides a solid foundation for ongoing research into the topic, and even where disagreements with Lohfink emerge, the debt of future researchers to his labors will remain immense.[59]

By Lohfink's acount there are 359 occurrences of *ʿam yhwh* or variants of the expression (*ʿam lĕyhwh*, *ʿammô*, etc.).[60] This number does not include the two Biblical occurrences of *ʿam ʾĕlōhîm* (Judg 20:2; 2 Sam 14:13), although both are important for the understanding of *ʿam yhwh*. The expression's frequency mandates a preliminary overview of the material, and here Lohfink's research yields interesting results. Most occurrences of *ʿam yhwh* belong to prophetic speech. By contrast, the expression is basically foreign to wisdom, law code, and simple narrative settings. In a more detailed investigation Lohfink identifies three discrete meanings of "Yahweh's people" in evidence for the reign of David: Yahweh's tribe *(Sippe)*; his militia; his wards.[61] It is his thesis that later uses of the expression derive from one of these founts; he restricts himself in the remainder of his essay to the development of the image of the deity's tribe.

Lohfink is chary of seeking a univocal origin of the expression, but his reluctance has not been universally shared. Recent writers have inclined to regard Yahweh's militia as its fundamental signification. This is implied in Rabin's suggestion that Yahweh's character as a "man of war" (Exod 15:3) made warfare the vehicle for Israel's becoming Yahweh's *ʿam(m)*.[62] Rudolf Smend justifies the priority of the military sense on different grounds - this is the meaning encountered in Israel's oldest poetry. He goes so far as to deny that "Israel" was *ʿam yhwh* in the earliest traditions of the Bible. For Smend, the identification of Israel and *ʿam yhwh* has its historical antecedent in the territorial incursion of the Rachel tribes *(ʿam yhwh)* into the realm of the Leah tribes (Israel). In the earliest Biblical traditions, Yahweh's "people" is not yet the amphictyonic league (Israel), but still no more than those who participated in the deities' wars.[63]

The priority of the meaning "Yahweh's militia" has recently been disputed by A. R. Hulst. Hulst cites with approval Roland de Vaux's observation that beduin tribes do not distinguish between the tribal militia and the tribe as a whole. Such an observation raises the question, is the military use of *ʿam yhwh* subsidiary to the concept of Yahweh's tribe? Hulst believes that it is. In conformity with insights expressed by Vriezen, Procksch, and many others, he conceives *ʿam yhwh* to be an extended family and finds an etymological underpinning for this view: the "people" of Yahweh perpetuates an early connotation of the noun, "family, tribe, those who are related."[64] One must ask whether the influence of etymology (correct or incorrect) is not excessively present here and in Lohfink's vision of the tribe of Yahweh. The textual evidence for finding in *ʿam yhwh* an extended family or sib proves on close inspection to be unimpressive. Hulst cites Deut 14:1; 32:5.19; Hos 11:1; Deut 1:31; Isa 1:2; 30:1.9; Jer 3:14.19; Isa 43:6. Lohfink's references expand the list to include 2 Sam 7:24; Isa

63:8.14; Jer 4:22; 31:1; Hos 1:9; 2:1.3.25. A distinction must be made between texts which reflect a familial relationship between deity and worshippers and texts which both reflect such a relationship and use the expression *ʿam yhwh*. Only the latter are relevant to the expression's study, and most of the texts alluded to by Hulst and Lohfink are therefore not germane to the topic. Deut 14:1 has been discussed previously. Of all remaining texts, only Isa 1:2; Deut 32:5.19; Isa 63:9; Jer 4:22; Hos 1:9; 2:1.3.25 join the expression and the family image. At Isa 1:2 and Deut 32:5.19, the relationship between Yahweh and his people is expressed in family language originating not in a traditional image of *ʿam yhwh* but rather in the forensic vocabulary of the prophetic lawsuit (see below). Jeremiah's reproach of Israel (Jer 4:22) draws on wisdom terminology for the image of foolish sons and not on the concept of Yahweh's people. Isa 63:8 belongs to an amalgamation of oracles which purposefully contrasts Yahweh's people and the descendants of Abraham. The image of Yahweh the father, his worshipper the son serves this contrast, which must be seen to have functioned against the background of a growing emphasis on pure descent in the definition of the post-Exilic religious community. To judge from the verbal similarity between Isa 63:8 and Hos 2:1, third Isaiah manipulated Hoseanic themes in pursuing his own objectives. We are left with Hosea as the earliest and the only writer independently to join the noun phrase "Yahweh's people" and the image of the divine-human family. Was Hosea's understanding of Yahweh's people already traditional? It is more easily imagined that he developed the family metaphor through reflection on the themes of marriage and the naming of children, themes founded in personal experience. In short, there does not seem to be much evidence that the people of Yahweh were conceived as the deity's clan. This is an observation brought into striking profile by the straightforward presentation at Num 21:29 of *ʿam kĕmôš* as the sons and daughters of that Moabite deity. The difference lies not in Israel's spiritualized view of Yahweh, for the metaphor of the deity's family is well attested in Israel's literature. Indeed, the issue is not whether Israel had a vision of the family of God and man. What is at stake is the relevance of that vision for a semantic appreciation of "Yahweh's people," and we are inclined to regard that relevance as marginal at best.

The sheer bulk of pertinent material is a major obstacle to the study of *ʿam yhwh*. To trace historically the development of its use is a task well beyond the scope of this volume. Here, attention will be confined to problems centering on the expression's earliest settings. Israel's ancient poetry is an obvious source of information about these early settings, but this limited corpus of texts is by no means the only witness to remote Israelite usage. Amidst the surfeit of later materials there occur recognizable patterns in usage which perhaps point to identifiable origins in the life of the nation. These later materials assist the interpretation of earlier texts, which taken by themselves can be the source of widely diverging images of *ʿam yhwh*. Lohfink has indicated some of the later patterns of use. He correctly locates the expression in the *nāgîd*-titulary, about which detailed comments are offered below. He situates the Covenant Formula in the streams of Yahweh's people traditions, but the formula enjoyed an independent history and has therefore been treated separately. Lohfink's most important observation concerns the concentration of *ʿam yhwh* in the realm of Yahweh's saving acts. To this realm belong the function of the *nāgîd*, psalmic pleading for deliverance, and an important core of prophetic functioning. In what follows we shall find repeated confirmation of the centrality of this sphere.

One of the clearer examples of the use of *ʿam yhwh* in a formula is the expression's repeated attachment to the idiom "to restore (?) the fortunes (?)," *šûb šĕbût*. Psalm 14:7 offers a characteristic instance of the attachment:

> Would that Israel's salvation would come from Zion!
> When Yahweh restores (?) the fortunes (?) of *his people*,
> let Jacob rejoice, let Israel be glad!

The verse and psalm are repeated as Psalm 53, at which point the noun *ʾĕlōhîm* is substituted for *yhwh* in accordance with the habit of the Elohistic psalter.

The idiom *šûb šĕbût* presents formidable problems of interpretation. Occasional *ktib-qre* variations breed doubts about the preferability of reading *šĕbût* instead of *šĕbît*. The etymology of the noun *šĕbût* remains undecided. Derivation from either √ šwb or √ šby is possible. Both have been proposed, and these alternatives do not exhaust the range of poosibilities. The noun's meaning must be determined from its use, but its occurrences do not point to an unequivocal definition. The problem has been the subject of a special literature.[65] The sense "fortunes" suits the Biblical evidence. The verb *šûb* is also difficult. It is sometimes replaced by *hēšîb*, and indeed the latter with its transitive meaning "return" fits the idiom "to restore the fortunes" better than the usually intransitive verb *šûb*.[66]

These problems in meaning and diction of the idiom are compounded by the obscurity of its origin. Hos 6:11 probably gives the earliest use of the construction:

> If I change *my people's* fortunes, if I heal Israel, then Ephraim's guilt is laid bare along with the evils of Samaria. Hos 6:llff.

The prophet means that when times are good, Israel is evil. Apart from this passage, the idiom is not securely attested in pre-Exilic writings. It occurs as a divine promise at the end of the book of Amos (Amos 9:14), but the text is thought secondary to the authentic traditions of the pre-Exilic prophet. The date of Ps 14/53 is also in doubt, although its parallel transmission in both the Davidic and Elohistic psalters raises doubts about the late date to which it is customarily assigned. Within the psalm, verse 7 stands apart thematically from the preceding verses. This gives the impression that the verse and its use of the expression are formulaic. This impression is confirmed by a striking verbal congruence of Hos 6:11 and Ps 14:7:

bĕsûbî šĕbût ʿammî...	*wĕniglâ ʿăwōn ʾeprayim*
bĕsûb yhwh šĕbût ʿammôˇ	*yāgēl yaʿăqōb*

Syntactically, these formulations are closely related; an intriguing paronomasia links their apodoses. Where the psalm proclaims "let Jacob rejoice *(gyl)*," Hosea complains, "Ephraim's guilt is laid bare *(gly)*." Hosea seems to have transformed a salvation formula and made it the heading for a reproach. It is possible that Hosea's action belonged traditionally to the role of the prophet. This seems to be implied at Lam 2:14:

Your prophets had visions for you, false and worthless.
They did not reveal your guilt to restore your fortunes
(wĕlōʾ gillû ʿal-ʿăwōnēk lĕhāšîb šĕbûtēk ktib: *šĕbîtēk).*

Verbal similarities with Hos 6:11 and Ps 14:7 are self-evident. The role of the prophet is to expose the guilt of the people, whereby will be accomplished the restoration of their fortunes. What does this signify concretely? The imagery of the dirge (chapter 2) is martial; the song responds to the Babylonian defeat and subjugation of Jerusalem. The restoration of fortunes can imply success in or recovery from a military venture, an act of salvation.

The expression *ʿam yhwh* occurs frequently in connection with the idiom "to restore the fortunes" (Ps 14/53:7; 85:2; Jer 30:3; Hos 6:11; Amos 9:14). "To restore the fortunes" may be predicated of other nations (Jer 49:6.39), and it is proper to think of *ʿam yhwh* as a designation for the deity's nation, a synonym of "Israel" (ideally both northern and southern states, Jer 33:7; Ezek 39:25). The formulaic use of *šûb šĕbût* opens the possibility of an early origin of restoring the fortunes of Yahweh's people. Despite the idiom's absence from early writings, its occurrence in both northern and southern texts (Hos; Lam, Ezek) makes an early genesis of the formula conceivable. We conclude that here *ʿam yhwh* belongs to the realm of Yahweh's saving acts and designates the nation for whom he operates.

*

*   *

Less obvious at a glance than the association of *ʿam yhwh* and *šûb šĕbût* is the regularity with which the noun phrase occurs in what have been called "covenant lawsuit" texts. Rib-prophecy has been the subject of an extensive literature conveniently summarized by Robert North.[67] The fundamental insight with which this literature is working is the observation that a number of Biblical texts, both prophetic and psalmodic, presuppose the situation of a legal dispute. The configuration of *dramatis personae* in this situation - Yahweh as judge (?), jury (?), prosecutor (?) - as well as the Israelite setting of the form have been argued, but the correctness of inferring a forensic situation appears certain. Within the corpus of legal dispute or Rib texts, H. Huffmon has attempted to identify a smaller core of material for which the issue of the dispute is Israel's violation of her covenant with Yahweh.[68] In a Rib text, whenever heaven and earth are summoned to hear the controversy, the text has its inspiration in covenant law and practice. The justification for using the appeal to heaven and earth as a covenant touchstone is provided by the occurrence of the phenomena of heaven and earth as witnesses to a variety of ancient Near Eastern treaties. Huffmon reasons that the natural phenomena invoked as witnesses were expected to participate in the blessings and curses that safeguard a treaty's observation. These natural phenomena correspond to the Biblical merismus heaven and earth, hence the invocation of heaven and earth (or their equivalent "mountains" and "foundations of the earth," Mic 6:1ff.) in a Biblical lawsuit implies a covenant situation. Thus analyzed, the Bible offers a handful of covenant lawsuits: Isa 1:2ff.; Mic 6:108; Jer 2:4-13 (?); Deut 32; Ps 50.

Huffmon's analysis of the role of heaven and earth has been challenged, but the observation that the summons to heaven and earth associates with a covenant Rib has much to commend it. The association is explicitly made at Ps 50:4-5:

> He summons the heavens above, and the earth to the judgment of *his people*:
>
> > "Gather to me, my covenant faithful, those who make sacrificial covenant with me."

Having summoned heaven and earth, Yahweh gathers his covenant community. To such an explicit linkage have been added less explicit evidences of the association. G. Ernest Wright has offered a detailed form-critical investigation of Deut 32, a text opening with a call to heaven and earth, and satisfactorily shown the covenant connections of the poem.[69] We shall not pursue the issue, for it leads away from the study of *ʿam yhwh*. The origins of the form may be sought whether or not the legal basis of the covenant Rib was in fact covenantal.

The expression *ʿam yhwh* occurs in every text designated a covenant lawsuit. It appears as part of a common vocabulary by which Yahweh's indicted partner is heralded. Yahweh's "servants" are invoked only in Deut 32, the "house of Israel" and the "house of Jacob" only in Jer 2. Even "Israel" is not used in all texts, but "Yahweh's people" is found in every covenant Rib. This usage is not accidental. *ʿam yhwh* is an expression at home in the covenant lawsuit, and the study of the lawsuit will promote an understanding of the noun phrase.

The temporal origin of the covenant Rib is not easily defined. Isaiah's career provides a *terminus a quo* for the form. Of the remaining texts both Deut 32 and Ps 50 may antedate the eighth century. Although the psalm offers little objective material for assigning it a date, the poem at Deut 32 has tantalized exegetes with veiled references to historical events and the consequent possibility of fixing the date of its composition. But these historical references are sufficiently vague to have permitted the advancing of widely disparate dates for its creation. Eissfeldt[70] and Albright[71] have advocated a high date, setting the poem in the period of the judges and tying its composition to disaster at the hands of the Philistines. But the history of Israel is dotted with calamities, and a trail of subsequent dates and subsequent disasters has been advanced. Despairing of an historical anchor and relying on stylistic evidence, Wright allows that the composition of the poem falls anywhere between 900 and 600. The period he intuitively prefers - toward the end of the ninth century - may be conveniently used to peg the text. More important than the absolute date of the poem is its geographical home. Its affinities with other material in Deut, with Exod 19:8 (?), and with Hosea offer substantial evidence that the text belongs to the literature of northern Israel.[72] Given the solid grounding of the covenant lawsuit in Judah as well, suspicion must be aroused that the covenant Rib originated in the unified life of Israel, either in the brief span of the united monarchy or in the period of the judges. Literary chronology also suggests an early genesis. For Judah, no prophetic writings antedate those of Isaiah. The date and authorship of Mic 6:1-8 are disputed,[73] but when the form reappears in Jeremiah its structure and style are exceptional, marking the genre as otiose.[74] In northern writings the form is found only in Deut 32, a text probably earlier than the career of Hosea. From such a pattern one would not infer that the covenant lawsuit was in creative use in the eighth century. On the contrary, one would guess that by the time of Isaiah it was an atrophying genre. This must be taken into account when the origins of the form are sought.

The form itself has been reconstructed by Harvey and ideally includes a call to heaven and earth, a declaration of Yahweh's propriety of action and an accusation of the people, an interrogation, a contrastive recital of the benevolence of Yahweh and the malevolence of the people, a rejection of foreign gods and sacrificial rites, threats or a positive decree.[75] This much is immediately clear, that the form is the outline of a legal process. Where to locate the process in ancient Israel becomes clear only when some of the details of the Rib texts are examined. In Ps 50, a text holding forth the possibilities of acquittal or conviction, the alternative outcomes of the trial are tied to alternative actions on the part of Yahweh. The eventuality of acquittal is expressed thus:

> Call on me (Yahweh) in your day of trouble and I shall
> rescue you, and you will honor me. v. 15

The moment for which the lawsuit exists is a "day of trouble" on which Israel may expect deliverance, either from or into adversity. In Ps 81, a text with close ties to the covenant lawsuit corpus, the day of trouble is clarified:

> Would that my people would listen to me,
> that Israel would walk in my ways!
> I would quickly subdue their enemies,
> and turn my hand against those who *trouble* them.
> vv. 14-15

Those who cause troubles are Israel's enemies; a day of troubles may have been a battle day, by extension any conflict with adversaries. It is Israel's position *vis à vis* her national enemies that Isa 1:2ff. and Deut 32 address, where images of defeat and dearth respond to the idea that Yahweh has condemned his people. The impression that one gains is that the judgment of Yahweh's people portends military consequences, concrete acts of salvation or subjugation. Isaiah made the terms of his covenant Rib perfectly clear:

> If you willingly obey, you will eat the good of the land.
> But if you refuse and rebel, you will be devoured by sword. Isa 1:18-20

The imagery of some of the covenant lawsuit texts is consistent with the idea that their subject, ultimately, can be combat. Ps 50 begins with a theophany of the warrior deity:

> Our god comes, he will not be silent.
> A fire burns before him, round about him it storms greatly.
> v. 3

Entirely similar is the deity's declaration at Deut 32:22:

> For a fire has broken out in my nostril,
> and it consumes as far as Sheol beneath.

The spectre of the fire-breathing god draws its inspiration from a stock of mythological vanguard motifs.[76] The deity will do battle, but in the case of Deut 32 the condemnation of Israel causes him to fight against his own people. Now it could be thought that the deity's war belongs to the covenant lawsuit as simply one of a variety of penalties against Israel for her misconduct. But it is to be recognized already in Harvey's outline of the form of the lawsuit that the condemnation of Israel is not a necessary outcome of the lawsuit, since some of the texts end in a positive decree implying victory. Especially Marina Mannati has shown that a Rib may end in acquittal (Ps 50).[77] It therefore appears that the military consequence of a covenant lawsuit is not simply the enactment of a treaty penalty, but perhaps of more central importance to the form.

Certainly the comparative materials indicate the centrality of warfare in the Rib. Harvey has gathered a series of Near Eastern texts from the Late Bronze Age that show striking similarities to the Biblical covenant Rib.[78] What the Near Eastern texts share among themselves is that they constitute the announcement of a just war. An important text is a letter from Yarim-Lim to Yašub-Yahad of the city Dir. Georges Dossin has published the text, and we follow his translation in understanding the relevant sections to mean:

> May Shamash inquire into my conduct and yours, and may he judge! *I* am like a father and a brother to you, but *you* are an evildoer and an enemy!

A contrastive account of Yarim-Lim's benevolence and Yašub-Yahad's malevolence leads to:

> I swear to you by Addu, the god of my city, and Sin, my personal god, that I shall not cease before I destroy you and your country. So, when spring arrives, I shall come. I shall march through the opening of your fortress door.[79]

The structure of the letter is congruent with that of the covenant lawsuit. A noteworthy feature of its language is the use of the image of the dutiful father in contrast with the evil-doer; Biblical reflexes of this forensic vocabulary occur at Deut 32:5.19 and Isa 1:2, where they have little to do with a traditional concept of the family of Yahweh. The message of Yarim-Lim's letter is clear: a just war has been announced.

In combination with the Biblical evidence, the Near Eastern materials point strongly to a place in the military life of Israel for the covenant Rib. A difference between Israel and her neighbors is immediately observable in the standard against which judgment is assessed. In the Near Eastern texts assembled by Harvey, justice stands on the side of the conflicting party whose behavior *vis à vis* its adversary has been correct. In the Biblical covenant Rib, no reference is made to the rival claims of disputing parties. The vital issue is Israel's comportment in her relationship with Yahweh. In this we find a transformation of the common setting of the lawsuit, yet we are not led away from the sphere of warfare in ancient Israel for two reasons. First, a remembrance of the military setting of the covenant Rib is maintained by the Biblical texts themselves which, as we saw, sometimes carry the language of holy war and a vision of the crisis of battle. Second, there is ample evidence that judgment in Israel was sometimes a military affair. This evidence must be reviewed, since it provides a concrete life setting out of which the literary covenant lawsuit appears to have sprung.

In Judg 11, Jephthah's second letter from Mizpah to an unnamed Ammonite king has features of vocabulary and form in common with the covenant lawsuit. The letter itself does not belong to its present context. It presupposes a land dispute with Moab, and has only redactionally been made to suit the context of an Ammonite war. Thus, at v. 15 a later hand has appended the words "and the land of the sons of Ammon" to the sentence "Israel has not taken Moab's land." Wüst's attempt to make the original letter address the Ammonites is unconvincing.[80] The extent of the Moab letter has been misjudged by recent exegetes. It extends through and includes v. 27, which has been altered to meet contextual demands, "the sons of Ammon" being substituted for "Moab." The exclusion of v. 27 led Richter incorrectly to analyze the form of the letter, which he described as an *Argumentation*.[81] With the inclusion of v. 27, it is clear that the text is a Rib, a call for a just war. The letter recites the historical background to a land dispute, justifies Israel's possession of Gilead, contrasts Israel's innocence of wrongdoing and Moabite guilt, and concludes with an appeal, "Let Yahweh the judge judge between the sons of Israel and *Moab (corrected to: the sons of Ammon)." The text even includes the *terminus technicus* for the form: "Are you better than Balaq ben Sippor, king of Moab? Did *he* ever dispute *(rîb)* with Israel?" (v. 25). The letter's similarities with the covenant lawsuit texts are important. As in Ps 50, Yahweh is called the judge (v. 27), and as in all covenant Rib texts, Israel is Yahweh's people. The expression finds contextual motivation in the contrast between Kemosh and his people Moab, Yahweh and Israel (vv. 23-24).

Jephthah's letter stands closer to the Near Eastern lawsuit traditions than to the Biblical covenant Rib, for it envisions a judgment between Israel and Moab founded on the justice of Israel's claim to a disputed territory. In the covenant lawsuit, Israel' adversaries recede from vision and the judgment is a matter concerning Israel's relationship with her god.

A series of texts presuppose such a judgment. For our purposes it will suffice to notice the earliest, Ju 5. The text of this old poem can be improved by joining v. 11d to v. 13:

ʾz yrdw lšʿrym ʿm yhwh
ʾz yrd śryd lʾdyrym
ʿm yhwh yrd lw bgbwrym
Then Yahweh's militia descended from the gates
Then a remnant descended from the nobles
As warriors Yahweh's militia went down for him.[82]

The text of Ju 5 portrays an act of judgment as a prelude to a war. Its language is unmistakable.[83] Yahweh's "people" descend from the *gates* and *nobles* where they had gathered. The word pair can only refer to a place of judgment, as it does in Ugaritic.[84] The figure of the place of judgment is pursued by the poet. Israelite law-givers are present, seated on judgment seats (*mdyn*; vs. 10). At the place of judgment the "kerygma" proclaimed is not Yahweh's wonders *(niplāʾôt)* but rather his right actions (*ṣĕdāqôt*; vs. 11). This is a term of jurisprudence, found elsewhere only at 1 Sam 12 in Samuel's judgment and in Micah's covenant lawsuit (Mic 6:5). In short, the Song of Deborah points to an ancient ideology of war as judgment.

In the Song of Deborah, *ʿam yhwh* has the special sense "Yahweh's militia." But if, as we have suggested, the covenant lawsuit emerged from a vision of war as judgment, then there is some reason to suspect that the militia was thought to embody all Israel. The contrast between Yahweh's people and Kemosh's people in a later lawsuit reveals what certainly was true, that the outcome of battle was an affair of pan-Israelite and pan-Moabite significance. We are thus inclined to discount a rigid interpretation of the noun phrase. While the military context of its use brings a martial connotation, its wider sense appears not to have been fully eclipsed.

*

* *

A lively debate has focussed on the expression *nāgîd ʿal ʿam yhwh*, "leader over Yahweh's people." The phrase and its variants ("over Yahweh's inheritance," "over Israel") occurs as the title of an Israelite office standing between the period of the judges and the Israelite monarchy and continuing into monarchic times. Whether the *nāgîd* titulary is authentic or a later creation and the nature of the office are controversial.[85]

The title has the form *nāgîd ʿal x*. The unique occurrence of *nĕgîd ʿammî* (referent: Yahweh) is a comparatively late and unimportant deviation from the usual pattern (2 Kgs 20:5). *Nāgîd ʿal x* must be analyzed into two components, the noun *nāgîd* and the prepositional phrase *ʿal x* indicating the sphere of the officer's function. Nothing opposes assuming the possibility of an early use of the noun *nāgîd*. The word seems to have belonged to the common vocabulary of the region. It occurs already in the Nora Inscription (ninth century, Phoenician) where it denotes a military officer.[86] Its referent in the Sefire Inscription[87] and the Saqqara papyrus[88] is unclear, although both texts permit inferring a military function. Its meaning in an unpublished Ammonite ostrakon is uncertain.[89] The prepositional phrase which completes the title may be compared with a number of Biblical functions the titles of which consist entirely of the preposition followed by the domain of activity: *ʿal habbayit; ʿal haṣṣābāʾ; ʿal hammās; ʿal hanniṣṣābîm* (1 Kgs 4;4ff.). Such "titles" indicate no more than the sphere of activity, and perhaps derive from a formula of institution such as is attested in epigraphic Hebrew:

ṣwk ḥnnyhw ʿl bʾršbʿ (Arad 3.3-4)

Ḥananyahu has appointed you over Beer-sheba

In the *nāgîd* titulary, the officer's domain is given as "Yahweh's people" (1 Sam 13:14), "Yahweh's inheritance" (1 Sam 10:1), "Israel" (1 Sam 25:30), or, most commonly, "Yahweh's people Israel" (1 Sam 9:16, 2 Sam 6:21, etc.). From this pattern it should not be inferred that the "original" title consisted of the name of a single domain, or even of a conflation of names. We seem rather to encounter the use of *nāgîd* in association with a variety of designations for the *nāgîd*'s domain. The authenticity of this domain terminology must therefore be probed. In the case of "Israel," it goes without saying that at an early date the term was used in an appropriate sphere. We are therefore particularly interested in "Yahweh's people" and "Yahweh's inheritance."

The two expressions occur together in quite a number of texts (Deut 9:26.29; 32:9; 2 Sam 14:13ff.; 1 Kgs 8:51-52, etc.). This makes it seem that the *nāgîd* titulary's variations in domain terminology either captures or recreates a vocabulary which circulated together. Two questions remain: did the terminology circulate at the putative time of the office of the *nāgîd*, and did it represent spheres of activity suited to an office at the transition from the period of the judges to the era of Israelite kings?

2 Sam 14:13.16 brings us close to the time in question. The chapter belongs to the Succession Narrative, a composition

usually ascribed to an historian contemporary with the events he portrayed. The writer's use of *ʿam ʾĕlōhîm* and *naḥălat ʾĕlōhîm* (vv. 13, 16) in place of the more usual *ʿam yhwh* and *naḥălat yhwh* is not a troubling concern. The functional equivalence of the terms is not in doubt. God's people and his inheritance are spoken of as though the realm of King David's effective activity. By shunning reconciliation with Absalom, David endangers *ʿam ʾĕlōhîm* (v. 13). His advocacy can spare a woman and her son extermination from *naḥălat ʾĕlōhîm* (v. 16). One garners the impression that in tenth century parlance the deity's people and inheritance were a sacred royal trust. To the extent that the office of the *nāgîd* anticipates monarchy, its titulary accurately represents the emerging political vocabulary.

A greater antiquity of *ʿam yhwh* and *naḥălat yhwh* as sacral-political terminology is established by the Song of Miriam, Exod 15. The song may be the oldest poem in the Bible. Having celebrated Yahweh's triumph at the Reed Sea, the poet turned to the theme of guidance:

> You led with your faithfulness
>   the people whom you redeemed
> You guided with your strength
>   to your holy pasture.
>
> . . .
>
> You brought them (antecedent: *ʿam yhwh*), you planted them
>   in the mountain of *your inheritance.*
> A place for your dwelling
>   you have made, O Yahweh!
> My lord's sanctuary
>   your hands have stablished.
> Yahweh will rule
>   for ever and ever!   vv. 13,17

Yahweh's people have been brought to his inheritance, an event which issues in the exclamation "Yahweh will rule for ever and ever!" The deity is thus king, his domain being defined as both his people and his inheritance. The continuity in language between this text and the vocabulary of monarchical Israel is striking. Between the two in time, according to the tradition, stood the *nāgîd*. His titulary seems to be authentic, and it becomes increasingly difficult to assume that the titles of the *nāgîd*, transmitted as they are with casual but accurate variations in domain terminology, entered the narratives of 1 and 2 Samuel by retrojective design.

We have reserved until now an attempt to exploit the nagid titulary and related texts for the understanding of *ʿam yhwh*. Although a strong case has been made for seeing in the *nāgîd* a military savior, it appears that his domain must be thought more general than Yahweh's militia. When the Song of Miriam refers to Yahweh's people, more is intended than the weapon-bearing men. The same is true when the king is accused of menacing the welfare of the people of god. The military dimensions of the noun phrase *ʿam yhwh* need to be subordinated to the larger image of the people of Yahweh.

The attraction between *ʿam yhwh* and *naḥălat yhwh* has inspired the idea that these expressions imagine respectively Yahweh's family and family property.[90] This understanding seems to be only partly correct. That Yahweh's *naḥălâ* is, as it were, his inheritance property is plausible. But Yahweh's *ʿam(m)* does not relate to that property in the manner thought. A close look at the imagery of the Song of Miriam reveals that Yahweh's *ʿam(m)* is yet another chattel. It is redeemed *(gʾl)* and purchased (*qny*; *not* "created"), brought to the deity's pasture land (*nāweh*; vs. 13). We are not to imagine the redemption of an impoverished relative. Instead, redemption is to be understood an act of purchase made for the benefit of the enduring inheritance.[91] The kind of property Yahweh's *ʿam(m)* is to be construed as is abundantly clear in the poet's diction. They are led to pasture as though a flock. The verbs used with the meaning "lead" *(nāḥâ, nēhēl)* are perfectly suited to the function of the shepherd, and while the word "shepherd" is missing from the poem, we are nevertheless in the presence of the divine pastor. "To shepherd" appears quickly in association with the *nāgîd* titulary and the language of monarchical Israel:

> Yahweh said to you (David), "You will shepherd my *ʿam(m)* Israel, and you will be *nāgîd* over Israel." 2 Sam 5:2
>
> For all the time I travelled with the sons of Israel, did I (Yahweh) say a word to one of Israel's judges whom I had

> commanded to shepherd my *ʿam(m)* Israel saying, "Why haven't you built me a cedar temple?" 2 Sam 7:7

> He chose David his servant, and took him from the sheep pens.
> He brought him away from the ewes
> to shepherd Jacob his *ʿam(m)*
> and Israel his inheritance. Ps 78:70-71

To pursue this typology is unnecessary. Our concern is to have shown that the image originated at an early date for Israel.

The forces attracting divine guidance and royal shepherd themes are not self-evident. That which survived their union was the idea that Yahweh's people are a flock, his surrogate (whether *nāgîd* or king) a shepherd. The pastoral image should not be mistaken for a definition of *ʿam yhwh*. There is never any question that the referent of the noun phrase was that human group that used it. But it is not improper to infer that *ʿam(m)*'s broader referential possibilities either promoted the development of the image of the human flock or guided the choice of terminology in expressing the metaphor.

*
* *

The results of an inquiry into *ʿam yhwh* may be summarized in this manner: While the expression finds a comfortable early setting in military contexts, it is far from clear that "Yahweh's militia" was the original meaning of the noun phrase. All the evidence points to a rather developed concept of the people of Yahweh for the dawn of Israel's history. Thus, while the phrase is frequently to be found in the realm of Yahweh's saving acts and while those acts are frequently to be construed as bellicose, it is not likely that the military use of the expression should be allowed to eclipse its broader referent - the full people of Yahweh. The full people probably should not be imagined as the deity's family. Where an image does surface, that image can be of the human flock over whom Yahweh, *nāgîd*, or king is shepherd.

Chapter VI

CONCLUSION

Our final task is to synthesize the results of this inquiry and attempt to forge an understanding of what the Old Testament means by "people."

We commented in our introduction that the comparative Semitic evidence is capable of supporting a variety of understandings of the origin of the word *ʿam(m)*. The word occurs with singular and collective meanings in most of the Semitic languages. Indeed, with the possible exception of Ugaritic (where the use of *ʿm* as a collective cannot be regarded as certain), the word is found in every major West Semitic language with both a singular and a collective referent. The link between singular and collective meanings is sometimes clear (Amorite "head of the family," "family"), and it is possible to conclude that we are dealing with a single noun and not two separate words.

The noun's crucial semantic developments must have occurred in Proto-Semitic times. Ordinarily, this would block access to the process of development, but in the case of the noun *ʿam(m)* it seems possible to recover the course of semantic evolution. The assumption that the word arose through onomatopoesis gives the word a firm origin. That this assumption is correct is hinted by certain morphological and semantic evidences. The Arabic term *ʿamāʿim*, used as a plural of *ʿamm*, is important. It not only invites the inference of a verb meaning "to make the sound *ʿam*," but also points to a possible biliteral origin of the noun *ʿam(m)*. The Hebrew noun *ʿămît* is therefore also important, for it is to be analyzed as a biliteral noun base with a feminine nisba suffix *(ʿam + ît)*. The semantic evidence of an Arabic flock vocabulary built up from the consonant core *ʿm* enhances the likelihood both that the noun comes from the domain of flocks and that it originated with a simple pair of consonants. It is sometimes thought that the evidence of parallel semantic developments assists linguistic interpretation.

For the onomatopoetic genesis of *ʿam(m)* we may compare Hebrew *hāmôn*, which means "crowd of people" and probably arose from the sound **ham*. That a term from the sphere of flocks might ultimately refer to a kinsman is shown by Ugaritic *ary*, which seems to refer literally to a stable mate but is used as a synonym of "brother." But what is more important than the instruction provided by such parallels is the fact that *ʿam(m)* appears sometimes to have signified the flock. Here the Hebrew evidence may prove decisive, for in Hebrew the noun can refer to animal groupings as well as human. Now the priority of biliteral word formation over triliteral is clear. This allows concluding that the Epigraphic South Arabian and Arabic verbs meaning "to be general" are secondary to the noun, for the verbs exhibit the identical triliteral root √ʿmm, and thus while they attest a Proto-Semitic development they already presuppose the expansion of **ʿm* to the pattern *ʿmm*. Admittedly, the argument subordinating the verbs to the noun is fragile, but the nature of the evidence requires fragile argument or none at all.

In our estimation, the noun *ʿam(m)* first designated the flock. What is not clear is whether it simultaneously expressed the collective and the sense of a noun of unity. The Arabian noun *ʿîma* (< *ʿima* ?; "animal from the flock") has the appearance of an old noun of unity, as does Hebrew *ʿāmît*. In both cases the feminine termination (or feminine nisba termination) can be taken as the vehicle for creating the *nomen unitatis* and the noun from which it derives a collective. Whether or not the word originated with both a collective and a singular referent, it appears that by the time the noun was molded to the triliteral pattern *ʿamm* (or *ʿimm*) it could refer to a group or an individual from the group.

What was the makeup of the human company called *ʿamm*? Was it at first a clan? The evidence is ambiguous. The noun's widespread use without necessary connotation of kinship (Amorite, Hebrew, Phoenician, Aramaic, ESA [?]) suggests that in prehistoric times the word could be used of any human company. But the common experience must have been that the human group was in fact an agnatic company, and so the noun came to be used of kinsmen and kinsman. We are attracted to the idea that the transfer of a word meaning "flock" to a human association occurred in a pastoral setting, although direct evidence of such a process is not to be had. The noun's use to mean "kinsman" tells much about the relationship of individuals to one another within the collective "kin." The degrees of relationship which *ʿam(m)* came to express may be described by saying that the word could refer to any agnate for whom a separate Proto-Semitic designation was wanting. Thus, "father," "brother," "son" are not called *ʿam(m)*. But any paternal uncle, close or distant (Arabic, Aramaic [?], ESA), great grandfather, grandfather (Aramaic, pre-Classical Arabic [?]), and perhaps even cousin (Arabic) may be designated by the word. The use of *ʾʿmm* in ESA to refer to all ascendants other than fathers perpetuates an ancient linguistic situation.

The widespread use of the noun in military contexts (Amorite [?], Hebrew, Phoenician, Aramaic [?], Ugaritic [?], ESA, Arabic) poses a special problem. What motivated this phenomenon in prehistoric times is not immediately clear. In historical times we occasionally encounter what seems to be an explanation of this use of the term. Among the Arabs, martial obligations were an encumbrance of agnatic relationship. But when we see that the acceptance of military responsibilities creates, as it were, a cousin relationship, we are given cause to wonder whether this feature of Arab life is a primitive associate of the word *ʿam(m)*. The idea that warfare is a concern of the tribe is attractive. In a real sense, those who engage in combat are the tribe; they certainly determine the fate of the entire group. The possibility of using *ʿam(m)* for militias not properly tribal may suggest a similarity in the mode of existence between the nomadic tribe and its camp and the roving army. An army lives the tribal ideal expressed in the book of Ruth. It travels together, spends the night together, and, of course, may find a common death and burial. Whether one might even press to connect the martial *ʿam(m)* and the use of animal names ("gazelle," etc.) for "warrior" and assert the connection between troop and *troupeau* is difficult to judge.[1] At all events, the military connotations of *ʿam(m)* can be assumed an ancient heritage of the noun. Those who wish to infer a special social significance to the use of *ʿam(m)* for an army have the burden of showing that such a significance was felt by the users of the word. For the Arabs this can be done, but it must be admitted that for ancient Israel the possibilities for finding a sociological motivation of the use of "people" for "army" seem restricted.

Apart from its complex heritage from Proto-Semitic developments, the decisive factor in the semantic evolution of the noun *ʿam(m)* must have been the collected social experiences of the word's users. In each language area obsolete meanings of the term can be expected to have quickly disappeared, and in this respect the noun's separate courses in the Semitic languages are instructive. Among the Phoenicians the word most often refers to the population of a city. In contrast, the noun's potential for suggesting the bonds of kinship is virtually lost; it is only in Phoenician personal names that "kinsman" can be inferred as the term's meaning, and a glance at the meager collection of such names[2] shows an eclipsing even here. The nature of the Phoenician literature obligates a cautious appraisal of this pattern, but even when allowance is made for the small size and eccentric character of the Phoenician corpus, one must be struck by the logic underpinning these parallel semantic developments. In an urban civilization, the importance of the agnatic tribe is diminished. The slender documention of Amorite suggests that a similar, although not identical, interaction of social setting and word meaning occurred among the city states of Mesopotamia. Here the noun managed to retain its connotation of kinship by specializing in the sense "family," for unlike the pastoral tribe, the family had a place in the town and city society of the Tigris and Euphrates valley. To see these developments in perspective, one must compare the linguistic situation of the Arabs for whom city life was a comparatively late and not always fashionable mode of existence. Here feelings of tribal solidarity survived, albeit in the guise of the obligations of avuncular relationship. Cousins are the tribe. The specificity of *ʿamm* meaning "paternal uncle" is a thin veil over the breadth of tribesmen to whom the term can be applied.

Anyone attempting to portray Israel's conception of a "people" must be given pause both by the wealth of nuances which the Hebrew word *ʿam(m)* may have inherited and by the extent to which changing conditions of life in ancient Israel may have altered the Israelite conception. A single key will not unlock the meaning of "people" in the Hebrew Bible. If one compares Israel's use of the noun with that of her ancient neighbors, one is immediately struck by the conservatism of the Hebrew language. Most if not all of the variety of senses carried by the noun in other Semitic languages are attested in the literature of ancient Israel. A people may be a kindred association, but it may also be free from the bonds of kinship. It may be a pastoral band or the population of a city, and the links between such different significations are not indicated. It is therefore difficult to tell whether the population of a town was thought in some sense a tribe, or whether a tribe was thought in some way to be just a human conglomerate. Certain common ideas about the Biblical conception of a people should be set aside. To assume that a "people" is a consanguineous association is not always safe. A people can be consanguineous, but ideas of fraternity do not so dominate the use of the noun that one may presume without contextual indication a kinship component to the group called a people. Nor is it safe to contrast sharply a people and a nation. From an early date the people of Yahweh were a political entity, governed by divine or human king. In short, a proper understanding of ancient Israel's "people" will assume a complex, multifaceted conception.

When allowance has been made for the diversity of the Biblical notion, then it is possible to try to locate lines of development within the larger picture. We have been concerned throughout this study to identify the extent to which pastoral ideals inform the use of Hebrew *ʿam(m)*. In addition to a core of texts which present a people as the human herd, there are traces in Israel's traditions of the people imagined as a flock or as a nomadic company. With the passing of time, these imaginations seem to have given way. A stiff-necked *people* became, instead of a wandering herd, an uneducable nation. The Covenant Formula ceased to celebrate Yahweh's adoption of a tenting tribe and became a temple saying. In broad terms the surrender of such nuances represents a kind of sedentarization of Israel, although we must be cautious at this point. An already sedentary people can absorb and alter the traditions of pastoral groups, so that the assumption of a linear development of "Israelite" ideas of the people is not warranted. But a minimal assessment of the significance of the pastoral associations of Biblical *ʿam(m)* must probably reckon that a part of what became or was Israel passed through a stage of pastoral nomadism in which its self-image as a people was for a time rooted. A comparison of the "peoples" who were Israel's ancient neighbors in and around Palestine imposes this reckoning. The absence of pastoral associations from *ʿam(m)* in the Phoenician, early Aramaic, and Moabite literatures, scanty though they be, contrasts markedly with the state of the Biblical evidence.

A second, recurring theme of the Biblical material is the military implication of a people. Precisely how a "people" and its "militia" were conceived to relate is never specified, but that a people has a military aspect is evident early and often in the traditions of Israel. At the dawn of Israelite history Yahweh's "people" are his fighting force. By calling itself a stiff-necked "people," an early Israelite group may have intended to highlight its militant resolve. It is probably difficult to overestimate the place in ancient Israelite thought of the concerns of war and survival, and in the matrix of Israel's self-perception as a people an important field of martial sentiment must not be overlooked. In this Israel was probably no different from her neighbors. To read the Moabite stone is to recognize that a people, if only the population of a city, is a totality affected by war and peace. Just how thoroughly the martial image of the Israelite people mixed with other images is brought into focus by the *nāgîd* titulary, where a military function and the shepherd's role fused.

To overlook the fact that Israel as a people was a worshipping community would be amiss. A fundamental idea of the religion of Israel was that Israel is Yahweh's people. In the history of Israelite thought this appears to have been an increasingly weighty perception. The ultimate fate of every Biblical formula and noun phrase we examined save one ("the people of the land") was to impinge on the relationship between deity and worshippers. To a certain extent the nature of

Israel's literary production, and especially the fact that the Priestly Writer came late and with a sacerdotal outlook to Israel's traditions, dictates that this would appear so. It is therefore perhaps not surprising that the Kareth penalty and "to be gathered to one's *ʿammîm*" are used with a coloring decidedly more religious than their origins might recommend. But the process of making the Israelite people an essentially religious group was not restricted to Priestly circles or late times. It is significant that "the people of Yahweh" had an early use as political terminology. And the history of traditions of the "stiff-necked people" are, if we have understood them correctly, informative. The literary presentation of the stiff-necked people is consistently theological. In ancient Israel's literature there is either no knowledge or no care that the expression might have a neutral or even complimentary significance. What mattered was the way in which the epithet could be coupled with Israel's history of relations with Yahweh, and here the expression's location in wilderness traditions facilitated taking the noun phrase *sensu malo*.

It is difficult to know the degree to which the religious aspect of the ancient Israelite people resembled the thought of Israel's neighbors. It is true that Israel conceived Moab to be "the people of Kemosh," but an expression corresponding to "the people of god" has not been found among Israel's closest neighbors. This may be a literary accident. There are cultic affairs which concerned Phoenician and Punic peoples. The people of Carthage seem to have celebrated a Maioumas festival, and the people of *gwl* built temples. The people of Cadiz were slaves of their god Molkastart. From such data one might infer that there were other peoples among Israel's closest neighbors who thought themselves the people of a certain god. But the evidence to confirm the inference is wanting.

When the complexity of the Biblical conception of a people is seen, one begins to appreciate the difficulty of defining what "Israel" was at the dawn of the Biblical period. The range of possibilities currently enjoying favor (amphictyonic league, religious community, territorial federation, etc.) falls well within the bounds of the native conception. Indeed, the fact that a people had many recognized aspects - war alliance, community of faith, sib - foretells the variety of modern understandings of the identity of primitive Israel. This fact may also serve a warning against attempts to define too narrowly or with precision too great the collective nature of those who left as a monument of their experience a literature held sacred even in distant lands and in distant times.

NOTES

Chapter I

1. James Barr, *The Semantics of Biblical Language* (Oxford: Clarendon, 1961).

2. John Sawyer, *Semantics in Biblical Research* (SBT 2/24; London: SCM, 1972).

3. Without vocalic suffix the gemination of the letter *m* is not retained by all Semitic languages (e.g., Hebrew *ʿam*). We shall refer to the noun as either *ʿam(m)* or *ʿamm*, the latter particularly for languages retaining case endings.

4. C. H. J. de Geus, *The Tribes of Israel: An Investigation into Some of the Presuppositions of Martin Noth's amphictyony Hypothesis* (Studia Semitica Neerlandica 18; Assen: Van Gorcum, 1976).

5. W. Robertson Smith, *Kinship and Marriage in Early Arabia* (reprint; Boston: Beacon, *1885):37ff.

6. Theodor Nöldeke, ZDMG 40 (1886):172-173.

7. One of the first to define Hebrew *ʿam(m)* in personal names as "paternal uncle" was M. Krenkel, "Das Verwandtschaftswort *ʿam*," ZAW 8 (1888):280-284.

8. Julius Wellhausen, "Die Ehe bei den Arabern," *Nachrichten von der Königlichen Gesellschaft der Wissenschaften und der Georg-Augusts-Universität zu Göttingen* 49/11 (1893):431ff., 480-481.

9. Otto Procksch, "Über die Blutrache bei den vorislamischen Arabern," *Leipziger Studien aus dem Gebiet der Geschichte* 5/4 (1899):24, note 1. Procksch gives the noun the slightly more nuanced sense *"Vetterschaft."* Cf. Procksch, *Theologie des Alten Testaments* (Gütersloh: Bertelsmann, 1950): 505ff.

10. Fritz Hommel, *Aufsätze und Abhandlungen* (München: Lukaschik, 1900) No. 5, *Die südarabischen Altertümer des Wiener Hofsmuseums*, 155, note 1.

11. Hugo Winckler, "Polyandrie bei Semiten," *Verhandlungen der Berliner Gesellschaft für Anthropologie, Ethnologie und Urgeschichte* 30 (1898):29-30.

12. Hugo Winckler, "Arabisch-Semitisch-Orientalisch," MVAG 6/4 (1901):164ff.

13. Th. Juynboll, "Über die Bedeutung des Wortes *ʿamm*," FS Nöldeke, vol. 1:353-356. The Ammonite name etiology is recorded at Gen 19:30-38.

14. L. B. Paton, "*ʿamm, ʿammī*," *Hastings Encyclopaedia of Religion and Ethics*, vol. 1:386-388.

15. Brenda Z. Seligman, "Studies in Semitic Kinship I," BSO(A)S 3 (1923-1925):51-61.

16. J. Pedersen, *Israel: Its Life and Culture*, trans. A. Møller and A. I. Fausbøll (London: Cumberlege, 1926-1947): vol. 1:54ff., 506, note.

17. Martin Noth, *Die israelitischen Personennamen im Rahmen der gemeinsemitischen Namengebung* (BZAW 46; Stuttgart: Kohlhammer, 1928):76-82. Cf. George Kerber, *Die religionsgeschichtliche Bedeutung der hebräischen Eigennamen des Alten Testamentes* (Freiburg: Mohr, 1897):58-65; Joseph Scharbert, "People (of God)," *Bauer Encyclopedia of Biblical Theology*, vol. 2:652.

18. Leonhard Rost, "Die Bezeichnungen für Land und Volk im Alten Testament," FS Procksch, 141-144.

19. E. Dhorme, "Le dieu parent et le dieu maître," RHR 106 (1932):229-230; idem, *L'évolution religieuse d'Israël* (Bruxelles: Nouvelle société d'éditions, 1937) vol. 1, *La religion des Hébreux nomades*, 113, 271-272.

20. W. F. Albright, *From the Stone Age to Christianity* (Garden City, New York: Doubleday, 1957):244-245. Albright's previous studies, "The Name of Bildad the Shuhite," AJSL 44 (1928):32; idem, "The Land of Damascus between 1850 and 1750 B.C.," BASOR 83 (1941):34; idem, review of HUCA 16, JBL 64 (1945):291ff.; idem, "Northwest-Semitic Names in a List of Egyptian Slaves from the Eighteenth Century," JAOS 74 (1954): 226, note 26.

21. Nyberg published these thoughts in "Hoseaboken," UUÅ 1941:26ff. I have relied on Aage Bentzen's summary of the Swedish original, *King and Messiah* (Oxford: Blackwell, 1970): 45. Cf. H. S. Nyberg, "Studium zum Hoseabuche," UUÅ 1935/6:27, where he emphasizes the reciprocal relationship between *ʿamm*-god and *ʿamm*-worshippers of god. Cf. also Josef Scharbert, *Solidarität in Segen und Fluch im Alten Testament und in seiner Umwelt* (BBB 14; Bonn: Hanstein, 1958):263.

22. John Gray, *Joshua, Judges and Ruth* (Century Bible; London: Nelson, 1967):276.

23. G. Ryckmans, "Les noms de parenté en safaïtique," RB 58 (1951):388ff.

24. E. A. Speiser, "'People' and 'Nation' of Israel," JBL 79 (1960):157-163.

25. Richard Deutsch, "The Biblical Concept of the 'People of God,'" South East Asia Journal of Theology 13/2 (1972):4-13.

26. E. Nestle, *Die israelitischen Eigennamen nach ihrer religionsgeschichtlichen Bedeutung* (Haarlem, 1876):passim.

27. Nestle already recognized that a name like Rehoboam is not easily accommodated to the idea that *ʿam(m)* means "paternal uncle" or "kinsman."

28. Martin Noth, "Gemeinsemitische Erscheinungen in der israelitischen Namengebung," ZDMG 81 (1927):1-45.

29. Reported by Fritz Hommel, ZDMG 49 (1895):525ff.

30. See Hommel, *Aufsätze*, 149.

31. T. Fahd, *Le panthéon de l'Arabie centrale à la veille de l'Hégire* (Paris: Geuthner, 1968):45-46.

32. Hommel, *Aufsätze*, 154-155; idem, *The Ancient Hebrew Tradition as Illustrated by the Monuments*, trans. E. McClure and L. Crossle (New York: Young, 1897):48.

33. E.g., H. V. Hilprecht, *Explorations in Bible Lands* (Philadelphia: Holman, 1903):745, note 1; Ad. Neubauer, "On Some Newly-discovered Temanite and Nabataean Inscriptions," *Studia Biblica* 1 (1885):225-226.

34. C. C. Torrey, "*ʿamm*," *The Jewish Encyclopedia*, vol. 1:521.

35. G. B. Gray, "*ʿammi*," *Encyclopaedia Biblica*, vol. 1: 138-142; idem, *Studies in Hebrew Proper Names* (London: Black, 1896):41-60, 245, 254ff.

36. Th. Bauer, *Die Ostkanaanäer* (Leipzig: Asia Major, 1926):19.

37. Noth, *Personennamen*, 76, note 4.

38. For evidence from regions outside South Arabia, see Fahd, above note 31.

39. F. Lenormant, *Lettres assyriologiques* (Paris, 1872) vol. 2:84.

40. Marie-Joseph Lagrange, *Études sur les religions sémitiques* (Paris: Lecoffre, 1905):116-118.

41. Bauer, 61.

42. Ditlef Nielsen, *Der dreieinige Gott* (København: Nordisk, 1922) vol. 1, *Die drei göttlichen Personen*:77.

43. E. Dhorme, "Dieu parent," 235.

44. Gray, *Proper names*, 253.

45. Franz Praetorius, *Neue Beiträge zur Erklärung der himjaritischen Inschriften* (Halle, 1873):25; Hugo Winckler, "Einige semitischen Eigennamen," *Altorientalische Forschungen* 2 (1898):84.

46. Noth, *Personennamen*, 73-75.

47. Herrmann Vorländer, *Mein Gott: Die Vorstellungen vom persönlichen Gott im Alten Orient und im Alten Testament* (AOAT 23; Neukirchen: Neukirchener Verlag, 1975):180ff.

Chapter II

1. TM 75 G 336.

2. G. Pettinato and P. Matthiae, "Aspetti amministrativi e topografici di Ebla," RSO 50 (1976):13.

3. M. Dahood, "Ebla, Ugarit and the Old Testament," SVT 29 (1977):87.

4. An early advocate of the idea that the noun was known to East Semitic was P. Jensen, *Literarisches Zentralblatt* 1902:694-696, and I. J. Gelb (see note 12 below) holds the same view.

5. CAD 6 (H):58.

6. AHw I:315.

7. Von Soden, GAG, §23.

8. CAD 6 (H):68.

9. ARM 14:253. M. Stol first called my attention to this text.

10. E. A. Speiser, "Census and Ritual Expiation in Mari and Israel," BASOR 149 (1958):17-25.

11. The i-vowel in names of the form Ammiṣaduqa is a problem for interpretation; it is most often taken as a neutral helping vowel rather than a pronominal suffix or a grammatically significant case ending.

12. The relevant personal names have been collected by H. Huffmon, *Amorite Personal Names in the Mari Texts* (Baltimore: Johns Hopkins, 1965):196-198. Compare Th. Bauer, *Die Ostkanaanäer* (Leipzig: Asia Major, 1926), a work which remains a useful source. See also M. Noth, "Die syrisch-palästinische Bevölkerung des zweiten Jahrtausends vor Chr. im Licht neuer Quellen," ZDPV 65 (1942):23; J. J. M. Roberts, *The Earliest Semitic Pantheon: A Study of the Semitic Deities Attested before Ur III* (Baltimore: Johns Hopkins, 1972):6, 49; I. J. Gelb, *Glossary of Old Akkadian* (MAD 3; Chicago: University of Chicago, 1957):43; J. J. Stamm, *Die akkadische Namengebung* (Leipzig: J. C. Hinrichs, 1939):58; Gelb, *Computer-Aided Analysis of Amorite* (AS 21; Chicago: University of Chicago, 1980): 260-264.

13. Huffmon, 196.

14. The text appears in H. Rawlinson, *The Cuneiform Inscriptions of Western Asia*, vol. 5, plate 44, i:21-22. It is

a Kassite composition dating somewhat after 1000 B.C. (Kemal Balkan, *Kassitenstudien*, trans. Fr. R. Kraus [AOS 37; New Haven: American Oriental Society, 1954] vol.1:1-11). See the discussion of Huffmon, 196. The king list has often been studied in the context of the search for the meaning of the name Hammurapi: J. Halévy, "Notes assyriologiques iii," ZA 3 (1888):332-334; G. Hüsing, "Miszellen 10," OLZ 10 (1907):235-238; O. Weber, "Der Name Hammurabi in einer südarabischen Inschrift," OLZ 10 (1907):146-149; F. Thureau-Dangin, "Un nouveau roi de Hana," OLZ 11 (1908):93; A. Ungnad, "Miscellen," ZA 22 (1909):7-9; J. Prince, "The Name Hammurabi," JBL 29 (1910):21-24; D. D. Luckenbill, "The Name Hammurabi," JAOS 37 (1917):250-253; A. T. Clay, *The Empire of the Amorites* (YOS 6; New Haven: Yale, 1919):113-114; W. F. Albright, "The Amorite Form of the Name Hammurabi," AJSL 38 (1922):140-141; I. Charles and F. Jean, séance of 22 Mai, 1946 in GLECS 4:26; J.-R. Kupper, "Un gouvernement provincial dans le royaume de Mari," RA 41 (1947):155, note 1; Ch. Virolleaud, "Sur le nom de Hammurabi," JA 243 (1955):133-134; W. F. Albright, *From the Stone Age to Christianity*:244; W. von Soden, "Neubearbeitungen der babylonischen Gesetzessammlungen," OLZ 53 (1958):523, note 1; R. Borger, "Kleinigkeiten zur Textkritik des Kodex Hammurapi," Or 31 (1962):364; idem, review of H. Schmökel *Hammurabi von Babylon*, ZA 56 (1964):289; G. R. Driver and J. C. Miles, *The Babylonian Laws* (Oxford: Clarendon, 1955) vol. 2:117-118; W. von Soden, "Duplikate aus Ninive," JNES 33 (1974):340, note 1; M. Stol, "Hammu-rabi," unpublished manuscript (I am indebted to the author for furnishing a copy of this study).

15. F. Thureau-Dangin, "Un hymne à Ištar de la haute époque babylonienne," RA 22 (1925):173, 176 (line 36).

16. AHw I:317; CAD 6 (H):68. Contrast SAHG 236; Marie-Joseph Seux, *Hymnes et prières aux dieux de Babylonie et d'Assyrie* (Littératures anciennes du Proche Orient 8; Paris: du Cerf, 1976):39-42.

17. Anne Draffkorn Kilmer, "The First Tablet of *malku=šarru* Together with its Explicit Version," JAOS 83 (1963):421ff., line 158: *am-mu = ze-ru*; cf. CAD 1/2 (A):77.

18. P. E. van der Meer, *Syllabaries A, B' and B with Miscellaneous Lexicographical Texts from the Herbert Weld Collection* (OEC 4; London: Oxford University, 1938):#150, iii:42. For an alternate reading, AHw I:44.

19. CAD 1/2 (A):77.

20. The form *ʿmn* results from the addition of the elusive element -n and does not attest a triliteral origin of the preposition with those consonants.

21. Ch. Virolleaud, "Les noms de personnes à Ras-Shamra," GLECS 8 (1958):9.

22. Frauke Grøndahl, *Die Personennamen der Texte aus Ugarit* (Studia Pohl 1; Rome: PBI, 1967).

23. *Ibid.*, 108-109.

24. Compare the personal names *Ammi*yanu and *Hali*yanu, Grøndahl, 109, 138.

25. M. Dahood, "Ugaritic-Hebrew Syntax and Style," UF 1 (1969):25.

26. M. Dietrich, O. Loretz, and J. Sanmartín, "Zur ugaritischen Lexikographie xii," UF 6 (1974):44-45.

27. WUS #2537, 2002.

28. M. Dietrich and O. Loretz, "Ein Spottlied auf ʻAṯtar," UF 9 (1977):331.

29. J. de Moor, *The Seasonal Pattern in the Ugaritic Myth of Baʻlu* (AOAT 16; Neukirchen-Vluyn: Neukirchener Verlag, 1971): 203.

30. Dennis Pardee, "The Preposition in Ugaritic," UF 7 (1975):362, and UF 8 (1976):260.

31. Dahood, "Syntax and Style," 24-25,

32. J. A. Emerton, "Ugaritic Notes," JTS ns 16 (1965): 441-442; John Gray, *The Legacy of Canaan* (2nd edition; SVT 5; Leiden: E. J. Brill, 1965):66.

33. Gray, 66.

34. G. R. Driver, *Canaanite Myths and Legends* (Old Testament Studies 3; Edinburgh: T. and T. Clark, 1956):111.

35. ANET, 140.

36. A. Caquot, M. Sznycer, and A. Herdner, *Textes ougaritiques* (Littératures anciennes du Proche Orient 7; Paris: du Cerf) vol. 1:257.

37. M. Held, "The Action-Result (Factitive-Passive) Sequence of Identical Verbs in Biblical Hebrew and Ugaritic," JBL 84 (1965):280, note 36.

38. M. Astour, "New Evidence on the Last Days of Ugarit," AJA 69 (1965):257.

39. H. J. van Dijk, *Ezekiel's Prophecy on Tyre (Ez 26,1-28,19): A New Approach* (BibOr 20; Rome: PBI, 1968):9-10.

40. M. Dietrich, O. Loretz, and J. Sanmartín, UF 6 (1974): 44, note 18.

41. Pardee, UF 8 (1976):304

42. For the spellings of the place name and geographic information, see G. F. del Monte and J. Tischler, *Répertoire géographique des textes cunéiformes* (Wiesbaden: Reichert, 1978) vol. 6:237-238.

43. Compare the alternative given by E. Lipiński, "*skn* et *sgn* dans le sémitique occidentale du nord," UF 5 (1973):197.

44. *Ibid.*, 198. The proof comes from the Akkadian translation *DINGIR a-bi*, *Ugaritica* vol. 5:44ff.

45. CTA 29.1.2ff.; *Ugaritica* vol. 5:44ff.

46. W. F. Albright, *Yahweh and the Gods of Canaan* (reprint; Winona Lake, Indiana: Eisenbrauns, *1968):141, note 178.

47. K. Koch, "Die Sohnesverheissung an den ugaritischen Daniel," ZA 58 (1967):215.

48. Gray, 109, note 2.

49. Lipiński, 197.

50. M. Tsevat, "Traces of Hittite at the Beginning of the Ugaritic Epic of AQHT," UF 3 (1971):352.

51. M. H. Pope, "Notes on the Rephaim Texts from Ugarit," Finkelstein Mem, 164.

52. W. F. Albright, "The 'Natural Force' of Moses in the Light of Ugaritic," BASOR 94 (1944):35, note 30. For the evidence of personal names, see Huffmon, 252-254. The zi sign is now conventionally transcribed sí, but the consistency of zi spellings may support Albright's understanding.

53. *Ugaritica* vol. 5:564.

54. E. Lipiński, "Ditanu," FS Loewenstamm, 91ff.

55. Caquot, Sznycer, and Herdner, 219.

56. The verb *pāraʿ* means here as in Ugaritic "to go forth." The noun *pĕrāʿôt* means literally "locks," metaphorically (from the position of locks at the top of the head) "captains."

57. Frank L. Benz, *Personal Names in the Phoenician and Punic Inscriptions* (Studia Pohl 8; Rome: PBI, 1972):379.

58. M. Sznycer, "'L'assemblée du peuple' dans les cités puniques d'après les témoignages épigraphiques," Sem 25 (1975):47-68.

59. N. Sloush, "Representative Government among the Hebrews and Phoenicians," JQR 4 (1913):303-310.

60. To the bibliography cited in KAI, add Ch. Clermont-Ganneau, RAO 3:57; M. Sznycer, "Quelques observations sur la grande inscription dédicatoire de Mactar," Sem 22 (1972):25-44; A. van den Branden, "L'inscription néopunique de Mactar KAI 145," *Rivista di Studi Fenici* 1 (1973):165-172.

61. The relevant line is *hmzrḥ ʾš ldrt ʾš bnʾ mqdš* etc., "The *mzrḥ* of the cella (?) which built the sanctuary, etc."

62. M. P. Berger, "Mémoire sur la grande inscription dédicatoire et sur plusieurs autres inscriptions néo-puniques du temple d'Hathor-Miskar à Maktar," *Mémoires de l'Académie des Inscriptions et Belles-Lettres* 36/2 (1899):19.

63. See Sznycer's discussion, "Mactar," 39.

64. Clermont-Ganneau, RAO 3:30; KAI 126:7: *ʾš lpny ʾdrʾ ʾlpqy wʿm ʾlpqy*, "who is before the nobles of Leptis and Leptis' population."

65. KAI 68.1-2 (Carthage); KAI 170.3 (Lixus); KAI 173.1 (Bitia); KAI 19.8 (Tyre); etc.

66. Thus it was understood by Donner and Röllig, KAI 126.4-6.

67. KAI 51.RS.4 The context does not permit a certain interpretation: ...*bn lkn lkl ʿm šmš*.

68. Sznycer, "'L'assemblée,'" 61, note 2.

69. CIS 1:263.3-4. The meaning of *ʿmt* in the Mactar Inscription (KAI 145.2) is uncertain, although a preposition cognate with Hebrew **ʿumma* "juxtaposition" (used as a preposition "corresponding with") is likely.

70. KAI 62: *pʿl wḥdš ʿm gwl ʾyt šlš* [..., "The people of *Gwl* made and renewed three (sanctuaries)."

71. KAI 71.

72. Sznycer, "'L'assemblée,'" 56, collected the texts: CIS 270-275, 290, 291, 4908, 4909.

73. J.-G. Février, "Vir Sidonius," Sem 4 (1951-1952):18.

74. For the term Maioumas see Hölscher/Jacoby, "Maiumas," Pauly-Wissowa 14/1:610-613; E. Saglio, "Maiumas," *Dictionnaire des antiquités grecques et romaines* (Paris: Hachette, 1904): 1555-1556; E. Y. Kutscher, *Words and their History* (Hebrew; Jerusalem: Kiryath Sefer, 1961):4ff.; M. H. Pope, *Song of Songs* (Anchor Bible; Garden City, New York: Doubleday, 1977):216ff. According to our interpretation, the Carthaginian texts record votive acts accomplished at the occasion of the festival.

75. M. Sznycer, "'L'assemblée,'" 53-55. The texts are KAI 43:5; KAI 19.5-8; KAI 18.4-6; KAI 60.1; and (conjecturally) KAI 62.7-8.

76. KAI 40.2.

77. Sznycer, "'L'assemblée,'" 60-64. The texts adduced by Sznycer are KAI 68, 99, 170; CIS 264-267, 3707, 5606; Trip 35, 41; Antas 1-3. Add to this list Antas 17, and if Février is correct Sousse Stele 4.

78. CIS 281, 282, 283, etc.

79. C. T. Falbe and J. Chr. Lindberg, *Numismatique de l'ancienne afrique* (Copenhague: Bianco Luno, 1861): vol. 2:75, 81.

80. Wm. J. Fulco, "The Amman Theater Inscription," JNES 38 (1979):37-38.

81. At line 11 *ʿm* probably refers to the population of the city *ʿṭrt*: *wʾḥzh.wʾhrg.ʾt.kl.hʿm.hqr* "I captured and killed all the people (in the ?) city." At line 24 the noun refers to Qeriḥo's population: *wbr.ʾn.bqrb.hqr.bqrḥh.wʾmr.lkl. hʿm* etc., "There was no cistern in the city, in Qeriḥo, so I said to all the people, etc."

82. J. Hoftijzer and G. van der Krooij, *Aramaic Texts from Deir ʿAlla* (Leiden: E. J. Brill, 1976):190. These texts are included here because their linguistic position is in doubt.

83. A. Caquot and A. Lemaire, "Les textes araméens de Deir ʿAlla," *Syria* 54 (1977):194.

84. The more common form of the preposition is *ʿam(m)*, but *ʿim(m)* is encountered in Jewish Palestinian Aramaic.

85. The need for a study of Aramaic personal names is partially offset by J. K. Stark, *Personal Names in Palmyrene Inscriptions* (Oxford: Clarendon, 1971).

86. For convenience the vocalization of names follows that of CIS here.

87. Clermont-Ganneau, RAO 2:370ff. The family tree reconstructed for CIS 182 has been confirmed by more recent texts, J. T. Milik, "Nouvelles inscriptions nabatéennes," *Syria* 35 (1958):227-228.

88. CIS 2:118; R. Degen, NEph 2:96.

89. C. Kayser, *Die Canones Jacob's von Edessa* (Leipzig: Hinrichs, 1886):24, line 26; for the references, Carl Brockelmann, *Lexicon Syriacum* (Berlin: Reuther and Reichard, 1895): 252; Th. Nöldeke, ZDMG 40 (1886):172-173, 173 note 1.

90. J. J. Overbeck, *St. Ephraemi Syri, Opera Selecta* (Oxford: Clarendon, 1865):221, line 8.

91. S. E. Assemani, *Acta Sanctorum Martyrum Orientalium et Occidentalium* (Paris, 1748):vol. 2:275, line 24.

92. Hasan bar Bahlul (tenth century), *Lexicon Syriacum*, ed. Rubens Duval (Paris, 1888):1444.

93. Jibrāʾil al-Ḳardāḥī, *Al-Lobab, Dictionarium Syro-Arabicum* (Beirut, 1887-1891):vol. 2:272.

94. Leonhard Rost, "Die Bezeichnungen für Land und Volk im Alten Testament," 143, note 1, cites Assemani vol.1:152, line 21 for the use of *ʿam(m)* to denote a group of paternal relatives, but the text does not require this sense.

95. J. Teixidor, *Inventaire des inscriptions de Palmyre* (Beyrouth: Institut Français d'Archéologie de Beyrouth, 1965): vol. 11, #57.

96. J. Starcky and C.-M. Bennett, "Les inscriptions du téménos," *Syria* 45 (1958):64.

97. E. S. Drower and R. Macuch, *A Mandaic Dictionary* (Oxford: Clarendon, 1963):340.

98. KAI 232.

99. Read *ngdy* for KAI *ngry*, with J. Fitzmyer, *The Aramaic Inscriptions of Sefire* (BibOr 19; Rome: PBI, 1967):98.

100. Cf. Cowley #83.94,162.

101. Fitzmyer, 113.

102. On *ngd*, see below, Chapter V, "Yahweh's people."

103. KAI 222.A.30; 222.B.11; 223.C.16.

104. The reading is not certain; Cowley #83.94,162.

105. *rḥm ʿmh*: RÉS 674.7; 1103.10; 1144.11; *dy ʾḥyy* etc.: RÉS 83.11-13.

106. Clermont-Ganneau, RAO 2:375, note 2.

107. Drower and Macuch, 21.

108. For a special discussion of the preposition, see A. F. L. Beeston, *A Descriptive Grammar of Epigraphic South Arabian* (London: Luzac, 1962):59-60.

109. A. Jamme, *Sabaean Inscriptions from Maḥram Bilqīs* (Baltimore: Johns Hopkins, 1962):444.

110. Joan Kendrick, "A Dictionary of Old South Arabic, Sabaean Dialect" (Ph.D. dissertation, Harvard: 1978):s.v. *ʿmm*.

111. RÉS 4439; 4514.1-2 (Sab.).

112. Beeston, 54.

113. *ʿmt* occurs at CIH 562.3.

114. See G. Ryckmans, *Les noms propres sud-sémitiques* (Louvain: Bureaux du Muséon, 1934):passim, and G. Lankester Harding, *An Index and Concordance of Pre-Islamic Arabian Names and Inscriptions* (Near and Middle East Series 8; Toronto: University of Toronto, 1971):s.v. *ʿm* and passim.

115. St. Nilus, Ammanes, see Toufic Fahd, *Le panthéon de l'Arabie centrale à la veille de l'Hégire* (Paris: Paul Geuthner, 1968):45-46.

116. F. Hommel, *Aufsätze und Abhandlungen* (München: Lukaschik, 1900) vol. 5:149-165.

117. H. Winckler, "Arabisch-Semitisch-Orientalisch," MVAG 6/4 (1901):164ff.

118. A. Jamme, "Le panthéon sud-arabe pré-islamique," *Le Muséon* 60 (1947):62ff., especially 78-80.

119. N. Rhodokanakis, "Katabanische Texte zur Bodenwirtschaft," *Sitzungsberichte*, Akademie der Wissenschaften in Wien, Philosophisch-Historische Klasse 194/2 (1919):66, note 4.

120. Following the translation of Rhodokanakis, reported at RÉS 2687.3.

121. RÉS 3427.3, and see the discussion.

122. Perhaps a solar god, see Jamme, "Panthéon," 110-112.

123. For the translation, see the discussion of RÉS.

124. A. Jamme, *Sabaean and Hasaean Inscriptions from Saudi Arabia* (Studi Semitici 23; Rome: Istituto di Studi del Vicino Oriente, 1966):40-41 (Ja 1028).

125. G. Ryckmans, "Inscriptions sud-arabes," *Le Muséon* 66 (1953):285, 287, 294 (no. 507, line 10).

126. Kendrick, s.v. *ʿwm*.

127. A. van den Branden, *Les inscriptions thamoudéennes* (Bibliothèque du Muséon 25; Louvain: Heverle, 1950); idem, *Les textes themoudéens de Philby* (Bibliothèque du Muséon 39 and 41; Louvain: Publications universitaires, 1956); G. Ryckmans, CIS, vol. 5. The short collection of Lihyanite inscriptions, van den Branden, *Les inscriptions dédanites* (Beirut: Publications de l'Université Libanaise, section des études historiques, 1962), offers no instances of the noun *ʿamm* apart from personal names.

128. CIS vol. 5:2381.

129. E. Littmann, *Semitic Inscriptions* (Publications of an American Archaeological Expedition to Syria in 1899-1900, part 4; New York: Century, 1904):119, 160; G. Ryckmans, "Les noms de parenté en safaïtique," RB 58 (1951):387-388.

130. G. L. Harding, "Safaitic Inscriptions in the Iraq Museum," *Sumer* 6 (1950):124 (IM 49217), lines 5ff.

131. G. Ryckmans, "A propos des noms de parenté en safaïtique," RB 60 (1953):524-525.

132. W. G. Oxtoby, *Some Inscriptions of the Safaitic Bedouin* (AOS 50; New Haven, Connecticut: American Oriental Society, 1968):101.

133. In the Qur'an *ʿamm* (pl. *'aʿmām*) and *ʿamma* (pl. *ʿammāt*) occur only a few times and always mean paternal uncle(s), paternal aunt(s): IV:23; XXIV:61; XXXIII:50.

134. L. W. Lane, *Arabic-English Lexicon* (London: Williams and Norgate, 1863-1893):1/5:2148-2150.

135. See Ibn Qutayba, *ʿUyūn al-'Aḫbār* I:229-230, where ʿUbaydallāh speaks of his adoptive uncle Muʿāwiya using the noun.

136. See, for example, Jean Lecerf, "Note sur la famille dans le monde arabe et islamique," *Arabica* 3 (1956):31-60.

137. Rudolf Dvořák, "Über die Fremdwörter im Korân," *Sitzungsberichte der philosophisch-historischen Classe der Kaiserlichen Akademie der Wissenschaften, Wien* 109 (1885): 512ff.; cf. H. L. Fleischer, "Das Arabische in Geiger's Preisschrift: Was hat Muhammed aus dem Judenthume aufgenommen?" *Kleinere Schriften* (Leipzig: S. Hirzel, 1885-1888) vol. 2:137.

138. Th. Nöldeke, *Neue Beiträge zur semitischen Sprachwissenschaft* (Strassburg: Trübner, 1910):78.

139. Ibn Qutayba, *ʿUyūn al-'Aḫbār* I:239; meter: ṭawīl.

140. Th. Nöldeke, *Delectus Carminum Arabicorum* (Porta Linguarum Orientalium 13; Berlin: Reuther, 1890):86, line 12. Meter: ṭawīl; poet and caliph flourished in the early eighth century.

141. Al-Jāḥiẓ, *Al-Bayān wat-Tabyīn* I:4. Meter: ṭawīl.

142. Al-Mubarrad, *Kāmil*, 170. Meter: kāmil; the second syllable of *'anā* is metrically short.

143. *Ḥamāsa* (Freytag):676-677. Meter: ṭawīl. The verse contradicts the view attributed to the tenth century Basran grammarian al-'Aḫfash that the nisba of *ʿamm* is *ʿamawī* (*aṣ-Ṣiḥāḥ*, 317). Wellhausen refers to this verse as evidence of a collective (see above, Introduction, note 8).

144. *Al-Mufaḍḍalīyāt* I:100, 104; trans. II:35, 38. Meter: ṭawīl.

145. *Ḥamāsa* (Freytag):187. Meter: ṭawīl. The identity of al-Muthallam was not known to at-Tabrīzī.

146. Hudhayl (Kosegarten):102. Meter: ṭawīl. Liḥyān is reckoned a descendant of Hudhayl, but the poem's narrative *mise en scène* makes it clear that the issue in the relationship between Liḥyān and the Banū Sahm was the fact that the former were clients of the latter.

147. ZDMG 47 (1893):83-84, and see Goldziher's notes. The poet was a contemporary of Muhammad. Meter: wāfir.

148. Dīwān al-Farazdaq (Boucher), #19 (pp. 36-37; cf. trans., p. 85 + note 1 on ʿAmr). Meter: wāfir.

149. Maymun (Geyer), #58:1. Meter: ṭawīl.

150. Hudhayl (Wellhausen), #128:10 (trans., p. 116). Meter: ṭawīl. The poet is Abū Shihāb al-Māzinī.

151. See Th. Nöldeke, ZDMG 40 (1886):153, note 1; R. Murphy and L. Kasdan, "The Structure of Parallel Cousin Marriage," *The American Anthropologist* 61/1 (1959):17-29; G. A. Wilken, *Het Matriarchaat bij de Oude Arabieren* (1884):124ff.; Gertrude H. Stern, *Marriage in Early Islam* (London: Royal Asiatic Society, 1939); Jean Cuisinier, "Endogamie et exogamie dans le mariage arabe," *L'homme* 2/1 (1962):80-105.

152. CIS 5:4417, 4443; Drower and Macuch, 351, report an Arabic dialect preposition *ʿm*. Franz Praetorius, "Beiträge zur äthiopischen Grammatik und Etymologie," *Beiträge zur Assyriologie und vergleichenden semitischen Sprachwissenschaft* 1 (1890):26 opposes deriving *maʿa* from **ʿm*.

153. Ibn Māja, #2635.

154. An-Nasāʾī VII:113.

155. *Lisān* 19:331; cf. Lane, s.v. *ʿmy*.

156. *Lisān* 19:331. Meter: basīṭ. The verse is not in ar-Rāʿī's diwan; the poet lived in the eighth century.

157. *Al-Muzhir* I:178. As-Suyūṭī was a fifteenth century scholar.

158. Ibn Durayd I:114. Labīd (Brockelmann), #52.1. Meter: rajaz.

159. ʿUrwa (Nöldeke), #31.1-2. Meter: ṭawīl. I follow a reading suggested by Prof. F. Rosenthal in correcting Nöldeke's *iḏa* to read *iḏi*. One might alternatively correct *zuhhadu* to read *zuhhidū* and retain Nöldeke's translation, "when the people are wearied."

160. Labīd (Brockelmann), #51.1-2. Meter: ṭawīl.

161. Al-Jāḥiẓ, *Ḥayawān* II:360.

162. *Tāj al-ʿArūs*, s.v. *ʿima*.

163. *Lisān* 15:328.

164. *Ibid.*, the alternate imperfect *yaʿāmu* is given.

Chapter III

1. Leonhard Rost, "Die Bezeichnungen für Land und Volk im Alten Testament," FS Procksch, 142.

2. E. A. Speiser, "'People' and 'Nation' of Israel," *Oriental and Biblical Studies*, ed. J. J. Finkelstein and M. Greenberg (Philadelphia: University of Pennsylvania, 1967):161.

3. Rost, 143, note 4.

4. Speiser, 162.

5. CTA 5.5.19-21.

6. Speiser, 164.

7. Rost, 147.

8. G. W. Anderson, "Israel: Amphictyony: *ʿām; qāhāl; ʿēdāh*," FS H. G. May, 150; H. Brichto, "Kin, Cult, Land and Afterlife - A Biblical Complex," HUCA 44 (1973):9; R. Clements, "*Gōy*," TDOT 2:426ff., A. Cody, "When Is the Chosen People Called a *Gōy*?" VT 14 (1964):1-6; J. Hempel, *Das Ethos des Alten Testaments* (BZAW 67; Berlin: Töpelmann, 1938):77ff.; A. R. Hulst, "*ʿām/gōj*," THAT 2:290-335; E. Lipiński, "Recherches sur le livre de Zacharie," VT 20 (1970):45-46; T. Mettinger, *King and Messiah: The Civil and Sacral Legitimation of the Israelite Kings* (Lund: Gleerup, 1976):108-190; H. Schulz, *Das Todesrecht im Alten Testament: Studien zur Rechtsform der mot-jumat Sätze* (BZAW 114; Berlin: Töpelmann, 1969):102, note 65; G. Wallis, "Der Vollbürgereid in Deuteronomium 27, 15-26," HUCA 45 (1974): 47ff.

9. H. C. M. Vogt, *Studie zur nachexilischen Gemeinde in Esra-Nehemia* (Werl: Dietrich-Coelde, 1966):79.

10. Hulst, 301-302.

11. E. Würthwein, *Der ʿamm haʾarez im Alten Testament* (BWANT 69; Stuttgart: Kohlhammer, 1936):13-14.

12. Wallis, 47-63.

13. Mitchell Dahood, *Psalms* (Anchor Bible; Garden City, New York: Doubleday, 1965-1970):1:112-113, 283-284; 2:93, 316, 348, 368; 3:68, 116; idem, "Vocative Lamedh in the Psalter," VT 16 (1966):309; idem, "Hebrew-Ugaritic Lexicography VII," Bib 50 (1969):349.

14. Among those to reject Dahood's thesis have been M. Dietrich, O. Loretz, and J. Sanmartín, "Zur ugaritischen Lexikographie XII," UF 6 (1974):44-45; J. C. de Moor, "Ugaritic Lexicography," *Studies on Semitic Lexicography*, ed. P. Fronzaroli (Quaderni di semitistica 2; Firenze: Istituto di Linguistica e di Lingue Orientali, 1973):93, note 1. Dahood's student A. C. M. Blommerde has supported the thesis, *Northwest Semitic Grammar and Job* (BibOr 22; Rome: PBI, 1969):25.

15. H. J. van Dijk, "Consolamini, consolamini, popule meus?" VD 45 (1967):342-346; idem, *Ezekiel's Prophecy on Tyre (Ez 26:1-28:19): A New Approach* (BibOr 20; Rome: PBI, 1968): 101-103.

16. A. Zaborski, "Prefixes, Root-Determinatives and the Problem of Biconsonantal Roots in Semitic," *Folia Orientalia* 11 (1970):307-313; J. Kuryłowicz, *Studies in Semitic Grammar and Metrics* (London, 1973):6.

17. Dahood, *Psalms*, 1:113.

18. Cf. H.-P. Müller, "Magisch-mantische Weisheit und die Gestalt Daniels," UF 1 (1969):81.

19. J. A. Davies, "A Note on Job xii,2," VT 25 (1975): 670-671.

20. With suffixes the preposition reveals the root form *ʿimm*; the form with a first person suffix *ʿimmādî* is correctly taken as a compound of *ʿim(m)* and *yad* ("at hand"), see P. Joüon, "Etudes de philologie sémitique," MUSJ 5 (1911):395.

21. See in particular Frank Zimmermann, "Folk Etymology of Biblical Names," SVT 15 (1966):320; Andrzej Strus, *Nomen-omen: La stylistique sonore des noms propres dans le Pentateuque* (AnBib 80; Rome: PBI, 1978):71. For a discussion of the name Ammon, see L. Köhler, "Der Name Ammoniter," TZ 1 (1945): 154-156 and the response of J. J. Stamm, "Zum Ursprung des Namens der Ammoniter," ArOr 17 (1948):379-382.

22. To the list of Martin Noth, *Die israelitischen Personennamen im Rahmen der gemeinsemitischen Namengebung* (BZAW 46; Stuttgart: Kohlhammer, 1928):77, may be added Biblical *ʾnyʿm*, *ytrʿm*, *ʾlyʿm*, *ʿmyšdy*, *blʿm*, and epigraphic *ʿmšlm* (Arad 59:4) *ʾdnʿm* (Samaria 8:2, etc.).

23. N. Lohfink, "Beobachtungen zur Geschichte des Ausdrucks *ʿam yhwh*," FS von Rad, 291-292.

24. *ʾaḥărê* means here (vs. 14) "with," see on this meaning R. B. Y. Scott, "Secondary Meanings of *ʾaḥar, After, Behind*," JTS 50 (1949):178-179.

25. For the reading, see the note to BH^3.

26. E. A. Speiser, *Genesis* (Anchor Bible; Garden City, New York: Doubleday, 1964):104; but vv 10-11, rather than implying the capture of a fighting force, suggest that the defenders of the cities fled for safety, leaving defenseless persons to be taken. Note that Sodom's king was not captured.

27. S. Mowinckel, "General Oriental and Specific Israelite Elements in the Israelite Conception of the Sacral Kingdom," *The Sacral Kingdom* (Leiden: E. J. Brill, 1959):288; J. de Fraine, *L'aspect religieux de la royauté israélite* (AnBib 3; Rome: PBI, 1954):351ff.; W. W. Hallo, *Early Mesopotamian Royal Titles: A Philological and Historical Analysis* (AOS 43; New Haven, Connecticut: American Oriental Society, 1957):141; M.-J.

Seux, *Epithètes royales akkadiennes et sumériennes* (Paris: Letouzey et Ane, 1967):s.v. *re'u* and *sipa*; H. D. Preuss, "... ich will mit dir sein!" ZAW 80 (1968):159-160; V. Maag, "*Malkût Yhwh*," SVT 7 (Leiden: E. J. Brill, 1960):132ff.; P. de Robert, *Le berger d'Israël* (Cahiers théologiques 57; Neuchâtel: Delachaux et Niestlé, 1960):passim; J. J. Glück, "*Nāgîd*-Shepherd," VT 13 (1963):144-150.

28. C. H. J. de Geus, *The Tribes of Israel: An Investigation into Some of the Presuppositions of Martin Noth's Amphictyony Hypothesis* (Studia Semitica Neerlandica 18; Assen: Van Gorcum):147, for a different appreciation of the text.

29. R. de Vaux, *Ancient Israel*, trans. John McHugh (London: Darton, Longman and Todd, 1961):1:12-13.

30. This sense suits Lev 19:16.

31. De Geus, 138.

32. S. Talmon, "The Judaean *'Am Ha'areṣ* in Historical Perspective," *Fourth World Congress of Jewish Studies*, 75.

33. Speiser, 167.

34. John Gray, *I and II Kings* (OTL; 2d ed.; London: SCM, 1970):495-496.

35. H. Ringgren, "*Gā'al*," TDOT 2:352.

36. M. D. Goldman, "Concerning the Meaning of *'ām*," ABR 3 (1953):51.

37. M. H. Pope, *Job* (Anchor Bible; Garden City, New York: Doubleday, 1973):89.

38. Trans. Pope, 255.

39. Rost, 145.

40. A. Malamat, "Aspects of Tribal Society in Mari and Israel," *Mari and the Bible* (Jerusalem: Hebrew University, 1975):47-48.

41. De Vaux, 1:214.

42. O. Bächli, *Israel und die Völker* (ATANT 41; Zürich: Zwingli, 1962):115, note 6.

43. For the interpretation of *ḥōbēb* as cognate with Akkadian *ebēbu*, see P. Miller, *The Divine Warrior in Early Israel* (Harvard Semitic Monographs 5; Cambridge, Massachusetts: Harvard University, 1973):80. The term should be related to *tebibtum* census/muster.

44. N. H. Snaith, "Genesis xxxi:50," VT 14 (1964):373 restores "our clan" at that verse, without compelling reason.

45. Seemingly also in the difficult phrase *bĕrît ʿam*, Isa 42:6, and see J. J. Stamm, "*Bĕrît ʿAm*," RS von Rad, 510-524; D. R. Hillers, "*Bĕrît ʿam*: 'Emancipation of the People,'" JBL 97 (1978):175-182.

46. For the possible use of the noun for a host of angels, see V. S. Poythress, "The Holy Ones of the Most High in Daniel vii," VT 26 (1976):208-213.

47. G. Buccellati, *Cities and Nations of Ancient Syria: An Essay on Political Institutions with Special Reference to the Israelite Kingdoms* (StSem 26; Rome: Istituto di Studi del Vicino Oriente, 1967):13ff.

Chapter IV

1. The pre-Exilic origin of the formula is suggested on other grounds by Gen 28:21b, which seems to come from the Yahwist and to presuppose the Bundesformel.

2. CAD 10/1 (M):320.

3. Norbert Lohfink, "Beobachtungen zur Geschichte des Ausdrucks *ʿam yhwh*," FS von Rad, 297, note 79.

4. A. R. Hulst, "*ʿam/gōj*," THAT 2:305.

5. For the translation of *šākan* by "to tabernacle," see F. M. Cross, "The Priestly Tabernacle," BA 10/3 (September, 1947):45-68.

6. W. Zimmerli, "Ich bin Jahweh," *Gottes Offenbarung: Gesammelte Aufsätze zum Alten Testament* (München: Kaiser, 1963): 11-40.

7. G. von Rad, *Das Gottesvolk im Deuteronomium* (BWANT 47; Stuttgart: Kohlhammer, 1929):20ff.

8. Von Rad, "Verheissenes Land und Jahwehs Land im Hexateuch," *Gesammelte Studien zum Alten Testament* (München: Kaiser, 1958):91.

9. R. Smend, *Die Bundesformel* (ThSt Barth 68; Zürich: EVZ, 1963):25ff.

10. Lohfink, "Beobachtungen," 296-300; idem, "Dt 26,17-19 und die 'Bundesformel,'" ZKT 91 (1969):548-553.

11. A. Jepsen, "Berith: Ein Beitrag zur Theologie der Exilzeit," FS Rudolph, 171ff.

12. L. Perlitt, *Die Bundestheologie im Alten Testament* (WMANT 36; Neukirchen-Vluyn: Neukirchener Verlag, 1969):108.

13. Lohfink, "Dt 26, 17-19," 526, for the argument that this use of the Covenant Formula is not essentially Deuteronomistic.

14. What is said here pertains to language only, not to the possibility of there being a covenant in the reign of Jehoash. For the text, see Klaus Baltzer, *The Covenant Formulary*, trans. David E. Green (Philadelphia: Fortress, 1971):78ff.

15. G. von Rad, *Deuteronomy*, trans. D. Barton (OTL; Philadelphia: Westminster, 1966):161ff. Contrast Perlitt (above, note 12).

16. Smend, 11-12; E. Nestle, "Dtn 26,17.18," ZAW 28 (1908):149; G. Mercati, "Una singolare versione di deut. xxvi 17 e 18 e l'originale di essa," Bib 24 (1943):201-204; P. Joüon, "Deuteronome 16:17-18," MUSJ 4 (1910):20-21.

17. Joüon, "Deuteronome 26:17-18."

18. Lohfink, "Dt 26,17-19," 541-542.

19. For the literature, see Lohfink, "Dt 26,17-19," 544, note 82.

20. It is possible that Deuteronomy uses the noun in reliance on E or common northern traditions.

21. I am indebted to F. M. Cross for calling this to my attention.

22. Perlitt, 167ff.

23. H. Wildberger, *Jahweh's Eigentumsvolk* (ATANT 37; Zürich: Zwingli, 1960):14ff.

24. G. von Rad, *Deuteronomy*, 161-162.

25. The recent literature on the text includes R. Martin-Achard, "La nouvelle alliance selon Jérémie," RTP 3rd series 12 (1962):81-92; J. Coppens, "La Nouvelle Alliance en Jér 31,31-34," CBQ 25 (1963):12-21; J. Bright, "An Exercise in Hermeneutics: Jeremiah 31:31-34," *Interpretation* 20 (1966):188-210; P. Buis, "La Nouvelle Alliance," VT 18 (1968):1-15; R. Martin-Achard, "Quelques remarques sur la nouvelle alliance chez Jeremie (Jeremie 31:31-34)," in *Questions disputées d'Ancien Testament: Méthode et théologie*, ed. C. Brekelmans (BETL 33; Louvain: Leuven University Press, 1974):141-164; J. Swetnam, "Why Was Jeremiah's New Covenant New?" SVT 26 (1974):111-115.

26. Martin-Achard, "Quelques remarques," 162-164.

27. G. von Rad, *Genesis*, trans. J. H. Marks (OTL; Philadelphia: Westminster, 1972):200.

28. M. Weinfeld, *Deuteronomy and the Deuteronomic School* (Oxford: Clarendon, 1972):80.

29. W. Robertson Smith, *Kinship and Marriage in Early Arabia* (reprint; Boston: Beacon, *1885):48.

30. David Daube, "Über die Umbildung biblischen Rechtsgutes," *Symbolae Friburgenses in Honorem Ottonis Lenel*

(Freiburg, 1935):249. The bibliography for this topic is provided by W. Zimmerli, *Ezechiel* (BKAT 13/1; Neukirchen-Vluyn: Neukircher, 1969):302.

31. E. Fink, "Gedanken über die *Kareth*-Strafe," *Jeschurun* 4 (1917):383ff.

32. Daube, 249-255.

33. Zimmerli, *Ezechiel*, 302-314; idem, "Die Eigenart der prophetischen Rede des Ezechiel," ZAW 66 (1954):12-19.

34. Donald Wold, "The Meaning of the Biblical Penalty *Kareth*" (Ph.D. dissertation, University of California, 1978).

35. These observations were already made by S. Jampel, *Vorgeschichte Israels und seiner Religion* (1913), summarized by Fink (note 31).

36. The occurrences in Deut 32, if not from P, represent a borrowing of Priestly vocabulary.

37. For the literature on the idiom see the introduction to this volume, passim. The most important study of the expression is that of B. Alfrink, "L'expression *neʾĕsap ʾel-ʿammayw*," OTS 5 (1946):118-131. Cf. Bernhard Stade, *Geschichte des Volkes Israel* (Berlin: Grote, 1887-1888) vol. 1:421; Friedrich Schwally, *Das Leben nach dem Tode* (Giessen: Ricker, 1892): 54; Johannes Frey, *Tod, Seelenglaube und Seelenkult im alten Israel* (Leipzig, 1898):226; Carl Grüneisen, *Der Ahnenkultus und die Urreligion Israels* (Halle: Niemeyer, 1900):53; Gustav Hölscher, *Geschichte der israelitischen und jüdischen Religion* (Giessen: Töpelmann, 1922):31-32; E. Dhorme, "Le dieu parent et le dieu maître dans la religion des Hébreux," RHR 106 (1932): 230; G. Ryckmans, "Les noms de parenté en safaïtique," RB 58 (1951):389; E. Lipiński, "Ditanu," FS Loewenstamm, 97.

38. W. F. Albright connected the Ugaritic verb and the Biblical idiom, "New Canaanite Historical and Mythological Data," BASOR 63 (1936):28, note 16.

39. Wold, 189ff.

Chapter V

1. For the verb *hiqšâ* see R. R. Wilson, "The Hardening of Pharaoh's Heart," CBQ 41 (1979):18ff.

2. M. Weinfeld, *Deuteronomy and the Deuteronomic School* (Oxford: Clarendon, 1972):341; B. Gemser, *Sprüche Salomos* (HAT 16; Tübingen: Mohr, 1937):78.

3. Jean Malfroy, "Sagesse et loi dans le Deutéronome," VT 15 (1965):49-65.

4. F. Hesse, *Das Verstockungsproblem im Alten Testament* (BZAW 74; Berlin: Töpelmann, 1955):13. Cf. A. S. van der Woude, "*qšh*," THAT II: 691.

5. M. H. Goshen-Gottstein, "'Ephraim is a well-trained heifer' and Ugaritic *mdl*," Bib 41 (1960):64-66.

6. J. Greenfield, "Ugaritic *mdl* and its Cognates," Bib 45 (1964):527-534.

7. Arabic *dalla*, Aramaic *dallel*.

8. Reading with LXX.

9. Otto Bächli, *Israel und die Völker: Eine Studie zum Deuteronomium* (Zürich: Zwingli, 1962):115.

10. B. S. Childs, *The Book of Exodus* (OTL; Philadelphia: Westminster, 1974):557.

11. W. Beyerlin, *Herkunft und Geschichte der ältesten Sinaitraditionen* (Tübingen: Mohr, 1961):104-113.

12. G. W. Coats, *Rebellion in the Wilderness: The Murmuring Motif in the Wilderness Traditions of the Old Testament* (Nashville: Abingdon, 1968):186; Martin Noth, *Exodus*, trans. J. S. Bowden (OTL; Philadelphia: Westminster, 1962):244; Childs, 559; Lothar Perlitt, *Die Bundestheologie im Alten Testament* (WMANT 36; Neukirchen-Vluyn: Neukirchener Verlag, 1969):208; Sigo Lehming, "Versuch zu Ex xxxii," VT 10 (1960):50.

13. Hugo Gressmann, *Mose und seine Zeit* (Göttingen: Vandenhoeck and Ruprecht, 1913):199ff.

14. W. F. Albright, *Yahweh and the Gods of Canaan* (reprint; Winona Lake, Indiana: Eisenbrauns, *1968):43.

15. M. Dahood, "Poetic Devices in the Book of Proverbs," FS Loewenstamm, 10-11.

16. F. M. Cross, *Canaanite Myth and Hebrew Epic* (Cambridge, Massachusetts: Harvard University, 1973):198, note 20; Noth, 253.

17. Noth, 25.

18. Weinfeld, 34.

19. Childs, 486-487.

20. Otto Eissfeldt, "Lade und Stierbild," ZAW 58 (1940/1941):190-215.

21. José Loza, "Exode xxxii et la rédaction JE," VT 23 (1973):31-55.

22. P. B. Machinist, "The Epic of Tukulti Ninurta I" (Ph.D. dissertation, Yale University, 1978):120-121 (= col. v. 46'-47').

23. H. Tadmor, "'The People' in the Kingdom in Ancient Israel: The Role of Political Institutions in the Biblical

Period," in *Jewish Society through the Ages*, ed. H. H. Ben-Sasson and S. Ettinger (New York: Schocken, 1971):66.

24. Previous treatments of the literature may be found in E. Würthwein, *Der ʿamm haʾarez im alten Israel* (Stuttgart: Kohlhammer, 1936):1-7; S. Talmon, "The Judaean *ʿAm haʾares* in Historical Perspective," *Fourth World Congress of Jewish Studies* (Jerusalem, 1967) vol. 1:71; John McKenzie, "The 'People of the Land' in the Old Testament," in *Akten des vierundzwanzigsten Internationalen Orientalisten-Kongresses, München*, ed. H. Franke (Wiesbaden: Deutsche Morgenländische Gesellschaft, 1959): 206.

25. M. Sulzberger, *ʿAm-ha-aretz - The Ancient Hebrew Parliament* (Philadelphia: Greenstone, 1909).

26. N. Sloush, "Representative Government among the Hebrews and Phoenicians," JQR 4 (1913):303-310.

27. E. Auerbach, *"ʿam haʾareṣ," First World Congress of Jewish Studies* (Jerusalem, 1952):362-366.

28. L. Rost, "Die Bezeichnungen für Land und Volk im alten Israel," FS Procksch, 146; C. U. Wolf, "Traces of Primitive Democracy in Ancient Israel," JNES 6 (1947):107.

29. R. Gordis, "Sectional Rivalry in the Kingdom of Judah," JQR ns 25 (1934/1935):237-259.

30. A. Alt, "The Monarchy in Israel and Judah," in *Old Testament History and Religion*, trans. R. A. Wilson (Garden City, New York: Doubleday, 1967):326-327.

31. Weinfeld, 88, note 2.

32. K. Galling, *Die israelitische Staatsverfassung in ihrer vorderorientalischen Umwelt* (Leipzig: J. C. Hinrichs, 1929):23.

33. E. Klamroth, *Die jüdischen Exulanten in Babylonien* (Leipzig: J. C. Hinrichs, 1912):99-101.

34. M. Weber, *Gesammelte Aufsätze zur Religionssociologie* (Tübingen: Mohr, 1921): vol. 3 *Das antike Judentum*, 30ff.

35. E. Gillischewski, "Der Ausdruck *ʿam ha-areṣ* im Alten Testament," ZAW 40 (1922):137ff.

36. Würthwein (above, note 24).

37. R. de Vaux, "Le sens de l'expression 'peuple du pays' dans l'Ancien Testament et le rôle politique du peuple en Israël," RA 58 (1964):167-172.

38. A. Menes, *Die vorexilischen Gesetze Israels* (BZAW 50; Giessen: Töpelmann, 1928):68-70.

39. G. von Rad, *Deuteronomium-Studien* (Göttingen: Vandenhoeck and Ruprecht, 1948):43ff.

40. J. A. Soggin, "Der judäische *ʿAm-Haʾareṣ* und das Königtum in Judah," VT 13 (1963):187-195.

41. Talmon, 71-76 (Talmon's study appears in a somewhat fuller form, in Hebrew, in *Bêt Miqrâ* 31 [1967]:27-55).

42. V. Maag, "Erwägungen zur deuteronomischen Kultzentralisation," VT 6 (1956):10; Ihromi, "Die Königinmutter und der *ʿAmm haʾArez* im Reich Juda," VT 24 (1974):421-429; Soggin, 187-195; Masao Sekine, "Beobachtungen zu der josianischen Reform," VT 22 (1972):367-368; G. Wallis, "Jerusalem und Samaria als Königsstädte," VT 26 (1976):484, note 9.

43. Talmon, 71-76.

44. M. Greenberg, "Am Ha-areẓ," EnJud 2:843-844; M. H. Pope, "Am Haʾarez," IDB 1:106-107; A. R. Hulst, *"ʿam/Gōj,"* THAT 2:299-302.

45. E. W. Nicholson, "The Meaning of the Expression *ʿam hāʾāreṣ* in the Old Testament," JSS 10 (1965):59-66.

46. Talmon, 71.

47. The only text not to belong chronologically with the mass of evidence, Gen 42:6 (E?), refers the noun phrase to the population of Egypt.

48. S. R. Driver, *An Introduction to the Literature of the Old Testament* (reprint; Cleveland: Meridan, *1913):43; A. Cody, *A History of Old Testament Priesthood* (AnBib 35; Rome: PBI, 1969):101; R. de Vaux, *Ancient Israel*, trans. John McHugh (London: Darton, Longman, and Todd, 1961):vol 2:397-400.

49. A. Alt, "The Origins of Israelite Law," in *Old Testament History and Religion*, 144-146.

50. B. Stade, "Anmerkungen zu 2 Kö 10-14," ZAW 5 (1885): 279-288; P. Joüon, "Notes de critique textuelle (AT)," MUSJ 5 (1912):480-482; W. Rudolph, "Die Einheitlichkeit der Erzählung vom Sturz der Atalja," FS Bertholet, 473-478; F. W. Farrar, "Notes on the Reign of Joash," *Expositor* 1894b:81-98; G. Fohrer, "Der Vertrag zwischen König und Volk in Israel," ZAW 71 (1959): 13; Tadmor, 61; K. Baltzer, *The Covenant Formulary in Old Testament, Jewish, and Early Christian Writings*, trans. D. E. Green (Philadelphia: Fortress, 1971):78ff.

51. Stade, 279-288.

52. Rudolph, 473-478.

53. G. von Rad, *Deuteronomy*, trans. D. Barton (OTL; Philadelphia: Westminster, 1966):67-68, 101.

54. Perlitt, 173.

55. H.-J. Kraus, "Das heilige Volk," FS de Quervain, 50-61.

56. N. Lohfink, "Beobachtungen zur Geschichte des Ausdrucks *ʿam yhwh*," FS von Rad, 279, note 21.

57. *Ibid.*

58. Despite M. Greenberg's attempt to refute the connection between Hebrew *sĕgullâ* and Akkadian *sug/kullu*, that connection remains probable. Greenberg, "Hebrew *sĕgullâ*: Akkadian *sikiltu*," JAOS 71 (1951):172-174. Cf. E. A. Speiser, "Nuzi Marginalia," Or 25 (1956):2-3; F. Dreyfus, "Le thème de l'héritage dans l'Ancien Testament," RSPT 42 (1958):15-16; M. Held, "A Faithful Lover in an Old Babylonian Dialogue," JCS 15 (1961): 11-12.

59. Lohfink, "Beobachtungen" (above, note 56):275-305, with references to further literature.

60. Lohfink, 276, notes 4-7, 9. Included in the count is the Covenant Formula, treated separately here.

61. The term "wards" seems to capture the sense of the disparate texts referred to by Lohfink, 291-293, but the rubric is not used by him.

62. Ch. Rabin, "Judges v,2 and the 'Ideology' of Deborah's War," JJS 6 (1955):125-134.

63. Rudolf Smend, *Yahweh War and Tribal Confederation*, trans. M. G. Rogers (Nashville: Abingdon, 1970):passim; idem, *Die Bundesformel* (ThSt Barth 68; Zürich: EVZ, 1963):11ff.

64. Hulst, 291, 306.

65. Cf. KAI 224.24-25; E. L. Dietrich, *šûb šĕbût, die endzeitliche Wiederherstellung bei den Propheten* (BZAW 40; Giessen: Töpelmann, 1925); Erwin Preuschen, "Die Bedeutung von *šûb šĕbût* im Alten Testament," ZAW 15 (1895):1-74; Eberhard Baumann, "*šûb šĕbût*: Eine exegetische Untersuchung," ZAW 47 (1929):17-44; R. Borger, "Zu *šûb šĕbût*," ZAW 66 (1954):315-316; W. Holladay, *The Root šubh in the Old Testament* (Leiden: E. J. Brill, 1958).

66. BDB, 998.

67. Robert North, "Angel-Prophet or Satan-Prophet?" ZAW 82 (1970):31-67; Ernst Würthwein, "Der Ursprung der prophetischen Gerichtsrede," ZTK 4 (1952):1-16; Franz Hesse, "Wurzelt die prophetische Gerichtsrede im israelitischen Kult?" ZAW 65 (1953):45-53; B. Gemser, "The *Rib*- or Controversy-Pattern in Hebrew Mentality," SVT 3 (FS Rowley; 1955):120-137; H.-J. Kraus, *Die prophetische Verkündigung des Rechts in Israel* (ThSt Barth 51; Zollikon: Evangelischer Verlag, 1957); Herbert Huffmon, "The Covenant Lawsuit in the Prophets," JBL 78 (1959):285-295; G. E. Wright, "The Lawsuit of God: A Form-Critical Study of Deuteronomy 32," FS Muilenburg, 26-67; Julien Harvey, "Le 'rib-pattern,' réquisitoire prophétique sur la rupture de l'alliance," Bib 43 (1962):172-196; idem, *Le plaidoyer prophétique contre Israël après la rupture de l'alliance* (Studia, travaux

de recherche 22; Montréal: Bellarmin, 1967); Marina Mannati, "Le psaume 50 est-il un rib?" Sem 23 (1973):27-50; Kirsten Nielsen, *Yahweh as Prosecutor and Judge*, trans. F. Cryer (SJSOT 9, 1978).

68. Huffmon, "Lawsuit."

69. Wright, "Deuteronomy 32."

70. O. Eissfeldt, "Das Lied Moses Deuteronomium 32:1-43 und das Lehrgedicht Asaphs Psalm 78 samt einer Analyse der Umgebung des Mose-Lieds," *Verhandlungen der Sächsischen Academie der Wissenschaften* Leipzig, Philosophisch-historische Klasse 104/5 (1958).

71. W. F. Albright, "Some Remarks on the Song of Moses in Deuteronomy xxxii," VT 9 (1959):339-346; idem, *Yahweh and the Gods of Canaan*, 17-19; cf. E. Sellin, "Wann wurde das Moselied Dtn 32 gedichtet?" ZAW 43 (1925):161-173.

72. Wright, 40ff., 57ff.

73. James L. Mays, *Micah* (OTL; Philadelphia: Westminster, 1976):129ff.

74. Harvey, *Le plaidoyer*, 45-48.

75. *Ibid.*, 54-55.

76. T. Mann, *The Divine Presence and Guidance in Israelite Traditions* (Johns Hopkins Near Eastern Studies; Baltimore: Johns Hopkins University, 1976); P. D. Miller, *The Divine Warrior in Early Israel* (Harvard Semitic Monographs 5; Cambridge, Massachusetts, 1973):122.

77. Mannati, "Psalm 50."

78. Harvey, *Le plaidoyer*, 119-143.

79. Georges Dossin, "Une lettre de Iarîm-Lim, roi d'Alep, à Iašûb-Iaḫad, roi de Dîr," *Syria* 33 (FS Virolleaud, 1956):63-69.

80. Manfried Wüst, "Die Einschaltung in die Jiftachgeschichte Ri 11,13-26," Bib 56 (1975):464-479; cf. Siegfried Mittmann, "Aroer, Minnith, und Abel Keranim," ZDPV 85 (1969): 63-75; W. Richter,"Die Überlieferungen um Jephtah Ri 10,17-12,6," Bib 47 (1966):485-556.

81. Richter, "Jephtah," 530.

82. The preposition *l* is here construed to mean "from," as seems to be required by the sense of the passage.

83. Robert G. Boling, *Judges* (Anchor Bible; Garden City, New York, 1975):109ff.

84. CTA 19.1.22-23; CTA 17.5.6-7.

85. The *nāgîd* literature is immense. A. Alt, "Formation of the Israelite State," 254, 278ff.; C. F. North, "The Religious Aspects of Hebrew Kingship," ZAW 50 (1932):8-32; P. Joüon, "Notes de lexicographie hébraïque," Bib 17 (1936):229-233; J. van der Ploeg, "Les chefs du peuple Israël et leurs titres," RB 57 (1950):45-47; J. de Fraine, *L'aspect religieux de la royauté israelite* (AnBib 3; Rome: PBI, 1954):98ff., 104, 109; Martin Buber, "Die Erzählung von Sauls Königswahl," VT 6 (1956):127; Martin Noth, *Geschichte Israels* (3rd ed.; Göttingen: Vandenhoeck and Ruprecht, 1956):156, note 2; Hans Wildberger, "Samuel und die Entstehung des israelitischen Königtums," TZ 13 (1957):454; W. F. Albright, "Samuel and the Beginnings of the Prophetic Movement," Goldenson Lecture, Hebrew Union College, Cincinnati (1961):8, 15; T. C. G. Thornton, "Charismatic Kingship in Israel and Judah," JTS ns 14 (1963):1-11; J. A. Soggin, "Charisma und Institution im Königtum Sauls," ZAW 75 (1963): 58ff.; J. J. Glück, "*Nagid*-Shepherd," VT 13 (1963):144-150; W. Richter, "Die *nāgîd*-Formel: Ein Beitrag zur Erhellung des *nāgîd*-Problems," BZ nF 9 (1965):71-84; Horst Seebass, "Die Vorgeschichte der Königserhebung Sauls," ZAW 79 (1967):164, 167; G. Wallis, *Geschichte und Überlieferung* (Arbeiten zur Theologie II/13; Stuttgart: Calwer, 1968):62; F. Langlamet, "Les récits de l'institution de la royauté (I Sam, vii-xii)," RB 77 (1970): 188ff.; Ludwig Schmidt, *Menschlicher Erfolg und Jahwehs Initiative* (WMANT 38; Neukirchen-Vluyn: Neukirchener Verlag, 1970): 141-171; F. M. Cross, *Canaanite Myth and Hebrew Epic*, 220, note 5; E. Lipiński, "*nāgīd*, der Kronprinz," VT 24 (1974):497-499; Georg C. Macholz, "*Nagid* - der Statthalter, 'praefectus,'" *Sefer Rendtorff*, 59-72; T. Mettinger, *King and Messiah: The Civil and Sacral Legitimation of the Israelite Kings* (Coniectanea Biblica, Old Testament Series 8; Lund: Gleerup, 1976): 158ff.; Tomoo Ishida, *The Royal Dynasties in Ancient Israel: A Study of the Formation and Development of Royal-Dynastic Ideology* (BZAW 142; Berlin: de Gruyter, 1977):50.

86. KAI 46:7, reading *ngd* with Brian Peckham, "The Nora Inscription," Or 41 (1972):457-468.

87. KAI 224.10.

88. KAI 266.8, reading *ngd'* at line 8; see J. Fitzmyer, "The Aramaic Letter of King Adon to the Egyptian Pharaoh," Bib 46 (1965):44-45.

89. The text was announced by F. M. Cross, "An Epigraphic Perspective," November 15, 1979, annual meetings of AAR, SBL, ASOR.

90. Lohfink, "Beobachtungen," 285; Mettinger, 172.

91. H. Ringgren, "*gā'al*," TDOT 2:353-354.

Chapter VI

1. F. M. Cross, *Canaanite Myth and Hebrew Epic* (Cambridge, Massachusetts: Harvard University, 1973):122, note 34.

2. Frank L. Benz, *Personal Names in the Phoenician and Punic Inscriptions* (Studia Pohl 8; Rome: PBI, 1972):379.

BIBLIOGRAPHY

Ackroyd, Peter R. "The Composition of the Song of Deborah." VT 2 (1952):160-162.

Acquaro, E., et al. *Ricerche puniche ad Antas*. StSem 30. Rome: Istituto di Studi del Vicino Oriente, 1969.

Aistleitner, Joseph. *Wörterbuch der ugaritischen Sprache*. Berlin: Akademie-Verlag, 1960.

Albrecht, Karl. "Miscelle." ZAW 34 (1914):312-313.

Albright, William Foxwell. "Abram the Hebrew: A New Archaeological Interpretation." BASOR 163 (1961):36-54.

______. "The Amorite Form of the Name Hammurabi." AJSL 38 (1921-1922):140-141.

______. "A Catalogue of Early Hebrew Lyric Poems." HUCA 23 (1950-1951):1-39.

______. "The Earliest Form of Hebrew Verse." JPOS 2 (1922): 69-86.

______. "The Egyptian Empire in Asia in the Twenty-First Century B.C." JPOS 8 (1928):223-256.

______. *From the Stone Age to Christianity*. Garden City, New York: Doubleday, 1957.

______. "The Land of Damascus between 1850 and 1750 B.C." BASOR 83 (1941):30-36.

______. "The Name of Bildad the Shuhite." AJSL 44 (1927-1928): 31-36.

______. "The 'Natural Force' of Moses in the Light of Ugaritic." BASOR 94 (1944):32-35.

______. "New Canaanite Historical and Mythological Data." BASOR 63 (1936):23-32.

______. "New Egyptian Data on Palestine in the Patriarchal Age." BASOR 81 (1941):16-21.

______. "New Light on the Early History of Phoenician Colonization." BASOR 83 (1941):14-22.

______. "Northwest-Semitic Names in a List of Egyptian Slaves from the Eighteenth Century B.C." JAOS 74 (1954);222-233.

______. "Samuel and the Beginnings of the Prophetic Movement." The Goldenson Lecture, Hebrew Union College Cincinnati (1961).

______. "Some Remarks on the Song of Moses in Deuteronomy xxxii." VT 9 (1959):339-346.

______. "The Song of Deborah in the Light of Archaeology." BASOR 62 (1936):26-31.

______. "A Vow to Asherah in the Keret Epic." BASOR 94 (1944): 30-35.

______. *Yahweh and the Gods of Canaan*. Reprint. Winona Lake, Indiana: Eisenbrauns, *1968.

______. Review of HUCA 16. JBL 64 (1945):285-296.

Alfrink, Bern. "L'expression *neʾĕsap ʾel-ʿammāyw*." OTS 5 (1948):118-131.

______. "L'expression *šākab ʿim ʾăbōtāyw*." OTS 2 (1943):106-118.

Alt, Albrecht. "The Formation of the Israelite State in Palestine." In *Essays on Old Testament History and Religion*, trans. R. A. Wilson, pp. 225-309. Garden City, New York: Doubleday, 1967.

______. "The Monarchy in the Kingdoms of Israel and Judah." In *Essays*, 313-335.

______. "The Origins of Israelite Law." In *Essays*, 103-171.

Amadasi, M. G. G. *Le iscrizioni fenicie e puniche delle colonie in occidente*. StSem 28. Rome: Istituto di Studi del Vicino Oriente, 1967.

Andersen, Francis I. "Israelite Kinship Terminology." *The Bible Translator* 20 (1969):29-39.

______. "Who Built the Second Temple?" ABR 6 (1958):3-35.

Anderson, George W. "Israel: Amphictyony: *ʿām; qāhāl; ʿēdāh*." In *Translating and Understanding the Old Testament*, ed. H. T. Frank, W. L. Reed, pp. 135-151. Nashville: Abingdon, 1970.

Archi, Alfonso. "Associations des divinités hourrites." UF 11 (1979):7-12.

Artzi, P. "'Vox populi' in the el-Amarna Tablets." RA 58 (1964):159-166.

Assemani, S. E. *Acta Sanctorum Martyrum Orientalium et Occidentalium*. Paris, 1748.

Astour, M. "New Evidence on the Last Days of Ugarit." AJA 69 (1965):253-258.

Auerbach, Elias. "ʿam hāʾāreṣ." *First World Congress of Jewish Studies*, pp. 362-366. Jerusalem, 1952.

Azzi, Pierre. "La notion d'«assemblée» dans l'Ancien Testament." Melto 1 (1965):7-23.

Bächli, O. *Israel und die Völker*. ATANT 41. Zürich: Zwingli, 1962.

Balkan, Kemal. *Kassitenstudien*. Vol. 1, *Die Sprache der Kassiten*, trans. F. R. Kraus. AOS 37. New Haven: American Oriental Society, 1954.

Baltzer, Klaus. *The Covenant Formulary*, trans. D. E. Green. Philadelphia: Fortress, 1971.

Barton. G. A. *A Sketch of Semitic Origins*. New York: Macmillan, 1902.

Barr, James. *The Semantics of Biblical Language*. Oxford: Clarendon, 1961.

Bauer, J. B. "König und Priester, ein heiliges Volk (Ex 19,6)." BZ nF 2 (1958):283-286.

Bauer, H. Review of M. Noth *Die israelitischen Personennamen*. OLZ 33 (1930):588-596.

Bauer, Theo. *Die Ostkanaanäer*. Leipzig: Asia Major, 1926.

Baumann, Eberhard. "Das Lied Mose's (Dt xxxii 1-43) auf seine gedankliche Geschlossenheit untersucht." VT 6 (1956): 414-424.

______. "*šûb šĕbût*: Eine exegetische Untersuchung." ZAW 47 (1929):17-44.

Bea, A. "Epistula Aramaica Saeculo vii Exeunte ad Pharaonem Scripta." Bib 30 (1949):514-516.

Beeston, A. F. L. *A Descriptive Grammar of Epigraphic South Arabian*. London: Luzac, 1962.

Bentzen, Aage. *King and Messiah*. Oxford: Basil Blackwell, 1970.

Benz, Frank L. *Personal Names in the Phoenician and Punic Inscriptions*. Studia Pohl 8. Rome: PBI, 1972.

Berger, Philippe. "Mémoire sur la grande inscription dédicatoire et sur plusieurs autres inscriptions néo-puniques du temple d'Hathor-Miskar à Maktar." *Mémoires de l'Académie des Inscriptions et Belles-Lettres* 36/2 (1899).

Bernhardt, H.-H. *Das Problem der altorientalischen Königsideologie im Alten Testament*. SVT 8. Leiden: E. J. Brill, 1961.

Beyerlin, Walter. *Herkunft und Geschichte der ältesten Sinaitraditionen.* Tübingen: Mohr, 1961.

Birot, Maurice. *Lettres de Yaqqim-Addu gouverneur de Sagarâtum.* ARM 14. Paris: Geuthner, 1974.

______. "Trois textes économiques de Mari (ii)." RA 47 (1953): 161-174.

Blenkinsopp, Joseph. "Ballad Style and Psalm Style in the Song of Deborah: A Discussion." Bib 42 (1961):61-76.

Blommerde, A. *Northwest Semitic Grammar and Job.* BibOr 22. Rome: PBI, 1969.

Boling, Robert G. *Judges.* Anchor Bible. Garden City, New York: Doubleday, 1975.

______. "Some Conflated Readings in Joshua-Judges." VT 16 (1966);293-298.

Borger, R. "Kleinigkeiten zur Textkritik des Kodex Hammurapi." Or 31 (1962):364-366.

______. Review of H. Schmökel *Hammurabi von Babylon.* ZA 56 (1964):288-290.

______. "Zu *šûb šěbût.*" ZAW 66 (1954):315-316.

Boston, James R. "The Wisdom Influence upon the Song of Moses." JBL 87 (1968):198-202.

Boucher, R. *Divan de Fêrazdak.* Paris: Labitte, 1870.

Brichto, Herbert. "Kin, Cult, Land and Afterlife--A Biblical Complex." HUCA 44 (1973):1-54.

Bright, John. "An Exercise in Hermeneutics: Jeremiah 31:31-34." *Interpretation* 20 (1966):188-210.

Brockelmann, Carl. *Die Gedichte des Lebîd.* Leiden: E. J. Brill, 1891.

______. *Lexicon Syriacum.* Berlin: Reuther and Reicherd, 1895.

Buber, Martin. "Die Erzählung von Sauls Königswahl." VT 6 (1956):113-173.

Buccellati, G. *Cities and Nations of Ancient Syria.* StSem 26. Rome: Istituto di Studi del Vicino Oriente, 1967.

Buis, Pierre. "Comment au septième siècle envisageait-on l'avenir de l'Alliance?" In *Questions disputées d'Ancien Testament: Méthode et théologie*, ed. C. Brekelmans, pp. 131-140. Louvain: Leuven Un. Press, 1974.

______. "La Nouvelle Alliance." VT 18 (1968):1-15.

Burney, C. F. *The Book of Judges*. London: Rivington, 1920.

Cantineau, J. *Inventaire des inscriptions de Palmyre*. Beirut: Imprimerie Catholique, 1930-1933.

Caquot, A. "Remarques sur la tablette alphabétique R.S. 24.272." In FS Loewenstamm, pp. 1-6.

______ and Lemaire, A. "Les textes araméens de Deir ʿAllah." *Syria* 54 (1977):189-208.

______ and Sznycer, A., and Herdner, A. *Textes ougaritiques*. Littératures anciennes du Proche Orient 7; Paris: du Cerf, 1974.

Cazelles, H. "Déborah (Jud v 14), Amaleq et Mâkîr." VT 24 (1974):235-238.

Childs, B.S. *The Book of Exodus*. OTL. Philadelphia: Westminster, 1974.

Cintas, P. "Le sanctuaire punique de Sousse." Rev. Africaine 91 (1947):1-80.

Clay, A. T. *The Empire of the Amorites*. YOS 6. New Haven, Connecticut: Yale University, 1919.

Clements, R. E. "Gôy." TDOT 2:426-433.

Clermont-Ganneau, Ch. *Recueil d'archéologie orientale*. Paris: Leroux, 1888-1924.

Coats, G. W. *Rebellion in the Wilderness*. Nashville: Abingdon, 1968.

Cody, Aelred. *A History of Old Testament Priesthood*. AnBib 35. Rome: PBI, 1969.

______. "When Is the Chosen People Called a *Gōy*?" VT 14 (1964):1-6.

Coppens, J. "La Nouvelle Alliance en Jér 31,31-34." CBQ 25 (1963):12-21.

Cowley, A. *Aramaic Papyri of the Fifth Century B.C.* Oxford: Clarendon, 1923.

Cross, F. M. *Canaanite Myth and Hebrew Epic*. Cambridge, Massachusetts: Harvard University, 1973.

______. "An Interpretation of the Nora Stone." BASOR 208 (1972):13-19.

______. "The Priestly Tabernacle." BA 10 (1947):45-68.

Cuisinier, Jean. "Endogamie et exogamie dans le mariage arabe." *L'Homme* 2/1 (1962):80-105.

______ and Miguel, A. "La terminologie arabe de la parenté: Analyse sémantique et analyse componentielle." *L'Homme* 5/3-4 (1965).

Dahl, Nils Alstrup. *Das Volk Gottes*. Darmstadt: Wissenschaftliche Buchgesellschaft, 1963.

Dahood, Mitchell. "Ebla, Ugarit and the Old Testament." SVT 29 (1977):81-112.

______. "Hebrew-Ugaritic Lexicography vii." Bib 50 (1969): 347-356.

______. "Nest and Phoenix in Job 29,18." Bib 48 (1967):542-544.

______. "Poetic Devices in the Book of Proverbs." In FS Loewenstamm, pp. 7-17.

______. *Psalms*. Anchor Bible. Garden City, New York: Doubleday, 1965-1970.

______. "Ugaritic-Hebrew Syntax and Style." UF 1 (1969):15-36.

______. "Vocative *Lamedh* in the Psalter." VT 16 (1966):299-311.

Daiches, S. "The Meaning of *am-haaretz* in the Old Testament." JTS 30 (1929):245-249.

Daube, David. "Über die Umbildung biblischen Rechtsgutes." In *Symbolae Friburgenses in Honorem Ottonis Lenel*, pp. 245-258. Freiburg, 1935.

Davies, J. A. "A Note on Job xii,2." VT 25 (1975):670-671.

Degen, R., and Müller, W., and Röllig, W. *Neue Ephemeris für semitische Epigraphik*. Wiesbaden: Harrassowitz, 1972-1978.

Delcor, Matthias. "Reflexions sur l'inscription phénicienne de Nora en Sardaigne." *Syria* 45 (1968):323-352.

del Monte, G. F., and Tischler, J. *Répertoire géographique des textes cunéiformes*. Wiesbaden: Reichert, 1978.

Derenbourg, M. H. "Nouveaux textes yéménites inédits." RA 5 (1903):115-128.

Deutsch, Richard. "The Biblical Concept of the 'People of God.'" *Southeast Asia Journal of Theology* 13/2 (1972):4-13.

Dhorme, Edouard. "Le dieu parent et le dieu maître dans la religion des Hébreux." RHR 106 (1932):229-244.

______. *L'évolution religieuse d'Israël*. Bruxelles: Nouvelle Société d'Editions, 1937. Vol. 1, *La religion des Hébreux nomades*.

______. "Hammourabi-Amraphel." RB 5 (1908):205-226.

Diepold, Peter. *Israels Land*. BWANT 95. Stuttgart: Kohlhammer, 1972.

Dietrich, E. L. *Šub šĕbût, die endzeitliche Wiederherstellungen bei den Propheten*. BZAW 40. Giessen: Töpelmann, 1925.

Dietrich, M., and Loretz, O. "Ein Spottlied auf *ʿAṯtar*." UF 9 (1977):330-331.

______. "Bemerkungen zum Aqhat-Text: Zur ugaritischen Lexikographie xiv." UF 10 (1978):65-71.

______ and Loretz, O., and Sanmartín, J. "Ugaritisch *ilib* und hebräisch *ʾ(w)b* 'Totengeist.'" UF 6 (1974):450-451.

______. "Zur ugaritischen Lexikographie xii." UF 6 (1974):39-45.

Donner, H., and Röllig, W. *Kanaanäische und aramäische Inschriften*. Wiesbaden: Harrassowitz, 1969.

Dossin, Georges. "Une lettre de Iarîm-Lim, roi d'Alep, à Iašûb-Iaḫad, roi de Dir." *Syria* 33 (1956):63-69.

Dreyfus, François. "Le thème de l'héritage dans l'Ancien Testament." RSPT 42 (1958):3-49.

Driver, G. R. *Canaanite Myths and Legends*. Old Testament Studies 3. Edinburgh: T. & T. Clark, 1956.

______ and Miles, J. C. *The Babylonian Laws*. Oxford: Clarendon, 1955.

Driver, S. R. *An Introduction to the Literature of the Old Testament*. Reprint. Cleveland: Meridan, *1913.

Drower, E. S., and Macuch, R. *A Mandaic Dictionary*. Oxford: Clarendon, 1963.

Dupont-Sommer, André. "Nouvelle lecture d'une inscription phénicienne archaïque de Nora, en Sardaigne (CIS I, 144)." CRAIBL 1948:12-22.

______. "Un papyrus araméen d'époque saïte découvert à Saqqarah." Sem 1 (1948):43-68.

Dvořák, Rudolf. "Über die Fremdwörter im Koran." *Sitzungsberichte der philosophisch-historischen Classe der Kaiserlichen Akademie der Wissenschaften*, Wien 109 (1885):481-562.

Eissfeldt, Otto. "Das Lied Moses Deuteronomium 32:1-43 und das Lehrgedicht Asaphs Psalm 78 samt einer Analyse der Umgebung des Mose-Lieds." *Verhandlungen der Sächsischen Academie der Wissenschaften*, Leipzig, Philosophisch-historische Klasse 104/5 (1958).

______. "Lade und Stierbild." ZAW 58 (1940-1941):190-215.

Emerton, J. A. "Ugaritic Notes." JTS ns 16 (1965):438-443.

Fahd, Toufic. *Le panthéon de l'Arabie centrale à la veille de l'Hégire*. Paris: Geuthner, 1968.

Falbe, C. T., and Lindberg, J. Chr. *Numismatique de l'ancienne Afrique*. Copenhague: Bianco Luno, 1861.

Falkenstein, Adam, and Soden, W. von. *Sumerische und akkadische Hymnen und Gebete*. Zürich: Artemis-Verlag, 1953.

Farrar, F. W. "Notes on the Reign of Joash." *Expositor* 1894b: 81-98.

Février, J.-G. "La grande inscription dédicatoire de Mactar." Sem 6 (1956):15-31.

______. "Vir Sidonius." Sem 4 (1951-1952):13-18.

Fink, E. "Gedanken über die *Kareth*-Strafe." *Jeschurun* 4 (1917):383-393.

Fitzmyer, J. *The Aramaic Inscriptions of Sefire*. BibOr 19. Rome: PBI, 1967.

______. "The Aramaic Letter of King Adon to the Egyptian Pharaoh." Bib 46 (1965):41-55.

Fleischer, H. L. "Das Arabische in Geiger's Preisschrift: Was hat Muhammad aus dem Judenthume aufgenommen?" In *Kleinere Schriften*, vol. 2, pp. 107-138. Leipzig: S. Hirzel, 1885-1888.

Fohrer, Georg. "Der Vertrag zwischen König und Volk in Israel." ZAW 71 (1959):1-22.

Forshey, H. O. "The Hebrew Root *nḥl* and its Semitic Cognates." Th.D. dissertation: Harvard University, 1973.

Fraine, J. de. *L'aspect religieux de la royauté israélite*. AnBib 3. Rome: PBI, 1954.

Freytag, G. G. *Hamasae Carmina*. Bonn, 1827.

Fulco, William J. "The Amman Theater Inscription." JNES 38 (1979):37-38.

Galling, K. *Die israelitische Staatsverfassung in ihrer vorderorientalischen Umwelt*. Leipzig: Hinrichs, 1929.

Gelb, I. J. *Computer-Aided Analysis of Amorite*. Chicago: University of Chicago, 1980.

______. *Glossary of Old Akkadian*. MAD 3. Chicago: University of Chicago, 1957.

Gemser, B. "The Rîb- or Controversy-Pattern in Hebrew Mentality." In SVT 3 (FS Rowley), pp. 120-137. Leiden: E. J. Brill, 1955.

_____. *Sprüche Salomos*. HAT 16. Tübingen: Mohr, 1937.

Gerleman, Gillis. "Nutzrecht und Wohnrecht: Zur Bedeutung von *ʾăḥuzzâ* und *naḥălâ*." ZAW 89 (1977):313-325.

Geus, C. H. J. de. *The Tribes of Israel: An Investigation into Some of the Presuppositions of Martin Noth's Amphictyony Hypothesis*. Studia Semitica Neerlandica 18. Assen: van Gorcum, 1976.

Geyer, Rudolf. *Gedichte von Abû Baṣîr Maimûn ibn Qais al-ʾAʿšâ*. London: Luzac, 1928.

Gillischewski, Eva. "Der Ausdruck *ʿam hāʾāreṣ* im A. T." ZAW 40 (1922):137-142.

Ginsberg, H. L. "An Aramaic Contemporary of the Lachish Letters." BASOR 111 (1948):24-27.

Glaser, Eduard. "Punt und die südarabischen Reiche." MVAG 4/2 (1899).

Glück, J. J. "*Nāgîd*-Shepherd." VT 13 (1963):144-150.

Goldman, M. D. "Concerning the Meaning of *ʿam*." ABR 3 (1953): 51.

_____. "Lexicographic Notes on Exegesis." ABR 1 (1951):57-67.

Goldziher, Ignaz. "Der Dîwân des Ǵarwal b. Aus Al-Ḥuṭejʾa." ZDMG 46 (1892):1-53, and ZDMG 47 (1893):43-85.

Gordis, R. "Sectional Rivalry in the Kingdom of Judah." JQR ns 25 (1934-1935):237-259.

Goshen-Gottstein, M. H. "'Ephraim is a well-trained heifer' and Ugaritic *mdl*." Bib 41 (1960):64-66.

Gray, G. B. "*ʿammi*." *Encyclopaedia Biblica* (1899):I:138-140.

_____. *Studies in Hebrew Proper Names*. London: A. and C. Black, 1896.

Gray, John. *Joshua, Judges and Ruth*. Century Bible. London: Nelson, 1967.

_____. *I. and II Kings: A Commentary*. Second edition. OTL London: SCM (Philadelphia: Westminster), 1970.

_____. *The Legacy of Canaan*. Second edition. SVT 5. Leiden: E. J. Brill, 1965.

Greenberg, Moshe. "Am ha-areẓ." EnJud 843-844.

______. "Hebrew *sĕgullâ*:Akkadian *sikiltu*." JAOS 71 (1951): 172-174.

Greenfield, Jonas. "Ugaritic *mdl* and its Cognates." Bib 45 (1964):527-534.

Gressmann, Hugo. *Mose und seine Zeit.* Göttingen: Vandenhoeck and Ruprecht, 1913.

Grøndahl, Frauke. *Die Personennamen der Texte aus Ugarit.* Studia Pohl 1. Rome: PBI, 1967.

Grüneisen, Carl. *Der Ahnenkultus und die Urreligion Israels.* Halle: Niemeyer, 1900.

Halévy, J. "Notes assyriologiques iii." ZA 3 (1888):332-352.

Hallo, W. W. *Early Mesopotamian Royal Titles: A Philological and Historical Analysis.* AOS 43. New Haven, Connecticut: American Oriental Society, 1957.

Harding, G. L. *An Index and Concordance of Pre-Islamic Arabian Names and Inscriptions.* Near and Middle Eastern Series 8. Toronto: University of Toronto, 1971.

______. "Safaitic Inscriptions in the Iraq Museum." *Sumer* 6 (1950):124-129.

Harvey, Julien. *Le plaidoyer prophêtique contre Israël après la rupture de l'alliance.* Studia, Travaux de recherche 22. Montréal: Bellarmin, 1967.

______. "Le 'rîb-pattern,' réquisitoire prophétique sur la rupture de l'alliance." Bib 43 (1962):172-196.

Hasan bar Bahlul. *Lexicon Syriacum*, ed. Rubens Duval. Paris, 1888.

Healey, John F. "The Pietas of an Ideal Son in Ugaritic." UF 11 (1979):353-356.

Held, M. "The Action-Result (Factitive-Passive) Sequence of Identical Verbs in Biblical Hebrew and Ugaritic." JBL 84 (1965):272-282.

______. "A Faithful Lover in an Old Babylonian Dialogue." JCS 15 (1961):1-26.

Hempel, J. *Das Ethos des Alten Testaments.* BZAW 67. Berlin: Töpelmann, 1938.

Hesse, Franz. *Das Verstockungsproblem im Alten Testament.* BZAW 74. Berlin: Töpelmann, 1955.

______. "Wurzelt die prophetische Gerichtsrede im israelitischen Kult?" ZAW 65 (1953):45-53.

Hillers, D. R. "*Bĕrît ʿam*: 'Emancipation of the People.'" JBL 97 (1978):175-182.

Hilprecht, H. V. *Explorations in Bible Lands.* Philadelphia: Holman, 1903.

Hölscher, G. *Geschichte der israelitischen und jüdischen Religion.* Giessen: Töpelmann, 1922.

_____ and Jacoby, F. "Maĭumas." Pauly-Wissowa 14/1:610-613.

Hoftijzer, J., and van der Kroij, G. *Aramaic Texts from Deir ʿAlla.* Leiden: E. J. Brill, 1976.

Hommel, Fritz. *The Ancient Hebrew Tradition as Illustrated by the Monuments*, trans. E. McClure and L. Crosslé. New York: E. and J. B. Young, 1897.

_____. *Aufsätze und Abhandlungen.* München: Lukaschik, 1900. No. 5, *Die südarabischen Altertümer des Wiener Hofsmuseums.*

_____. "Miscellanea." OLZ 10 (1907):482-486.

_____. Review of F. Delitzsch *Assyriologische Bibliotek*, Band XI. ZDMG 49 (1895):522-528.

Huffmon, Herbert B. *Amorite Personal Names in the Mari Texts.* Baltimore: Johns Hopkins University, 1965.

_____. "The Covenant Lawsuit in the Prophets." JBL 78 (1959): 285-295.

Hüsing, G. "Miszellen." OLZ 10 (1907):235-238.

Hulst, A. R. *"ʿām/gōj."* THAT 2:290-325.

Ihromi. "Die Königinmutter und der *ʿamm haʾarez* im Reich Juda." VT 24 (1974):421-429.

Ishida, Tomoo. "*Nāgîd*: A Term for the Legitimation of the Kingship." Annual of the Japanese Biblical Institute 3 (1977):35-51.

_____. "'The People of the Land' and the Political Crises in Judah." Annual of the Japanese Biblical Institute 1 (1975):23-38.

_____. *The Royal Dynasties in Ancient Israel: A Study on the Formation and Development of Royal-Dynastic Ideology.* BZAW 142. Berlin: de Gruyter, 1977.

Jamme, A. "Le panthéon sud-arabe préislamique." *Le Muséon* 60 (1947):57-147.

_____. *Sabaean Inscriptions from Maḥram Bilqîs (Mārib).* Baltimore: Johns Hopkins University, 1962.

_____. *Sabaean and Hasaean Inscriptions from Saudi Arabia.* StSem 23. Rome: Istituto di Studi del Vicino Oriente, 1966.

Jean, Charles -F. "Lettres de Mari iv, transcrites et traduites." RA 42 (1948):53-78.

Jensen, P. Review of Luzac's Semitic Text and Translation Series II,III,VIII. *Literarisches Zentralblatt* 1902:694-696.

Jepsen, A. "Berith: Ein Beitrag zur Theologie der Exilzeit." In FS Rudolph, pp. 161-179.

Jibrā'il al-Ḳardāḥī. *Al-Lobab, Dictionarium Syro-Arabicum.* Beirut, 1891.

Joüon, Paul. "Etudes de philologie sémitique." MUSJ 5 (1911): 355-415.

______. "Etudes de sémantique arabe." MUSJ 11 (1926):1-36.

______. "Deutéronome 26,17-18." MUSJ 4 (1910):20-21.

______. "Notes de critique textuelle (AT)." MUSJ 6 (1912): 447-488.

______. "Notes de lexicographie hébraïque x." Bib 17 (1936): 229-233.

______. "Notes de lexicographie hébraïque vii." Bib 16 (1935):422-430.

Juynboll, Th. "Über die Bedeutung des Wortes *ʿamm*." In FS Nöldeke, Vol. 1:353-356.

Kayser, C. *Die Canones Jacob's von Edessa.* Leipzig: Hinrichs, 1886.

Kendrick, Joan Biella. "A Dictionary of Old South Arabic, Sabaean Dialect." Ph.D. Dissertation: Harvard University, 1978.

Kerber, Georg. *Die religionsgeschichtliche Bedeutung der hebräischen Eigennamen des Alten Testamentes.* Freiburg: Mohr, 1897.

Kilmer, Anne Draffkorn. "The First Tablet of *Malku=Šarru* together with Its Explicit Version." JAOS 83 (1963):421-446.

Klamroth, Erich. *Die jüdischen Exulanten in Babylonien.* Leipzig: Hinrichs, 1912.

Koch, Klaus. "Haggais unreines Volk." ZAW 79 (1967):52-66.

______. "Die Sohnesverheissung an den ugaritischen Daniel." ZA 58 (1967):211-221.

Köhler, L. "Der Name Ammoniter." TZ 1 (1945):154-156.

Kraus, Hans-Joachim. "Das Heilige Volk." In FS de Quervain, pp. 50-61.

______. *Die prophetische Verkündigung des Rechts in Israel.* ThSt (Barth) 51. Zollikon: Evangelischer Verlag, 1957.

Krenkel, M. "Das Verwandtschaftswort *ʿam*." ZAW 8 (1888):280-284.

Kupper, J.-R. "Un gouvernement provincial dans le royaume de Mari." RA 41 (1947):149-183.

Kuryłowicz, J. *Studies in Semitic Grammar and Metrics.* London, 1973.

Kutscher, E. Y. *Words and Their History.* Hebrew. Jerusalem: Kiryath Sefer, 1961.

Lagrange, Marie-Joseph. *Etudes sur les religions sémitiques.* Paris: Lecoffre, 1905.

Lane, L. W. *Arabic-English Lexicon.* London: Williams and Norgate, 1863-1893.

Langlamet, F. "Les récits de l'institution de la royauté (1 Sam., vii-xii)." RB 77 (1970):161-200.

Lecerf, Jean. "Note sur la famille dans le monde arabe et islamique." *Arabica* 3 (1956):31-60.

Lehming, Sigo. "Versuch zu Ex xxxii." VT 10 (1960):16-50.

Lemaire, A. "Une nouvelle inscription paléo-hébräique sur cruche." Sem 25 (1975):43-46.

Lenormant, François. *Lettres assyriologiques.* Vol. 2, Paris, 1872.

Lewy, Julius. "The Old West Semitic Sun God Ḥammu." HUCA 18 (1943-1944):429-488.

Lipiński, E. "Ditanu." In FS Loewenstamm, pp. 95-117.

______. "*Nāgīd*, der Kronprinz." VT 24 (1974):497-499.

______. "Recherches sur le livre de Zacharie." VT 20 (1970): 25-55.

______. "*skn* et *sgn* dans le sémitique occidental du nord." UF (1973):191-207.

Littmann, Enno. *Semitic Inscriptions.* Publications of an American Archaeological Expedition to Syria in 1899-1900, part 4. New York: Century, 1904.

Lohfink, Norbert. "Beobachtungen zur Geschichte des Ausdrucks *ʿam yhwh*." In FS von Rad, pp. 275-305.

______. "Dt 26,17-19 und die 'Bundesformel.'" ZKT 91 (1969): 517-553.

Loza, José. "Exode xxxii et la rédaction JE." VT 23 (1973): 31-55.

Luckenbill, D. D. "The Name Hammurabi." JAOS 37 (1917):250-253.

Lyall, Charles. *The Mufaḍḍalīyât.* Oxford: Clarendon, 1921.

Maag, Victor. "Erwägungen zur deuteronomischen Kultzentralization." VT 6 (1956):10-18.

______. *"Malkût Jhwh."* SVT 7 (1960):129-153.

Machinist, P. B. "The Epic of Tukulti Ninurta I." Ph.D. dissertation: Yale University, 1978.

Macholz, Georg Christian. "*Nāgīd*--der Statthalter 'praefectus.'" In *Sefer Rendtorff*, pp. 59-72.

McKenzie, John. "The 'People of the Land' in the Old Testament." In *Akten des vierundzwantigsten internationalen Orientalisten-Kongresses, München*, ed. Herbert Franke. Wiesbaden: Deutsche Morgenländische Gesellschaft, 1957, pp. 206-208.

Malamat, A. "Aspects of Tribal Societies in Mari and Israel." In *Mari and the Bible*, pp. 34-51. Jerusalem: Hebrew University, 1975.

Malfroy, Jean. "Sagesse et loi dans le Deutéronome." VT 15 (1965):49-65.

Mann, Thomas. *The Divine Presence and Guidance in Israelite Traditions.* Johns Hopkins Near Eastern Studies. Baltimore: Johns Hopkins University, 1976.

Mannati, Marina. "Le psaume 50 est-il un *rîb*?" Sem 23 (1973):27-50.

Martin-Achard, R. "La nouvelle alliance, selon Jérémie." RTP third series 12 (1962):81-92.

______. "Quelques remarques sur la nouvelle alliance chez Jérémie (Jérémie 31,31-34)." In *Questions disputées d'Ancien Testament: Méthode et théologie*, ed. C. Brekelmans, pp. 141-164. Louvain: Leuven Un. Press, 1974.

May. H. G. "'This People' and 'This Nation' in Haggai." VT 18 (1968):190-197.

Mays, J. *Micah.* OTL. Philadelphia: Westminster, 1976.

Menes, Abram. *Die vorexilischen Gesetze Israels.* BZAW 50. Giessen: Töpelmann, 1928.

Mercati, G. "Una singolare versione di deut. xxvi, 17 e 18 e l'originale di essa." Bib 24 (1943):201-204.

Mettinger, Tryggve. *King and Messiah: The Civil and Sacral Legitimation of the Israelite Kings.* Coniectanea Biblica, Old Testament Series 8. Lund: Gleerup, 1971.

Meyer, Rudolf. "Der *'Am hā-'Āreṣ*: Ein Beitrag zur Religionssoziologie Palästinas im ersten und zweiten nachchristlichen Jahrhundert." *Judaica* 3 (1947):169-199.

Milgrom, Jacob. "Priestly Terminology and the Political and Social Structure of Pre-Monarchic Israel." JQR 69 (1978): 65-81.

Milik, J. T. "Nouvelles inscriptions nabatéennes." *Syria* 35 (1958):227-251.

Miller, Patrick D. *The Divine Warrior in Early Israel.* Harvard Semitic Monographs 5; Cambridge, Massachusetts: Harvard University, 1973.

Mittmann, Siegfried. "Aroer, Minnith und Abel Keranim." ZDPV 85 (1969):63-75.

Moor, J. de. *The Seasonal Pattern in the Myth of Ba'lu.* AOAT 16. Neukirchen-Vluyn: Neukirchener Verlag, 1971.

Mowinckel, S. "General Oriental and Specific Israelite Elements in the Israelite Conception of the Sacral Kingdom." In *The Sacral Kingship*, pp. 283-293. Eighth International Congress for the History of Religions. Rome: April, 1955. Published in Leiden: E. J. Brill, 1959.

Müller, H.-P. "Magisch-mantische Weisheit und die Gestalt Daniels." UF 1 (1969):79-94.

Murphy, R., and Kasdan, L. "The Structure of Parallel Cousin Marriage." *The American Anthropologist* 61/1 (1959):17-29.

Nestle, E. "Dtn 26,17.18." ZAW 28 (1908):149.

______. *Die israelitischen Eigennamen nach ihrer religionsgeschichtlichen Bedeutung: Ein Versuch.* Haarlam, 1876.

Neubauer, Ad. "On Some Newly-Discovered Temanite and Nabataean Inscriptions." *Studia Biblica* 1 (1885):209-232.

Nicholson, E. "The Meaning of the Expression *'am hā'āreṣ* in the Old Testament." JSS 10 (1965):59-66.

Nielsen, Ditlef. *Der dreieinige Gott.* København: Nordisk, 1922, vol. 1, *Die drei göttlichen Personen.*

______. "Der sabäische Gott Ilmuḳah." MVAG 14/4 (1909).

Nielsen, Kirsten. *Yahweh as Prosecutor and Judge*, trans. F. Cryer. SJSOT 9, 1978.

Nöldeke, Theodor. *Beiträge zur semitischen Sprachwissenschaft.* Strassburg: Trübner, 1904.

______. *Delectus Veterum Carminum Arabicorum.* Porta Linguarum Orientalium 13. Berlin: Reuther, 1890.

______. *Die Gedichte des ʿUrwa ibn Alward.* Göttingen: Dieterichs, 1863.

______. *Neue Beiträge zur semitischen Sprachwissenschaft.* Strassburg: Trübner, 1910.

______. Review of W. R. Smith, *Kinship and Marriage.* ZDMG 40 (1886):148-187.

North, C. R. "Angel Prophet or Satan Prophet?" ZAW 82 (1970): 31-67.

______. "The Religious Aspects of Hebrew Kingship." ZAW 50 (1932):8-38.

Noth, Martin. "Das Amt des 'Richters Israels.'" In FS Bertholet, pp. 404-417.

______. *Exodus*, trans. J. S. Bowden. OTL. Philadelphia: Westminster, 1962.

______. "Gemeinsemitische Erscheinungen in der israelitischen Namengebung." ZDMG 81 (1927):1-45.

______. *Geschichte Israels.* Third edition. Göttingen: Vandenhoeck and Ruprecht, 1956.

______. *Die israelitischen Personennamen im Rahmen der gemeinsemitischen Namengebung.* BZAW 46. Stuttgart: Kohlhammer, 1928.

______. "Die syrisch-palästinische Bevölkerung des zweiten Jahrtausends v. Chr. im Licht neuer Quellen." ZDPV 65 (1942):9-67.

Nyberg, H. S. *Studien zum Hoseabuche.* UUÅ 1935/1936.

Oppenheimer, A. *The ʿAm ha-Aretz*, trans. I. H. Levine. Leiden: E. J. Brill, 1977.

Overbeck, J. J. *S. Ephraemi Syri, Opera Selecta.* Oxford: Clarendon, 1865.

Oxtoby, Willard Gurdon. *Some Inscriptions of the Safaitic Bedouin.* AOS 50. New Haven, Connecticut: American Oriental Society, 1968.

Pardee, Dennis. "The Preposition in Ugaritic." UF 7 (1975): 329-378, and UF 8 (1976):215-322.

Paton, Lewis Bayles. *"ʿAmm, ʿAmmi."* In *Hastings Encyclopaedia of Religion and Ethics*, vol. 1:386-388.

Peckham, Brian. "The Nora Inscription." Or 41 (1972):457-468.

Pedersen. J. *Israel, Its Life and Culture*, trans. A. Møller and A. I. Fausbøll. London: Cumberlege, 1926-1947.

Perlitt, Lothar. *Die Bundestheologie im Alten Testament.* WMANT 36. Neukirchen-Vluyn: Neukirchener Verlag, 1969.

Pettinato, G., and Matthiae, P. "Aspetti amministrativi e topografici di Ebla nel III millennio av. Cr." RSO 50 (1976):1-30.

Pope, M. H. "Am Ha'arez." *Interpreter's Dictionary of the Bible.* Vol. 1:106-107.

______. *Job.* Anchor Bible. Garden City, New York: Doubleday, 1973.

______. *Song of Songs.* Anchor Bible. Garden City, New York: Doubleday, 1977.

______. "Notes on the Rephaim Texts from Ugarit." In Finkelstein Mem, pp. 163-182.

Porteous, N. W. "Volk und Gottesvolk im Alten Testament." In *Theologische Aufsätze Karl Barth zum 50. Geburtstag,* ed. Ernst Wolf, pp. 146-163. München: Kaiser, 1936.

Praetorius, Franz. "Beiträge zur äthiopischen Grammatik und Etymologie." *Beiträge zur Assyriologie und vergleichenden semitischen Sprachwissenschaft* 1 (1890):21-47.

______. *Neue Beiträge zur Erklärung der himjaritischen Inschriften.* Halle, 1873.

Preuschen, Erwin. "Die Bedeutung von *šûb šĕbût* im Alten Testament." ZAW 15 (1895):1-74.

Preuss, H. D. ". . . ich will mit dir sein!'" ZAW 80 (1968): 139-173.

Prince, J. D. "The Name Hammurabi." JBL 29 (1910):21-23.

Pritchard, James, ed. *Ancient Near Eastern Texts Relating to the Old Testament.* Third edition. Princeton, New Jersey: Princeton University, 1969.

Procksch, O. *Theologie des Alten Testaments.* Gütersloh: Bertelsmann, 1950.

______. "Über die Blutrache bei den vorislamischen Arabern." Leipziger Studien aus dem Gebiet der Geschichte 5/4 (1899).

Rabin, Chaim. "Judges v,2 and the 'Ideology' of Deborah's War." *Journal of Jewish Studies* 6 (1955):125-134.

Rad, G. von. *Deuteronomium-Studien.* Göttingen: Vandenhoeck and Ruprecht, 1948.

______. *Deuteronomy,* trans. Dorothea Barton. OTL. Philadelphia: Westminster, 1966.

______. *Genesis,* trans. J. H. Marks. OTL. Philadelphia: Westminster, 1972.

______. *Das Gottesvolk im Deuteronomium.* BWANT 47. Stuttgart: Kohlhammer, 1929.

______. *Der heilige Krieg im alten Israel.* ATANT 20. Zürich: Zwingli, 1951.

______. "Verheissenes Land und Jahwehs Land im Hexateuch." In *Gesammelte Studien zum Alten Testament*, pp. 87-100. München: Kaiser, 1958.

Rawlinson, H. *The Cuneiform Inscriptions of Western Asia.* London: Bowler, 1861-1891.

Reymond, Philippe. "Sacrifice et 'spiritualité,' ou sacrifice et alliance?" TZ 21 (1965):314-317.

Rhodokanakis, Nikolaus. "Katabanische Texte zur Bodenwirtschaft." In *Sitzungsberichte*, Akademie der Wissenschaften in Wien, Philosophisch-historische Klasse, 194/2, 1919.

Richter, Wolfgang. "Die *nāgîd*-Formel: Ein Beitrag zur Erhellung des *nāgîd*-Problems." BZ nF 9 (1965):71-84.

______. "Die Überlieferungen um Jephtah, Ri 10,17-12,6." Bib 47 (1966):485-556.

______. "Zu den 'Richtern Israels.'" ZAW 77 (1965):40-72.

Robert, Philippe de. *Le berger d'Israël.* Cahiers théologiques 57. Neuchâtel: Delachaux and Niestlé, 1960.

Roberts, J. J. M. *The Earliest Semitic Pantheon: A Study of the Semitic Deities Attested before Ur III.* Baltimore: Johns Hopkins University, 1972.

Rossini, Carlo Conti. *Chrestomathia arabica meridionalis epigraphica.* Rome: Istituto per l'Oriente, 1931.

Rost, Leonhard. "Die Bezeichnungen für Land und Volk im Alten Testament." In FS Procksch, pp. 125-148.

Rothstein, D. J. W. *Juden und Samaritaner.* BWAT 3. Leipzig: J. C. Hinrichs, 1908.

Rudolph, Wilhelm. "Die Einheitlichkeit der Erzählung vom Sturz der Atalja (2 Kön 11)." In FS Bertholet, pp. 473-478.

Ryckmans, G. "A propos des noms de parenté en safaïtique." RB 60 (1953):524-525.

______. "L'épigraphie arabe préislamique au cours de ces dix dernières années." *Le Muséon* 61 (1948):197-213.

______. "Inscriptions sud-arabes (viii)." *Le Muséon* 62 (1949):55-124.

______. "Les noms de parenté en safaïtique." RB 58 (1951):377-392.

______. *Les noms propres sud-sémitiques.* Louvain: Bureaux du Muséon, 1934.

Saglio, E. "Maiumas." In *Dictionnaire des antiquités grecques et romaines*, pp. 1555-1556. Paris: Hachette, 1904.

Sawyer, John. *Semantics in Biblical Research.* SBT 2/24. London: SCM, 1972.

Scharbert, Josef. *Solidarität in Segen und Fluch im Alten Testament und in seiner Umwelt.* BBB 14. Bonn: Hanstein, 1958.

Schmidt, Hans. "Die Ehe des Hosea." ZAW 42 (1924):245-272.

Schmidt, Karl Ludwig. "Die Verstockung des Menschen durch Gott." TZ 1 (1945):1-17.

Schmidt, Ludwig. *Menschlicher Erfolg und Jahwehs Initiative.* WMANT 38. Neukirchen-Vluyn: Neukirchener Verlag, 1970.

Schulz, Hermann. *Das Todesrecht im Alten Testament: Studien zur Rechtsform der mot-jumat Sätze.* BZAW 114. Berlin: Töpelmann, 1969.

Schwally, Friedrich. *Das Leben nach dem Tode.* Giessen: Ricker, 1892.

Scott, R. B. Y. "Secondary Meanings of *ʾaḥar*: After, Behind." JTS 50 (1949):178-179.

Seebass, Horst. "Die Vorgeschichte der Königserhebung Sauls." ZAW 79 (1967):155-171.

Sekine, Masao. "Beobachtungen zu der josianischen Reform." VT 22 (1972):361-368.

Seligman, Brenda Z. "Studies in Semitic Kinship I." BSO(A)S 3 (1923-1925):51-68.

Sellin, Ernst. "Wann wurde das Moselied Dtn 32 gedichtet?" ZAW 43 (1925):161-173.

Serjeant, R. B. "Kinship Terms in Wadi Hadramaut." In *Der Orient in der Forschung*, ed. W. Hoenerbach, pp. 626-633. Spies Festschrift. Wiesbaden: Harrassowitz, 1967.

Seux, M.-J. *Epithètes royales akkadiennes et sumériennes.* Paris: Letouzey and Ane, 1967.

______. *Hymnes et prières aux dieux de Babylonie et d'Assyrie.* Littératures anciennes du Proche Orient 8. Paris: du Cerf, 1976.

Sloush, N. "Representative Government among the Hebrews and Phoenicians." JQR 4 (1913):303-310.

Smend, Rudolf. *Die Bundesformel.* ThSt (Barth) 68. Zürich: EVZ-Verlag, 1963.

Smend, R. *Yahweh War and Tribal Confederation*, trans. M. G. Rogers. Nashville: Abingdon, 1970.

Smith, W. R. *Kinship and Marriage in Early Arabia*. Reprint. Boston: Beacon, *1885.

Snaith, N. H. "Genesis xxxi:50." VT 14 (1964):373.

Soden, W. von. "Duplikate aus Ninive." JNES 33 (1974):339-344.

______. *Grundriss der akkadischen Grammatik*. Analecta Orientalia 33/47. Rome: PBI, 1969.

______. "Neubearbeitungen der babylonischen Gesetzessammlungen." OLZ 53 (1958):517-527.

Soggin, J. Alberto. "Charisma und Institution im Königtum Sauls." ZAW 75 (1963):54-65.

______. "Der judäische *ʿAm-Haʾareṣ* und das Königtum in Juda." VT 13 (1963):187-195.

Speiser, E. A. "Census and Ritual in Mari and Israel." BASOR 194 (1958):17-25.

______. *Genesis*. Anchor Bible. Garden City, New York: Doubleday, 1964.

______. "Nuzi Marginalia." Or 25 (1956):1-23.

______. "'People' and 'Nation' of Israel." JBL 79 (1960):157-163 (= pp. 160-170 in *Oriental and Biblical Studies*, ed. J. J. Finkelstein and M. Greenberg. Philadelphia: University of Pennsylvania, 1967).

Stade, Bernhard. "Anmerkungen zu 2 Kö. 10-14." ZAW 5 (1885): 275-297.

______. *Geschichte des Volkes Israel*. Berlin: Grote, 1887-1888.

Stamm, J. J. "*Bĕrīt ʿAm* bei Deuterojesaja." In FS von Rad (1971), pp. 510-524.

______. *Die akkadische Namengebung*. Leipzig: Hinrichs, 1939.

______. "Zum Ursprung des Namens der Ammoniter." ArOr 17 (1948):379-382.

Starcky, J., and Bennett, C.-M. "Les inscriptions du téménos." *Syria* 45 (1958):41-66.

Stark, J. K. *Personal Names in Palmyrene Inscriptions*. Oxford: Clarendon, 1971.

Stern, Gertrude H. *Marriage in Early Islam*. London: Royal Asiatic Society, 1939.

Strus, Andrzej. *Nomen-omen: La stylistique sonore des noms propres dans le Pentateuque.* AnBib 80. Rome: PBI, 1978.

Sulzberger, M. *Am-ha-aretz--The Ancient Hebrew Parliament.* Philadelphia: Greenstone, 1909.

Swetnam, James. "Why was Jeremiah's New Covenant New?" SVT 26 (1974):111-115.

Sznycer, Maurice. "'L'assemblée du peuple' dans les cités puniques d'après les témoignages épigraphiques." Sem 25 (1975):47-68.

______. "Quelques observations sur la grande inscription dédicatoire de Mactar." Sem 22 (1972):25-44.

Tadmor, Hayim. "'The People' and the Kingship in Ancient Israel: The Role of Political Institutions in the Biblical Period." In *Jewish Society through the Ages*, ed. H. H. Ben-Sasson and S. Ettinger, pp. 46-68. New York: Schocken, 1971.

Talmon, Shemaryahu. "The Judaean *ʿAm haʾareṣ* in Historical Perspective." *Fourth World Congress of Jewish Studies*, Vol. 1:71-76. Jerusalem, 1967.

Teixidor, Javier. *Inventaire des inscriptions de Palmyre, xi.* Beyrouth: Institut Français d'Archéologie de Beyrouth, 1965.

Thornton, T. C. G. "Charismatic Kingship in Israel and Judah." JTS ns 14 (1963):1-11.

Thureau-Dangin, F. "Un hymne à Ištar de la haute époque babylonienne." RA 22 (1925):169-177.

______. "Un nouveau roi de Ḫana." OLZ 11 (1908):93.

Torrey, C. C. "ʿamm." In *The Jewish Encyclopedia* (1901):Vol. 1:521.

Tsevat, M. "Traces of Hittite at the Beginning of the Ugaritic Epic Aqht." UF 3 (1971):351-352.

Ungnad, A. "Miscellen." ZA 22 (1909):6-16.

van den Branden, A. "L'inscription néopunique de Mactar, KAI 145." *Rivista di Studi Fenici* 1 (1973):165-172.

______. *Les inscriptions dédanites.* Beyrouth: Publications de l'Université Libanaise, sections des études historiques 8, 1962.

______. *Les inscriptions thamoudéennes.* Louvain: Université, 1950.

______. *Les textes thamoudéens de Philby.* Bibliothèque du Muséon, 39,41. Louvain: Publications universitaires, 1956.

van der Meer, P. E. *Syllabaries A, B' and B with Miscellaneous Lexicographical Texts from the Herbert Weld Collection.* OET 4. London: Oxford University, 1938.

Van der Ploeg, J. "Les chefs du peuple Israël et leurs titres." RB 57 (1950):40-61.

van der Woude, A. S. *"qāšâ."* THAT Vol. 2:689-692.

van Dijk, H. J. "Consolamini, consolamini, popule meus?" VD 45 (1967):342-346.

______. *Ezekiel's Prophecy on Tyre (Ez 26,1 - 28,9): A New Approach.* Bib Or 20. Rome: PBI, 1968.

Vaux, Roland de. *Ancient Israel*, trans. John McHugh. London: Darton, Longman, and Todd, 1961.

______. "Le sens de l'expression 'peuple du pays' dans l'Ancien Testament et le rôle politique du peuple en Israël." RA 58 (1964):167-172.

Virolleaud, Ch. "Les noms de personnes à Ras Shamra." GLECS 7 (1954-1957):109-110.

______. "Les nouveaux textes mythologiques et liturgiques de Ras Shamra." In *Ugaritica* Vol. 5, pp. 546-595.

______. *Le palais royale d'Ugarit*, Vol. 5. Paris: Klincksieck, 1965.

______. "Sur le nom de Hammurabi." JA 243 (1955):133-134.

______. "Le vrai nom de Hammurabi." GLECS 7 (1954-1957):1.

Vogt, Hubertus. *Studie zur nachexilischen Gemeinde in Esra-Nehemia.* Werl: Dietrich-Coelde, 1966.

Vorländer, Herrmann. *Mein Gott: Die Vorstellungen vom persönlichen Gott im alten Orient und im Alten Testament.* AOAT 23. Neukirchen-Vluyn: Neukircher Verlag, 1975.

Wallis, G. "Jerusalem und Samaria als Königsstädte." VT 26 (1976):480-496.

______. "Der Vollbürgereid in Deuteronomium." HUCA 45 (1974): 47-63.

Waters, John W. "The Political Development and Significance of the Shepherd-King Symbol in the Ancient Near East and the Old Testament." Ph.D. dissertation: Boston University, 1970.

Weber, Max. *Gesammelte Aufsätze zur Religionssoziologie. Das antike Judentum.* Tübingen: Mohr, 1923.

Weber, Otto. "Der Name Hammurabi in einer südarabischen Inschrift." OLZ 10 (1907):146-149.

Weil, H. M. "*ʿAmmî* 'compatriote, consanguin,'" Revue des Etudes Sémitiques et Babyloniaca (1941-1945):87-88.

Weinberg, J. P. "Der *ʿam ha-areṣ* des 6.-4. Jh v.u.Z." Klio 56 (1974):325-335.

Weinfeld, Moshe. *Deuteronomy and the Deuteronomic School.* Oxford: Clarendon, 1972.

Weippert, Helga. "Das Wort vom neuen Bund in Jeremia xxxi 31-34." VT 29 (1979):336-351.

Weiser, Artur. "Das Deboralied: Eine gattungs- und traditionsgeschichtliche Studie." ZAW 71 (1959):67-97.

Wellhausen, J. "Die Ehe bei den Arabern." *Nachrichten von der Königlichen Gesellschaft der Wissenschaften und der Georg-Augusts Universität zu Göttingen* 49/11 (1893):431-481.

______. *Skizzen und Vorarbeiten.* Berlin: Reimer, 1884.

Wildberger, Hans. *Jahwehs Eigentumsvolk.* ATANT 37. Zürich: Zwingli, 1960.

______. "Samuel und die Entstehung des israelitischen Königtums." TZ 13 (1957):442-469.

Wilken, George Alexander. *Het Matriarchaat bij de oude Arabieren.* 1884.

Wilson, John A. "The Assembly of a Phoenician City." JNES 4 (1945):245.

Wilson, R. R. "The Hardening of Pharaoh's Heart." CBQ 41 (1979):18-36.

Winckler, Hugo. "Arabisch-Semitisch-Orientalisch." MVAG 6/4 (1901):151-373.

______. "Einige semitische Eigennamen." In *Altorientalische Forschungen* Vol. 2:84-86. Leipzig: Pfeiffer, 1898.

______. "Polyandrie bei Semiten." *Verhandlungen der Berliner Gesellschaft für Anthropologie, Ethnologie und Urgeschichte* 30 (1898):29-30.

Wold, Donald. "The Meaning of the Biblical Penalty *Kareth.*" Ph.D. dissertation: University of California, 1978.

Wolf, C. Umhau. "Traces of Primitive Democracy in Ancient Israel." JNES 6 (1947):98-108.

Wright, G. Ernest. "The Lawsuit of God: A Form-Critical Study of Deuteronomy 32." In FS Muilenburg, pp. 26-67.

Wright, W. *The Kāmil of El-Mubarrad.* Leipzig: Kreysing, 1864.

Würthwein, E. *Der ʿAmm haʾarez im Alten Testament.* BWANT 69. Stuttgart: Kohlhammer, 1936.

______. "Der Ursprung der prophetischen Gerichtsrede." ZTK 4 (1952):1-16.

Wüst, Manfried. "Die Einschaltung in die Jeftachgeschichte, Ri 11,13-26." Bib 56 (1975):464-479.

Zaborski, A. "Prefixes, Root-Determinatives and the Problem of Biconsonantal Roots in Semitic." *Folia Orientalia* 11 (1970):307-313.

Zimmerli, W. "Die Eigenart der prophetischen Rede des Ezechiel." ZAW 66 (1955):1-26.

______. *Ezechiel*. BKAT. Neukirchen-Vluyn: Neukirchener Verlag, 1969.

______. "Ich bin Jahwe." In *Gottes Offenbarung: Gesammelte Aufsätze zum Alten Testament*, pp. 11-40. München: Kaiser, 1963.

Zimmermann, Frank. "Folk Etymology of Biblical Names." SVT 15 (1966):311-326.

DATE DUE
